BLESSED IS HE WHO READS

BLESSED IS HE WHO READS

A Primer on the Book of Revelation

Second Edition

Larry E. Ball

Fountain Inn, South Carolina 29644

"Proclaiming the kingdom of God and teaching those things which concern the Lord Jesus Christ, with all confidence."
(Acts 28:31)

Blessed Is He Who Reads: A Primer on the Book of Revelation
by Larry E. Ball
Copyright Second Edition © 2015 by Larry E. Ball

All rights reserved. No part of this book may be reproduced in any form or by any means, except for brief quotations for the purpose of review, comment, or scholarship, without written permission from the publisher.

Unless otherwise noted, Scripture references are taken from the New American Standard Bible, (c) 1960, 1962, 1963, 1968, 1971, 1972, 1973, 1975, 1977 by The Lockman Foundation. Used by permission.

Published by Victorious Hope Publishing
P.O. Box 1874
Fountain Inn, South Carolina 29644

Website: www.VictoriousHope.com

Printed in the United States of America

ISBN: 978-0-9826206-6-3

VICTORIOUS HOPE PUBLISHING is committed to producing Christian educational materials for promoting the whole Bible for the whole of life. We are conservative, evangelical, and Reformed and are committed to the doctrinal formulation found in the Westminster Standards.

DEDICATION

To my children and grandchildren:
May each of them love the Lord God Almighty
and serve him to the end of their days

TABLE OF CONTENTS

Preface ix
Introduction 1
1. Historical Limitations 7
2. Temporal Expectation. 19
3. Coming with the Clouds. 41
4. The Letters to the Seven Churches. 57
5. The Sealed Book. 77
6. Seven Seals Broken. 97
7. Seven Trumpets and Three Woes. 117
8. Three Enemies of the Early Church. 135
9. The Seven Bowls of Wrath. 155
10. A Post-mortem Analysis and a Victory March. 173
11. The Final Judgment. 191
12. The Future of God's People.. 211
Summary 233
Appendix 237
Scripture Index. 239
Subject and Name Indices 247

PREFACE

What is a Primer?

This book is intended to be a primer (pronounce like "prim and proper") on the book of Revelation. A primer is a book for beginners, presenting the most basic elements of a field of study. It is a first step toward understanding something more complicated. Actually, a primer assumes you know very little about a particular subject. It is an introduction to a particular topic that may encourage you to pursue your own study in more detail and depth.

This book is not a commentary. It is not a word-by-word, verse-by-verse explanation of Revelation. I am mainly interested in moving through Revelation at a fairly fast pace without getting all bogged down in the details. If I move too slowly, I believe you will tend to lose the big picture and get lost quickly. On the other hand, if I move too fast, then you may not retain much of what you read. I will explore Revelation in chronological order (chapter by chapter). Sometimes I will cover several chapters at a time when I think it is more helpful.

From Sermons to a Book

This book is the result of a series of sermons that I preached at Bridwell Heights Presbyterian Church in Kingsport, Tennessee from June 2010 to April 2012. Years ago as a young minister, I thought to myself that I would never preach through Revelation. I considered it just too difficult. It is full of images, symbols, and metaphors. Who can decipher such a mysterious book? Besides, I am not a literary person. I find stories such as *Peter Pan* and *The Chronicles of Narnia* boring. I majored in mathematics and physics in college. Later on I became a Certified Public Accountant (CPA). I have a very logical mind. I like numbers. I like debits and credits. I seldom read novels. Thus, I do not have a natural propensity toward a study of Revelation, a book that includes descriptions of crazy-looking monsters and creatures full of eyes with horns on their heads.

I have found two extreme perspectives in the church in regard to this last book of the Bible. First, I have found that many church leaders in some churches spend a great amount of their time on this book. They believe they have solved the riddles and have developed numerous charts which in their minds present a plausible answer to the book's mysteries. They specialize in Revelation and prophecy.

On the other hand, I find that church leaders from many Christian denominations (including my own) mostly avoid this book. In very few of these churches will you find pastors who have either preached through Revelation or taught it in a Bible class. I think the reason may be the same reason that I avoided it for so many years. I was afraid of it. I did not believe I was competent to deal with the book. There are so many views on how to interpret it; who was I to even challenge the experts?

However, a few things changed my mind. I was near the end of thirty years of preaching through the Bible at the church where I was the pastor. This is not to say I had covered the entire Bible, but I had preached a large number of sermons from many books of the Bible over this period. My style was exposition. That is to say, I generally preached through a book of the Bible verse by verse. Actually, my style was more expositional/topical. From most verses that I was interpreting, my sermon usually resulted in focusing on some topic that was related to the text.

After thirty years of preaching Sunday after Sunday, I was looking for a different challenge. One of the leaders of the church suggested that I attempt preaching through Revelation. He gave me some audio lectures by Dr. Kenneth Gentry and some audio sersmons by Dr. Greg Bahnsen on Revelation. Listening to these tapes gave me the confidence I needed to preach through Revelation. For two years, I preached almost every Sunday morning from this book. Some folks wearied of it, but I persevered and they did too. They were very gracious.

While listening to one of Dr. Bahnsen's sermons, I was convicted that it was a dereliction of duty for preachers to ignore Revelation since it is a part of the Holy Scriptures. "All Scripture is inspired by God and is profitable for teaching, for reproof, for correction, for training in righteousness; so that the man of God may be adequate, equipped for every good work" (2 Tim. 3:16-17).

If a man is to preach the whole counsel of God, this should include preaching through Revelation. Since Revelation is part of God's Word, there is much benefit in it for God's people. We are commanded to heed the words written in the book. "Blessed is he who reads and those who hear the words of the prophecy, and heed the things which are written in it; for the time is near" (Rev. 1:3). Hence, the name of this book — *Blessed Is He Who Reads*. I concluded that indeed it would be a dereliction of duty for me to withhold from my congregation a series of either sermons or lectures on Revelation. I believed that it would be a mistake to withhold this blessing.

This primer comes from the notes I used for my sermons, but it is not simply my sermons transcribed into a book. I decided that the most profitable use of my time (and yours as the reader) was to concentrate on the main verses in the various chapters that demonstrate the theme of Revelation as a whole.

This is a book for the so-called "man in the pew." Other material on Revelation by other writers is available for the more scholarly reader. I believe there is a need for a concise and direct appeal to the average person in the church who is simply afraid to deal with Revelation. I took the jump and dived into the book. After jumping into what I thought was over my head, I actually came up breathing more easily than I had expected. I discovered it is not as difficult as it initially appears. As a result, I have been greatly blessed. I no longer believe it is a book to be feared or avoided. I pray that this primer which is in your hands will be likewise a blessing for you the reader.

A Word of Thanks

I want to thank the many folks who have helped me in writing this book, including Claire Shackelford, who helped me organize the sermon notes; and Harold Walma, who was a patient editor after I completed my first draft. I would also like to thank my dear wife Brenda, who sat at the computer reading each sentence with me and helping me through my second draft. A word of thanks must be given to Suzanne Rhodes, Richard Bridwell, and Rob Elder who assisted me significantly. Special gratitude belongs to the members of Bridwell Heights Presbyterian Church, who endured a prolonged sermon series on Revelation every Sunday for almost two years.

Dedication

I would like to dedicate this book to my children Titus, Timothy, and Sarah. I thank my children and their spouses for being a blessing to me. Of course, as a grandfather, I also would like to dedicate this book to my grandchildren, with the hope that it will have an impact on their lives. I am thankful that my grandchildren are being raised in the faith once for all delivered to the saints (Jude 3). I am a rich man indeed! My prayer is that each of them may love the Lord God Almighty, serve him to the end of their days, and help pass that love of God on to consecutive generations.

Larry E. Ball
Kingsport, Tennessee
2014

INTRODUCTION

"All Scripture is inspired by God and profitable for teaching, for reproof, for correction, for training in righteousness; so that the man of God may be adequate, equipped for every good work." (2 Tim. 3:16-17)

My Primary Sources

Anyone in my theological circles will notice that my interpretations, for the most part, are not original. I learned and borrowed most of them from other men. I want to recognize at the very beginning my indebtedness to Dr. Kenneth Gentry and Dr. Greg Bahnsen. From listening to their sermons, tapes, and reading their books, I have gleaned much from these men. I do differ with them on the interpretation of certain parts of Revelation; therefore, not everything I say will reflect their views. They are the scholars. I am the man who stands between the scholars and the people in the pew. I believe this is part of my calling in life — to study the giants and bring their teaching down to the level of the Christian who is not so well-versed.

Assumptions

Anyone who reads the Bible brings certain presuppositions with him when he opens its pages. By the word "presuppositions," I mean assumptions we take for granted and seldom question. For example, we all assume that the sun will rise tomorrow. We don't think much about that, but we assume it as we live day by day. The probability is high that the sun will rise tomorrow, but we cannot be one-hundred percent sure apart from the promises of God. We presuppose it. One plus one equals two. This is not something we think much about when we are counting money or even performing complicated mathematical calculations; however, we do assume it.

We never ask the question why one plus one equals two. It is a presupposition.

We all have certain assumptions in mind when we set our eyes on God's Word. These presuppositions or attitudes may have come from previous teachers, from previous church associations, from personal experiences; or even from our own personalities. If a man was raised in one particular denomination, then he probably believes the doctrinal distinctives of that denomination. If he was not raised in church at all, then his impressions of the Bible may be affected by his interaction with other Christians. Also, he may have heard bits and pieces quoted from the Bible in various venues such as the television or the news media.

It is my experience that none of us has a mind that is like a clean, unstained slate when we approach anything, and that includes the Bible. We all have our biases from the get-go. There are assumptions and presuppositions already written on our minds that affect both how we approach the Bible and how we interpret it. You may not accept this as being true of you, but at least this is what I learned about myself.

In my Christian life, I have experienced times when I discovered something new about the Bible that was really plain all the time but that I had never previously seen. How could I have missed this or that truth when it was so obvious? I would be very confident of my position until someone or something challenged me to reconsider my assumptions. I was open to listening to different perspectives, and at times my views changed. Remember this as you read my book. I may challenge some of your assumptions. It is never easy to have them questioned. As a matter of fact, it is very uncomfortable. However, this may turn out to be a blessing.

Approaches to the Bible

In regard to the nature and character of the Bible itself, there are a number of different views people embrace. Some believe the Bible is good literature but nothing more. They believe the Bible is no more than an interesting book composed by men who were inspired just as good poets might be inspired to write eloquent poetry. They believe the writings of the Bible are excellent in style and content when compared with other literature. They might also say the Bible contains principles that will be profitable if they live by them, such as the teachings of Jesus found in the Sermon on the Mount.

No doubt there are many other approaches to the Bible. Before I begin the interpretation of Revelation, I will first summarize my view of the Scriptures. What assumptions do I have before I even open the Bible, especially Revelation, which is probably the most difficult book of the Bible? This will help you understand my approach as you read this primer. You will probably guess my assumptions early in your reading, but let me be up-front about them at the beginning.

My Assumptions

My basic assumption is that the Bible is the inerrant and infallible Word of God. It is "God breathed." This is the testimony of the Bible regarding itself (2 Tim. 3:16). In the Greek language (the original language of the New Testament) the word usually translated as the English word "inspired" is better translated "God-breathed." Although the Bible was written by men, yet it was ultimately breathed by the mouth of God — every word of it. It is God's Holy Word. God breaks into history and speaks to man in the words of the Bible. This is my basic assumption and one reason I believe the interpretation of the Bible must be handled with care.

The original books of the Bible were the actual documents written by their authors in the original languages of either Hebrew or Greek (and a few verses of Aramaic). For example, when Paul wrote the letter to the Christians at Ephesus, it was written in the Greek language on papyrus (the writing material of that day) and sent to the church in that city. That original copy was inspired by the Holy Spirit (the third person of the Trinity). It had no errors (such as grammatical or historical errors) because Paul was under the direct and supernatural influence of the Holy Spirit. God makes no mistakes. Every word written by Paul was the exact and perfect word intended by God himself. The Holy Spirit was using Paul's ability and personality to pen the words on the papyrus; but since Paul was "moved by the Holy Spirit" (2 Pet. 1:21), the words he used were actually God's words. Thus, his letter (or book as we often call it) was inerrant (without error) and infallible (incapable of error).

The original copy of Paul's letter (autograph) to the church at Ephesus is no longer in existence. However, ancient copies of the original letter still exist today. These copies of the books of the Bible are almost exact duplicates of each other except for a few variations (mistakes made by those who transcribed the copies). The variations are so few and minor that essentially when a person reads the Bible in a good translation, it can be said with confidence that he is reading the inerrant and infallible Word of God. For more in-depth studies on this, see *The Infallible Word: A Symposium by the Members of the Faculty of Westminster Theological Seminary*.[1]

Because I believe the Bible is the inerrant and infallible Word of God, I also believe it is a record of accurate history. It begins with the creation of the world in Genesis 1, and its writers take us through history down to the apostolic age (the lifetime of the apostles). Also, it certainly tells us some things about the future beyond the apostolic age, as we will see in Revelation. It tells us about life after death.

I suppose God could have dropped a book from heaven that was a summary of Christian doctrine. He could have ordered to appear out of thin air a book that contained truths and songs of praise about himself. Instead, he used a book written over many hundreds of years by numerous authors describing the history of the events unfolding his work on this earth from the beginning of the world down through the apostolic age. The Bible is mostly a historical narrative. It gives us the names of particular people, particular families, and particular nations, and it tells us what happened to

---

[1] N. B. Stonehouse and Paul B. Woolley, eds., *The Infallible Word: A Symposium by the Members of the Faculty of Westminster Theological Seminary* (Phillipsburg, N.J.: P & R, 2003).

them. God's Word gives us stories about how people responded to the events God brought into their lives. It also reads like a novel. It has a beginning and an end with an overarching theme. In addition to containing acts of love and sacrifice, it contains stories about wars, calamities, murders, adultery, and betrayal. Its style varies from historical narrative to poetry.

Because I believe the Bible is the inerrant and infallible Word of God, I also believe it is more than a record of accurate history or a book about how to live. The Bible is more than good literature. It is the story of the fall of man into sin, the curse of God upon sin, and the grace of God in sending his Son, Jesus Christ, to save man from his lost condition. It is a book about the plight of man and how God came to deliver man from his misery. The Bible is a history book, but it is more than a history book. It is also a story about how God redeems his people in history. God reveals who he is in the Bible, and God reveals in the Bible how he deals with man and the problem of sin and death. Yes, the Bible teaches us eternal truths that never change, but maybe as important, the Bible is a window into the very character of God himself.

Newspapers and Current Events

As you read through this book, one thing I hope you will notice are the sources I use for interpretation. The present practice of most prophecy experts is to read the newspapers about current events in our world, and then use those events to explain the meaning of Revelation. My main source will be the Scriptures themselves. I quote a great deal of the Bible in my interpretation of Revelation. I believe most of the answers to the mysteries in Revelation can be found in other parts of the Scriptures.

I believe that a person's view of the future is very important. If the church believes that the events in Revelation will yet occur in the future, she will tend to focus on prophecy. If the church takes a different position such as the one I hold, then she will focus on kingdom-building in the present age. The modern church basically has become irrelevant to the world around her. Because much of the church has focused on prophecy, she has lost a truly biblical, prophetic voice which seeks to bring Christianity to bear on all areas of life, including education, politics, science, etc. This is the sad state of the modern church, and I believe her view of the future has contributed greatly to her irrelevance in the culture in which we live.

Conclusion

What do I believe about the Bible? I believe the Bible is the inerrant, infallible Word of God. This is my assumption as I read the Bible, and as I write this book. According to traditional Christian theology, my belief is a result of the influence of the Holy Spirit upon me. Only the supernatural influence of the Holy Spirit can enable a person to accept the truth that the Bible is the Word of God.

Now you know my assumptions in my approach to Revelation. As I move on to the first chapter, I will challenge you to consider a principle of interpretation that seems quite obvious; however, I would guess that you probably have not given it much thought. This principle will provide the foundation for the rest of my book.

The quotes from the Bible in this book are from the New American Standard Version (NASB) of the Bible (Copyright 1996 by The Lockman Foundation). *Italics* in Scripture quotes indicate words which are not in the original Hebrew, Aramaic, or Greek but implied by it. Other words or phrases in *italics*, I have added myself, and noted by [emphasis added]. CAPS in New Testament quotes are used to indicate Old Testament quotations or obvious inferences to the Old Testament texts.

1
HISTORICAL LIMITATION

"When you come bring the cloak which I left at Troas with Carpus, and the books, especially the parchments." (2 Tim. 4:13)

Introduction

In this chapter I will consider something very important. It is critical for understanding Revelation. This may be the shortest chapter of my book, but it may also be the most important. I think Christians have failed in general to understand or recognize what I am about to say. If you are a Christian, my intention is to help you understand some assumptions you hold, assumptions about which you probably have never given much thought. Hold on, this may prove difficult! The point is this: "The Bible was not written *to us* but *for us.*" This statement may sound dangerous. At first it sounded a little alarming even to me when I read what I wrote. Though it may sound dangerous, I am convinced it is not. It is a plain biblical principle that I ignored for years, a principle that simply describes what is obviously true.

Think about it. Most of the Old Testament was written to Old Covenant Israel. The Pentateuch was the Law of God given to Israel through Moses. The Psalms were songs to be used in the worship of God by Israel. The Prophets spoke warnings to Israel. Most of the New Testament was written to various early apostolic churches or to men like Timothy and Titus. Indirectly, we benefit from those writings, but we were not the original target audience. They were not written to us, but they were written for us.

What Is Historical Limitation?

Remember that the Bible was written in a historical context, and much of it was written to those who lived in a particular time in history. The Bible often limits its message to the time in which it was written. I call this *historical limitation*. This means that an event that happened in history cannot happen again. The event is limited to a particular time in history. For example, Jesus died on the cross one time. It cannot happen again in history. His death on the cross is historically limited. This is a basic principle that Christians assume when they read the Bible, and it is a principle that I will assume as I approach Revelation. I am not denying that God may speak to us through the work of the Holy Spirit as we read the Bible or hear it preached. This is a different issue. The point here is that the Bible originally was not written to us, but for us.

Examples of Historical Limitations

For example, Paul concludes his letter to Philemon by writing: "At the same time also prepare me a lodging, for I hope that through your prayers I will be given to you" (v. 22). Was this written directly to Larry Ball? Obviously not! I do have an extra bedroom in my house, but I cannot prepare lodging for the Apostle Paul. Paul is no longer living on this earth. This letter was written by Paul to Philemon and not to me. This particular text provides an example of historical limitation. This does not take away from the authority of the Word of God, but it simply recognizes that this was written at a particular time in history in a specific geographical area to a person who is no longer living on this earth. God evidently wanted me to know about Paul's need for lodging during this trip because he had it written in the Bible. I can make a number of applications from this text for a sermon (such as the importance of hospitality). However, I cannot prepare a room for Paul. Such texts are written for us, but not directly to us. It will be important for you to understand this distinction as I take you through Revelation, especially the first and last chapter.

This principle of historical limitation is so important that I will provide several other examples from the Bible. In 2 Timothy 4:11, Paul writes to Timothy: "Only Luke is with me. Pick up Mark and bring him with you, for he is useful to me for service." Now, this is something I personally cannot do living in the twenty-first century. Mark is in heaven and I am on earth. This letter was written to Timothy, and it was an instruction to him given by the Apostle Paul. Timothy could pick up Mark and bring him to Paul, but I cannot. This is another example of historical limitation. Consider Paul's words in 2 Timothy 4:13: "When you come bring the cloak which I left at Troas with Carpus, and the books, especially the parchments." Here again, the words are not directed to me in particular. I doubt this particular cloak is still in existence today. There may be some clothing items in museums that are very old, but I doubt that Paul's cloak is in any of them or that his cloak is still at Troas. Even if it were in Troas, I do not believe God expects me to make a trip there to pick it up. That was a command limited to Timothy.

In Luke 18:22, when Jesus was speaking to the rich young ruler, he said to him: "One thing you still lack; sell all that you possess and distribute it to the poor, and you shall have treasure in heaven; and come, follow me." Most of us would argue that Jesus was talking to the rich young ruler here and that this is not a command for everyone who reads the text. Otherwise, we would have no choice but to sell all we have and give it to the poor. Again, this is an example of historical limitation. All these examples are fairly easy applications of the principle. Now let us move on to some more difficult texts.

Luke 12:33 and Historical Limitation

In Luke 12:33, Jesus says: "Sell your possessions and give to charity; make yourselves money belts which do not wear out, an unfailing treasure in heaven, where no thief comes near nor moth destroys." This poses a more difficult situation because the words were addressed to the followers of Christ, and the directives in much of the context of this verse parallel the Sermon on the Mount as it was recorded in the book of Matthew.

Usually, Christians read the Sermon on the Mount as if it were written directly to them. Is Jesus here in Luke 12 telling all Christians in the twenty-first century to sell all they have and give it to the poor? This is a big question! Did the Roman Catholic monks get it right when they sold all their belongings and took a vow of poverty? Is this not a command for everyone who reads the text? The language of the text intimates that this is not just a suggestion Jesus made to those who heard him, but that it was a command.

I have heard many sermons by numerous preachers who have had a very difficult time dealing with this text and applying it to the lives of those in their own congregations. The plain meaning of the text has been so "spiritualized" that the obvious meaning of the words are made to mean something totally different than what it literally says. Why then should we not sell all of our possessions and give the proceeds to the poor if this is a command of Christ spoken directly to those of us living today? One dilemma arising from actually doing this is that such action will cause serious problems for every Christian. How shall a Christian feed his own family? Will he not have to go on welfare himself? If all Christians sell all they have and give it to the poor, then who will support the church and Christian ministries?

Jesus here did not say we are to give the proceeds to the church but rather to the poor. This is not an instruction to form a social commune. Did not Jesus realize the consequences? How then can we extricate ourselves from this interpretative quandary if as Christians we want to be faithful to Christ?

The answer to interpreting this difficult text is not "spiritualizing" it to mean that all of us in some general sense should be committed to Christ. This is true for all of us, but this is not what the text commands. The text requires the disciples to sell all they have and give the proceeds to the poor. This is plain and simple. How do we deal with such a dilemma? The answer once again is historical limitation. Again, do not misunderstand me — the Bible is God's inspired Word and all of it speaks to us. However, not every command is a command directly intended for those of us living in the twenty-first century.

There are two important things to note about this text. First of all, in Luke 12:22, Jesus was speaking to his twelve disciples. "And he said to his disciples: 'For this reason I say to you, do not worry about *your* life, *as to* what you will eat; nor for your body, *as to* what you will put on.'" Later in the same chapter, Peter is confused about to whom this should be applied. Was it meant for the twelve disciples or for all the disciples who were following Jesus? Peter said: "Lord, are You addressing this parable to us, or to everyone *else* as well?" (Luke 12:41). According to the commentator Matthew Henry, Jesus intended this for all the disciples: "What I say to you, I say to all. Be on the alert!" (Mark 13:37). Thus the intended audience was all the disciples who were following Jesus.

Secondly, the context of this particular command is the coming destruction of Jerusalem (A.D. 70) by Christ himself, who will use the armies of Rome to destroy Jerusalem. Shortly after Jesus commanded his disciples to sell all their possessions, he says: "You too, be ready; for the Son of Man is coming at an hour that you do not expect" (Luke 12:40). Jesus is telling his disciples to prepare for persecution by the Jews, for the loss of all their property, and for his coming. His coming will be in judgment using the Roman armies. He is not here speaking about his Second Advent, which will be personal and visible. In his reference in this text, he will come using the armies of Rome as the instrument of his judgment. We will look at this interpretation of the coming of Christ later in this book.

Soon, because of the persecution from the Jews, his disciples will have nothing. Once the Roman soldiers are finished with Jerusalem, all surviving citizens will be reduced to poverty. Better to sell everything now and give it to charity because they would soon lose it all anyway. Better to have treasure in heaven than treasure on earth that will soon be taken away and is always subject to decay anyway. This particular historical limitation is the only honest way I could ever extricate myself personally from responding to the words of Christ by selling all I have and giving it to the poor.

Indeed, the text can be applied to any generation because materialism is always idolatry. Every generation must remember that possessions are temporary, and these possessions must not become gods because in the end such idols will fail to save them. This is true for all Christians in any age, but in the text of Luke 12:33, the command literally demands that the disciples sell all they possess and give it to the poor. A spiritual application does not solve the problem that appears to exist in a literal application of this text.

I do not believe this text should be limited to a spiritual application, nor is it a command for every Christian in every age to take a vow of poverty. It is a text written to followers of Christ living before the destruction of Jerusalem in A.D. 70 with the expectation that they should indeed sell all they owned and give it to the poor before the destruction of Jerusalem. The text is historically limited.

The principle of historical limitation is critical for interpreting some of the more difficult texts of the Bible. Think about it — although the whole Bible speaks to us personally and although there are principles in every text that apply to us, unless we apply

Blessed Is He Who Reads 13

historical limitation, we can at times put ourselves in a difficult situation. Not only do we find ourselves commanded to do things impossible (bring the cloak), but we also find ourselves liable to do things most difficult and unwise such as selling all our possessions and giving them to the poor. Christian poverty seems to be the only alternative if we embrace Luke 12:33 as a text speaking directly to us who live in the twenty-first century.

Matthew 24:34 and Historical Limitation

Let me challenge another assumption you may hold. This one deals with the things we have been taught about the events leading up to the end of the world. In Matthew 24, after Jesus spoke of a number of events that have traditionally been associated with the end of the world (false prophets, wars and rumors of wars, the great tribulation), he says in verse 34: "Truly, I say to you, this generation will not pass away until all these things take place." If I interpret the word "generation" here as I do in other parts of the Scriptures, then what did Jesus mean?

Some have translated the Greek word in this verse for "generation" as the word "race," but after studying the original languages and comparing Scripture with Scripture, I do not believe this is possible. By the word "generation," Jesus meant that all the events of which he spoke prior to verse 34 were to happen within the time span of that generation. That generation was the time period in which the twelve disciples of Jesus lived. That is what it says if we take it literally, and if we interpret the word generation to mean exactly what it means in other parts of the Bible.

Therefore, the reader should believe that those wars, rumors of wars, and the great tribulation have already happened. They occurred before the apostolic generation died. Now this may create problems with what you have been taught about the end times. It may create problems in regard to identifying when and how these events occurred in the generation of the apostles, but those problems can be solved.

There is much written on this issue. You can begin by reading *Israel and the New Covenant* by Roderick Campbell.[1] It is the book that first challenged my assumptions about what I had been taught concerning the end of the world. Gary DeMar has written extensively on this and other similar topics. For further study, I recommend going to the website www.americanvision.org. For a list of books written from this perspective, see Appendix.

Thus, the preceding discussion of the meaning of the word "generation" demonstrates my position that Matthew 24:34 imposes a historical limitation on the reader. All of those events leading up to verse 34 have already happened. Not only have they already happened in history, but they happened before that generation died to whom Jesus spoke these words.

I will not deal with this further nor seek to answer your many questions here, but I will examine this issue again, especially as I move into chapter 1 of Revelation. Actually, this principle will determine how I interpret the entire book of Revelation, and it is why I say this chapter of my book may prove to be the most important. My goal for now is simply to point out the importance of the principle of historical limitation.

Misapplication of Historical Limitation

Of course there is a danger of misapplying the principle of historical limitation, just as there is a danger with any good thing that is abused. Historical limitation has been used to support many teachings that are contrary to the Word of God. For example, it is common today in our feminized society for women to assume the

---

[1] Roderick Campbell, *Israel and the New Covenant* (Phillipsburg, N.J.: P&R Publishing, 2010).

office of elder or even pastor of a church. The argument is made that any restriction against women holding office in the church is controlled by the principle of historical limitation. It is often argued that the restriction of women holding ordained teaching offices in the church is a truth limited to Bible times only and that the limitation does not apply today. The case is made that modern man is so much more advanced. We live in the days of egalitarianism (total equality in every area of life). Also, Paul said in Galatians 3:28: "There is neither Jew nor Greek, there is neither slave nor free man, there is neither male nor female; for you are all one in Christ Jesus." Did not Paul himself free women from the early New Testament restrictions in regard to holding offices of leadership in the church?

Again, this is an abuse of the principle of historical limitation. Obviously, the same Paul who penned Galatians 3:28 also penned 1Timothy 2:12: "But I do not allow a woman to teach or have authority over a man, but to remain quiet."

Paul's intent in the phrase "neither male nor female" in Galatians was not to erase the distinction between the two genders nor to contradict what he said in other parts of the Bible. Rather, he was simply recognizing that all persons — regardless of position, race, or gender — have access to the same forgiveness that is in Christ.

Creation Ordinance

There is another important tool of biblical interpretation that legislates against the preceding misapplication of the principle of historical limitation. A *creation ordinance* is an ordinance (a rule or law) made when the world was created by God that does not change. It was put into effect before the fall of man into sin, and thus is tied to the act of creation itself. In a sense, a creation ordinance trumps historical limitation. A creation ordinance is a rule that remains the same down through history; for example, the regulation that only a man and a woman may be joined together in marriage. A creation ordinance was legislated at the time of creation and cannot change. The principle of historical limitation cannot change it. Notice that Paul appeals to the creation ordinance itself when he states his position regarding women not holding teaching positions in the church where he goes on to say in the next verse: "For it was Adam who was first created *and* then Eve" (1 Tim. 2:13). Obviously, this limitation on women holding the ordained office of teacher in the church is rooted in creation itself. It cannot be classified as unique to the generation of the early church since it is a creation ordinance. Therefore, there is no historical limitation to the teaching that relegates the ordained teaching ministry to males only. The restriction of ordaining males only for ruling and teaching positions is rooted in a creation ordinance and is not limited to the age of the New Testament. It is still a creation ordinance today.

Conclusion

When reading the Bible, everyone needs to ask the question: "Is every verse in the Bible written directly to me?" For years, I read the Bible with the assumption that every verse of the Bible was written directly to me. I don't deny that the Word of God speaks to me when I read it or hear it preached. However, I did learn somewhere along the way that there are clearly a number of texts in the Bible that are restricted by historical limitation. Many of these texts were written to those who lived in the apostolic age and not to me. It is wrong of me to think that I am responsible to carry out every directive the Bible makes. I cannot take parchments to Paul. I am not responsible to sell all that I have and follow Christ.

There is a popular teaching in some church circles called "neo-orthodoxy" which takes the position that the Bible is not God's infallible, inerrant Word, but that God speaks his Word separately through a Bible that is full of mistakes. In this view, the Bible becomes God's Word only as it has an effect on the hearer. This is not what I am teaching. I believe the Bible in written form is the inerrant and infallible Word of God, regardless of whether it has an effect on the reader. At the same time, I do believe that the Bible is historically limited.

The principle of historical limitation in no way denies the truth that God is speaking through the Bible to me by his Holy Spirit as I read it. Indeed, the Bible was written for us. Paul makes this assertion in the book of Romans where he says: "For whatever was written in earlier times was written *for our instruction* [emphasis added], so that through perseverance and the encouragement of the Scriptures we might have hope" (Rom. 15:4).

The concept of historical limitation does limit the directives of some texts of the Bible to the generation to which it was written. Yes, this principle can be abused; however, to deny this principle is to deny the obvious teaching of the Word of God itself. To say that everything that happened in the Bible can happen today is a fallacy. The principle of historical limitation is very important. It is critical as I approach Revelation, especially as I examine chapter 1.

2
TEMPORAL EXPECTATION

"The Revelation of Jesus Christ, which God gave Him to show to His bond-servants, the things which must soon take place; and He sent and communicated it by His angel to His bond-servant John, who testified to the word of God and to the testimony of Jesus Christ, even to all that he saw. Blessed is he who reads and those who hear the words of the prophecy, and heed the things which are written in it; for the time is near." (Rev. 1:1-3)

Introduction

These particular verses contain one of the most important keys to understanding the entire book of Revelation. Thus, it is critical that you follow my reasoning in this chapter. Understanding these verses will remove much of the mystery of the book.

It is the testimony of many Christians that Revelation has always frightened them. I know some Christians who live in constant fear because of what they have been taught about this book of the Bible. They live every day of their lives as if total chaos and bedlam will break out on the earth at any moment. They fear that all of the strange creatures in Revelation will come to earth, and the end result will be a world filled with pandemonium and mayhem. It will be a little like the movie *Jurassic Park*. Unless we are raptured from earth, it will be a dreadful place to be.

I do not believe that God intends for Christians to live this way. I don't think that Jesus died on the cross to leave us here on earth living our days full of apprehension and anxiety. This is not a necessary consequence of studying Revelation. On the contrary, if you stay with me through this study, I believe I can help you to remove these fears from your heart and to replace them with encouragement and hope.

However, no matter what assumptions are present as a person studies Revelation, he still needs to maintain some degree of fear and awe. Also, no matter what assumptions a person takes with himself as he approaches the book, there will be some speculation. This is unavoidable. Although I do believe that speculation can be reduced considerably, it would be arrogant of me to think I have an answer to every question.

Getting a grip on Revelation depends a great deal on how a person deals with the first three verses of chapter 1. If we do not agree about this, then maybe you have wasted the cost of this book. However, if you stay with me, I believe the meaning of the mysterious texts and metaphors will become clearer as I go through Revelation. At least this has been my own experience. The point I will make from these texts is that most of the events described in Revelation have already happened. To establish this point, I will apply the principle of historical limitation as I described it in the previous chapter. If I have not persuaded you of the validity of this principle, then Revelation probably will become an exercise in pure speculation on the one hand, or, on the other, simply a pep talk for the discouraged. I believe its central message is more than either of these.

Transition Events in My Own Life

If I can convince you of my perspective on Revelation, it may be a dramatic change for most of you from your previous views. Dramatic changes in biblical views happen sometimes in our lives. We assume something all of our lives, and then suddenly we see things differently. Views of marriage before and after tying the wedding knot might qualify as an example of this kind of transition!

In my own life there have been times when my views on the Bible were dramatically changed. Maybe it was a book I read or a sermon I heard. Regardless of what changed my mind, the transition was one from darkness to light. As I alluded to in the previous chapter, I was amazed at what was clearly always there in the Scriptures, and yet I had not seen it.

This includes periods of transitions for me such as the first time I learned about the doctrine of justification by faith alone. That was a life-changing event. The forgiveness of my sins is not based on anything I do or can do, but is based on the work of Christ alone. My forgiveness is ultimately not a matter of how good I am, or how religious I am, or even how much faith I have, but on the work of Christ alone. The righteousness of Christ is credited (imputed) to my account. I wear his robe of righteousness, and when God looks at me, he sees the perfection of Christ rather than me. I did not earn that robe. I could not earn it. I accept this new position in Christ through the instrument of faith alone, and even that faith is a gift of God. This is my only hope for salvation.

Another period of transition for me included the time I first learned of the doctrines of grace. This followed my acceptance of the doctrine of the sovereignty of God. Both of these were life-changers. Also, at another time in my life, my eyes were opened to see the application of God's law to all spheres of life — to the family, to the church, and even to the civil magistrate. This paralleled my move to an optimistic view of the future as was held by the Puritans at the time they settled America.

The most recent shining light that changed my perspective on the Bible was studying and preaching through Revelation and finding that there are answers to most of the deep and dark mysteries that lie within it. Meaning can be found in these (sometimes awful) images, which John describes throughout the book. Revelation need not be a book that remains a mystery to the people of God nor a book we dread. As I mentioned in my introduction, as a minister of a particular local church, I tried to avoid dealing with Revelation as long as I could. It just seemed too difficult for me. After thirty years of preaching at the same church, I was encouraged by others to jump in and preach on Revelation. I did, and this book is one result of those sermons. Preachers do not need to avoid Revelation. Neither do we need large and complicated charts to understand it.

A Short Review

Before I look at the first few verses of Revelation chapter 1, I will review the principle of historical limitation that I described previously. Even though the Bible is written *for us,* not everything in the Bible is written *to us.* This is not being disrespectful to the Bible, nor does it deny that God through the ministry of the Holy Spirit can speak to us in his Word as we read it or hear it preached. It is simply being honest in recognizing that the Bible as a whole was not written directly to us. I will apply this to Revelation, but first I need to clarify a few things, and consider some significant points made by John in the first few verses of Revelation. Afterwards I will return to our main premise about how historical limitation applies to this text.

Apocalypse

The word "revelation" (apocalypse) means "revealed" and not hidden. Revelation means to unveil or uncover, not to hide and cover over. Think of an architect's drawing of a newly-proposed city hospital that is to be presented at a special fund-raising event. The drawing often is covered by a drape until the final moment the picture is to be revealed. The drapery is removed, and the picture of the proposed hospital is visible to the eyes of everyone present. Likewise, the purpose of the book of Revelation is not to hide truth but to reveal it. My goal is to dispel the mystery of the book by removing the drapery in order to reveal the events that were to take place during the apostolic age. Every Christian should approach Revelation with the expectation of uncovering its meaning and therefore understanding it. Jesus never intended that it remain a covered mystery to all generations down through history.

God's intention for us to comprehend Revelation is also reflected in John's words in verse 1 when he writes: "The Revelation of Jesus Christ, which God gave Him to show to His bond-servants the things which must soon take place." The word "show" demonstrates the intent of uncovering or exposing. John was told to show or display to the readers that which he received from Jesus Christ. The word show also means to show by means of a sign. John intends to show the readers through signs (metaphors) what will soon happen. John assumes that the readers will understand the meaning of the signs or metaphors. Once again, I say Revelation should not be a mystery.

Heeding the Words

Another underlying principle is that not only can the content of Revelation be understood, but it is also very important that it be understood. Later in verse 3, John demonstrates the importance of comprehending the book when he says: "Blessed is he who reads and those who hear the words of the prophecy, and heed the things which are written in it; for the time is near." As the original readers understood Revelation, they were responsible to heed and obey God as he spoke in the book. Understanding Revelation was important to the early readers so that they might know how to obey God. I believe the same is true for us in the twenty-first century.

Historical Limitation:
"The Time is Near"

Now, I will return to the main point of these first three verses of Revelation and to one of the keys to understanding the entire book. Notice in verses 1 and 3, John gives an example of historical limitation (restricting the events to the age of the apostles). In these verses, John was writing to the seven churches, which are identified in Revelation chapters 2 and 3. These were real churches in real cities with real people in those churches. The members of those churches had names, families, homes, jobs, and the common things we all have today that identify who we are. We tend to forget this when we think of the Bible as a book written only to us today.

Imagine yourself receiving this letter from the Apostle John by someone who carried it from John to the churches. Take, for example, the congregation at Philadelphia. The leader (or reader) of that congregation would have shared Revelation (a scroll) with the members living at that time in that particular church. Maybe he let the members read the original letter themselves. Maybe the letter was passed around from house to house. Maybe duplicates were made so the Christians would have their own copies. Regardless, the point is that the letter was written to a particular people at a particular time in history. It was written directly to them and only indirectly to us in the twenty-first century. When I read Revelation, I read what was directly written to someone else.

Notice that the words in verse 1 speak about the things "which must soon take place." Also notice the words in verse 3 where John writes "for the time is near." John makes clear the meaning of "soon" by using a second phrase, "for the time is near." He leaves no doubt as to his meaning. Now, I ask you, if you were hearing these words as a member of the church at Philadelphia, what would you think about the timing of the events predicted to occur in Revelation? What would have been your reaction as you were there in midst of the congregation? Well, I think all of those hearing or reading the words would have thought that Revelation was written to describe something that was to happen very soon, in the generation of the reader himself. The time was near.

The word "soon" or "shortly" is a translation from the Greek word *en tachei*. Luke uses this word when he describes Festus being in a hurry to leave Caesarea after the chief priests and the leading men of the Jews tried to bring charges against Paul. "Festus then answered that Paul was being kept in custody at Caesarea and that he himself was about to leave *shortly* [emphasis added]" (Acts 25:4). The Greek word for "near" is *engus*. Matthew uses this word to describe the nearness of summer following the springtime. "Now learn the parable from the fig tree: when its branch has already become tender and puts forth its leaves, you know that summer is *near* [emphasis added]" (Matt. 24:32).

To the church in Smyrna, John wrote in Revelation 2:10: "Do not fear what you are about to suffer. Behold, the devil is about to cast some of you into prison, so that you will be tested, and you will have tribulation for ten days. Be faithful until death, and I will give you the crown of life." Most interpreters will explain this text as something that was about to happen to the church at Smyrna. They are assuming the principle of historical limitation. John was not talking about something that was going to happen two thousand years in the future. We should assume that suffering did happen to the church at Smyrna. Persecution has happened to various generations down through the history of the church; however, I think it is only proper to apply this particular suffering to the church at Smyrna. I believe the church in that city took the language literally. They did not think, "Oh, the word soon must mean more than two thousand years into the future, so we have nothing to worry about." No, the text is historically limited. In Revelation 3:11 to the church at Philadelphia, we read: "I am coming quickly; hold fast what you have, so that no one will take your crown." The readers of these words knew that in some sense Christ was coming quickly in their own generation. In Revelation 6:10, the question is asked by recently martyred saints in heaven: "How long, O Lord, holy and true, will You refrain from judging and avenging our blood on those who dwell on the earth?" The answer to that question in the same chapter is "*a little while longer.*" Notice what John says in verse 11: "And there was given to each of them a white robe; and they were told that they should rest for a little while longer, until *the number* of their fellow servants and their brethren who were to be killed even as they had been, would be completed also." Here again, the picture is one of Christians who have just shed their blood for the faith and are in heaven asking God how long must they wait to see vengeance against their persecutors who are still on the earth. The answer is, "a little while longer." The answer is, in essence — soon.

A common argument against my position in regard to the time-restrictions is a reference to 2 Peter 3:8 where Peter says: "But do not let this one *fact* escape your notice, beloved, that with the Lord one day is like a thousand years, and a thousand years like a day." The argument goes as follows. God views time differently than we do, so when John makes a reference to "the time is near" or "soon," actually these terms could mean thousands of years. I don't believe that I need to spend much time refuting this argument. Following is part of Gentry's response:

> "In the first place, Peter is *talking about God*, whereas John is *giving directives to men*. Peter makes a theological statement regarding God and his perception of time; John provides an historical directive to men regarding their unfolding hardships.

We must not confuse theological truth about God with historical directives to men."[1]

If the martyred saints would not see vengeance shortly, then I have a real problem with the integrity of the text and the integrity of God. In my mind, a 2000-year delay would be a denial of the promise of God to the martyrs in heaven who were crying out for vengeance. Such a delay would nullify any hope of those Christians being delivered from the persecution of apostate (fallen away from the faith) Jews. If I do not interpret such an event as happening soon after Revelation was written, then God's promise is empty. How can anyone trust his promises? This is the reason I believe emphatically that the integrity of the entire Scriptures is at stake if I interpret these texts in any way other than being historically limited to the apostolic age.

Mistakes in Generations of the Past

Another example of historical limitation appears in the last chapter of Revelation. The time-restrictions appear both at the beginning and at the end of the book (and in the body of the book as well). In Revelation 22, John writes in five separate verses:

> "And he said to me, 'These words are faithful and true'; and the Lord, the God of the spirits of the prophets, sent His angel to show to His bond-servants the things which must soon take place" (v. 6).

> "And behold, I am coming quickly. Blessed is he who heeds the words of the prophecy of this book" (v. 7).

---

[1] Kenneth L. Gentry, Jr., *The Book of Revelation Made Easy* (American Vision Press: 2008), 41.

"Do not seal up the words of the prophecy of this book, for the time is near" (v. 10).

"Behold I am coming quickly, and My reward is with Me, to render to every man according to what he has done" (v. 12).

"He who testifies to these things says, 'Yes, I am coming quickly. Amen. Come, Lord Jesus'" (v. 20).

Think about it — these words have been interpreted by almost every generation since they were written as promises to be fulfilled in their own generation. This probably has been going on since the apostolic age. Most of us read them the same way in our own generation as those who read them in previous generations before us. For years I read them in the sense that the Second Advent of Christ is imminent. Maybe he will come today! Maybe he will come tomorrow!

Yet, at some point, it also dawned on me that probably for nearly two thousand years Christians have been reading these verses the same way I was reading them. The Second Advent did not happen — and it has not happened. All those generations that expected an imminent return of Christ did not see it happen. They were all wrong! Now take this to heart as I say it again. They were all wrong! I concluded that something was not right in my understanding of the imminent return of Christ. I had to reconsider whether my interpretation of the text was correct. If John was referring to the distant future, then as each generation before me was wrong, maybe I was wrong too. How could we all be wrong? That's when I discovered the principle of historical limitation in the Bible. These texts actually restricted the timing of these events to the apostolic age.

If you had lived — let's say 1500 years ago — would you have read these verses the same way as most people read them today? Would you have been wrong if you had interpreted these words as predicting an imminent return of Christ in your lifetime? What about — let's say 500 years ago — if you had been living then and had read these words, what would you have thought? What about 100 years ago? My point is, if we interpret these words "I am coming quickly" to mean the Second Advent of Christ, then either John is incorrect or John is deceiving us. Neither of these two options can be true. God forbid!

The only other solution is the one I am presenting in this book, which is that Revelation in these passages is not referring to the visible and personal return of Christ, but rather to the coming of Christ in judgment on Jerusalem in A.D. 70 using the instrument of the armies of Rome. The year 70 would have been soon for those living in the generation of the apostles, as it would have been for the readers sitting in the seven churches, or even as it would have been for the martyrs in heaven crying out for vengeance. The words of Revelation predicting the coming of Christ as happening soon should then be read as actually being true to the generation to whom it was written. Again, let me say that if this assertion is incorrect, then it creates an ethical problem for me with the Bible itself and makes me doubt the integrity of the Word of God. This is one reason I have written this book.

Defeating the Liberal Argument

One major criticism of the Bible by liberals is that the Bible cannot be true because apostles like Paul and John were expecting Christ to return in their day, and it did not happen. Liberals believe this is obvious from the language in the Bible. There are many other texts in the New Testament that present the same issue as found here in Revelation. For example, consider 1 John 2:18: "Children, it is the last hour; and just as you heard that antichrist is coming, even now many antichrists have appeared; from this we know that it is the last hour." Now if John here did not mean that the readers were living in the last hour, then he should have been clear about that.

His language certainly implies they were living in the last hour of something. If the last hour meant the end of the world, then we have a major problem. We would have to conclude that the Bible is in error since the end of the world did not come. This is the argument of liberals. It would appear that they win the argument. The Scriptures would be in error. The world did not end as Paul and John had predicted, and Christ did not return personally and visibly soon. However, we have an answer to their criticism. The answer is the principle of historical limitation.

Again, this does not mean that we no longer believe in the visible and personal coming of Christ. It just means that over the years, Christians have misinterpreted these words in Revelation and other books in the New Testament as referring to the Second Coming when actually they refer to the destruction of Jerusalem in A.D. 70. Jesus came again during the time period of A.D. 67–70 using the instrument of the Roman armies to bring destruction on the city of Jerusalem. This is the only way to resolve the problem raised by liberals. R. C. Sproul alludes to this in his book on Revelation, *The Last Days According to Jesus*.[1]

The same issue is found in the Gospel of Matthew. For example, in Matthew 24:29–41, Jesus pronounces woes on the Jews at Jerusalem. After describing a number of judgments that will happen to them, he concludes in verse 34: "Truly I say to you, all these things will come upon this generation." Here we have the destruction of Jerusalem predicted by Christ himself long before John penned the words of Revelation. Jesus informs the Jews that Jerusalem's end will come upon that generation. As a result, those disciples who heard Jesus' words could conclude with confidence

---

[1] R. C. Sproul, *The Last Days according to Jesus* (Grand Rapids: Baker, 2000).

that Christians suffering persecution at the hand of the Jews would be relieved of Jewish persecution in their own generation.

Jesus predicted the end of Jerusalem in the Gospel of Luke. "When He approached *Jerusalem*, He saw the city and wept over it, saying: 'If you had known in this day, even you, the things which make for peace! But now they have been hidden from your eyes. For the days will come upon you when your enemies will throw up a barricade against you, and surround you and hem you in on every side, and they will level you to the ground and your children within you, and they will not leave in you one stone upon another, because you did not recognize the time of your visitation'" (19:41–44). I believe those Jews who heard these words actually understood that this would happen in their own generation.

A Personal Example

Does the concept of historical limitation in the first few verses of Revelation seem difficult to understand or accept? I will use a personal example to help illustrate my point. If my wife were stranded on a mountainous highway without any gasoline in her car, she would probably call me on her cell phone to come and help her. If she were to call and request that I come quickly (for there are bears in these hills in northeast Tennessee), then I would probably say something to the effect that I am coming quickly. The time is near. I would hop into my SUV and drive to rescue her. What then would she expect of me? She would expect me to be there within a few minutes or maybe within a few hours depending on how far away she was from me. She would expect me to come very soon. That is the ordinary way we use these time references. Soon means soon. The phrase "the time is near" means that something is going to happen shortly. My point is that the first readers of Revelation, if we take these words and phrases literally, would have expected the events predicted in Revelation to happen quickly, at least in their own generation. These words are historically limited.

If my wife called me for help, and I were to show up over 2000 years later, then what would she think of me? Can you imagine me arriving 2000 years later and how she might respond? "Larry, where have you been? You said you were coming soon, and I have been waiting here for 2000 years. You're a joke! After forty years of marriage (actually at that time it would be 2040 years of marriage), I find out you are not trustworthy."

Now carry this example over to those who first read Revelation. If by "soon" or "the time is near," John meant a few hundred years into the future, or even a few thousand years into the twenty-first century, then what would the readers think? If I were sitting there listening to the letter being read with the hope of help coming soon, and then if I were to learn that "soon" meant 2000 years or more after I was dead, what would I think? I will tell you what I would think. I would say, "This thing called Christianity is a sham!" To this I can only respond as Paul did in Romans 9:14, "May it never be!" God forbid! Actually, to tell someone that relief of suffering is shortly to come — knowing that the relief is not coming soon — is cruel. That's all I can say — it is cruel! The good news is that neither John nor God is cruel. The help did come soon in that generation. Otherwise, I have a moral problem with both John and God. I hope the reader understands why, based upon the content of Revelation 1: 1–3, I do not see any other option but to believe that the events described in Revelation occurred in the generation of the apostles. My faith in the integrity of God depends on it.

Another Argument

Also, one more argument should be made at this juncture. It should be pointed out that even though most of Revelation is written in metaphorical language, these particular verses (1–3) are not. These verses should be read literally. That will not always be the case in Revelation. There are no pictures or metaphors here to interpret. There are no wild animals with seven heads and ten horns. I take John literally here for what he said, and I believe that the readers in the seven churches were comforted that some relief from their persecution would come quickly.

Four Different Views on the Book of Revelation

My view is not new. It is one of several common views held today. Revelation traditionally has been interpreted in one of four ways: 1) the historical view, 2) the idealist view, 3) the preterist view, and 4) the futurist view. The *historical view* interprets Revelation as if it covers major events in the history of the church down through the ages, at least up to the apostasy of the Roman Catholic Church and the Reformation. It gets a little confusing after that. The pope at times has been considered to be the Antichrist. This view considers Revelation as a panorama of church history since the apostolic age. The *idealist view* interprets Revelation apart from any historical events. It claims that Revelation is about spiritual principles without considering church history. It sees the events of the book as describing persecution and victory that the church always faces, regardless of any particular time in church history. Revelation is simply a book to comfort believers in any age. The *preterist view* (the word "preterist" in Latin means "gone by") interprets Revelation as if the major events in the book happened before the end of the apostolic age. This view holds that Revelation's main theme is the destruction of Jerusalem in A.D. 70 and the consequential relief of persecution against Christians of that age. However, the comfort given to early Christians can be applied to any age.

There is also a movement falsely associated with historical preterism that believes the Bible teaches that the resurrection of the dead, the final judgment, and the end of Satan — all of these events happened in A.D. 70. This is a small movement that I call the hyper-preterist view. I do not believe this. Some people, in order to distinguish my view from the hyper-preterist view, have renamed my preterist view as the partial-preterist view. I do not feel the need to do this since the radical hyper-preterist view has so few followers, and is contrary to historic Christian orthodoxy. So I will continue to use the word preterist as long as the reader understands that my views must be distinguished from hyper-preterist views. The *futurist view* interprets the events of Revelation as if they are yet to happen. The futurist view is very popular in some Bible-believing circles today.

As I have stated, I have adopted the preterist view, believing that Revelation applies primarily to the fall of Jerusalem in A.D. 70 and the events leading up to the end of that city. Obviously, I have a highly emotional commitment to this view. As I mentioned before, it is so important that to deny it, at least for me, is to deny the integrity of the Bible.

The Help of Josephus

It is helpful in the preterist approach to Revelation to have some knowledge of Jewish and Roman history of the first century. Providentially, that history was recorded by a man named Josephus in his *Wars of the Jews*. His complete writings are available to us in *The Works of Josephus*. Josephus is described as follows in *Eerdmans Handbook to the History of Christianity*:

"Josephus, the Jewish historian, was born in A.D. 37 of a priestly Jewish family. He was well educated, and followed the Pharisaic form of Judaism. In 64 he visited Rome as a member of a Jewish embassy. Although Josephus claimed to have advised against the armed revolt against the Romans during the Jewish revolt (A.D.

66–70) he commanded a Jewish force in Galilee with some success. Besieged at Jotapata, he was captured by the Romans, and then devoted his energies to helping the Romans and trying to persuade the remaining Jews to come to terms. After the end of the Jewish revolt, he went to Rome with Titus, and lived there until his death about A.D. 100. Josephus became a close friend of Emperors Vespasian and Titus, and took the family name, Flavius."

Josephus had a bird's-eye view of the events that happened in the destruction of Jerusalem, and he recorded those events in his book. As one reads from his works about the events of the fall of Jerusalem and compares them to the descriptions in Revelation, it becomes much easier to make sense of many of the mysterious metaphors found in it.

I believe we have no other option but to apply the principle of historical limitation to the first few verses of Revelation chapter 1. As we do this, in my mind, it is an inevitable conclusion that most of the events described in Revelation occurred in the apostolic age. They have already happened. Revelation describes those events in metaphorical form, and Josephus describes them from a historian's perspective in simple historical prose.

G. A. Henty

Another source one might find helpful in understanding the nature of the events that happened from A.D. 66–70 is the novel written by G A. Henty, *For The Temple: A Tale of the Fall of Jerusalem*,[1] written in the nineteenth century. This book chronicles the events of the fall of Jerusalem through the eyes of a young boy. It is a

---

[1] G A. Henty, *For The Temple: A Tale of the Fall of Jerusalem* (CreateSpace, 2010).

novel, but it is based on the history as recorded by Josephus. In Henty's novel, he helps the reader understand the life and times of those living during that particular era. He gives a vivid description of the war, the horrific conditions, the great suffering, and the final calamity of Jerusalem.

The Dating of the Book

Another important point pertinent to this discussion is the dating of the writing of Revelation. It is a historical fact that the city of Jerusalem was destroyed in A.D. 70 after some three and a half years of war with the Roman soldiers. No one disputes that. My interpretation is based upon the presupposition that Revelation was written before A.D. 70, and that it predicted the destruction of Jerusalem. If Revelation was written after 70, then the preterist theory collapses. It cannot be a prediction of Jerusalem's fall in 70 if the city had already been destroyed before Revelation was written.

The majority view of theologians today is that Revelation was written around A.D. 95 during the reign of the Roman Emperor Domitian, although the popularity of this position is changing. There are good men who hold different views on this topic. I believe Revelation was written before A.D. 70, and that it *had* to be written before A.D. 70. If the words of Revelation were not a prophecy of some major event shortly to happen, then I have a problem with the integrity of the writers and the integrity of God. In this case, they should not have used words like "shortly" or "soon." They were giving the Christians living at that time a false hope.

My position, drawn from the principle of historical limitation, is that the events of which John speaks must have happened in the apostolic age. Those occurrences must have been those that described the fall of Jerusalem. There is no other major event in the apostolic age that could be the subject of these prophecies. I do not have time to list all the arguments for the early dating of Revelation. If you want to study a defense of this position from a much more scholarly perspective, then I would recommend reading Kenneth Gentry's book on the dating of Revelation, *Before Jerusalem Fell: The Dating of the Book of Revelation*.[1] This was his doctoral thesis. He clearly lays out a convincing argument for the early dating of the book.

More Dating Arguments

As I will show in the next chapter, Revelation uses metaphors and in some places contains interpretations of its own metaphors. In these instances, I am not left in doubt as to the meaning of the metaphor since God interprets it himself. These interpretations give us hints in regard to the dating of the book. For example, in Revelation 11:8, John tells us the city which is mystically called Sodom and Egypt is actually "the place where also their Lord was crucified." This is obviously the city of Jerusalem in the apostolic age. I suppose the futurists could apply this verse to some reconstructed future Jerusalem, but that still would not be the place or city where our Lord was crucified 2000 years ago. The place where Jesus was crucified was the Jerusalem of the apostolic era. The city of Jerusalem was still standing when the book of Revelation was written. This supports the preterist view.

Also, in Revelation 17:9, this is another place where John interprets a metaphor: "Here is the mind of wisdom. The seven heads are seven mountains on which the woman sits." It is quite

---

[1] Kenneth L. Gentry, Jr., *Before Jerusalem Fell: Dating the Book of Revelation* (3d. ed.: Fountain Inn, S.C.: Victorious Hope, 2010). See also: John A. T. Robinson, *Redating the New Testament* (Philadelphia: Westminster, 1976).

obvious that anyone living in the time of John would have identified the seven mountains (hills) with the city of Rome. As we shall see, Rome had a part to play in the events described in Revelation. The ancient city of Rome was built on seven hills. The names of those hills were Aventine, Caelian, Capitoline, Esquiline, Palatine, Quirinal, and Viminal. To the early readers of Revelation, it would have been clear that the City of Seven Hills was the Rome that existed in their own day. This is another argument for the preterist view.

According to Josephus, the city of Jerusalem was destroyed in almost exactly forty-two months or in three and one-half years (from ca A.D. April 67 to ca August 70). Also, in Revelation 17:10, John speaks of seven kings. These kings can be matched with the first seven emperors of Rome.

Conclusion

As you read the rest of this book, you will notice how much easier it is to interpret the pictures and metaphors in Revelation if the events described therein have a reference to events that happened in the generation of those to whom John wrote. Jerusalem was the hub of Judaism. The Jews were persecuting Christians. "Saul was in hearty agreement with putting him [Stephen] to death. And on that day a great persecution began against the church in Jerusalem, and they were all scattered throughout the regions of Judea and Samaria, except the apostles" (Acts 8:1). If Jerusalem was destroyed, then the nemesis of Christians would be dealt a heavy blow.

Also, those of you who have been influenced by the futurist view can be relieved of many of your fears and anxieties. Revelation speaks of the fall of Jerusalem 2000 years ago. Revelation was predicting the relief of persecuted Christians by unbelieving Jews. Annihilate the hub and you end much of the persecution. The apostate Jews had a large presence in Asia Minor, the location of the seven churches. This was the comfort that John was communicating to the seven churches and to all other Christians of that era who would read or hear the book read. The response of Christians would be something similar to the response of the Allies in World War II when they took Berlin, thus ending the war in the major theater of Europe. It would be a time of joy and relief.

Again, does this mean the book of Revelation has no meaning for us in the twenty-first century as we read about those events that happened nearly 2000 years ago? Not at all. We can take comfort too. As God delivered his people from persecution when they cried out to him, we should believe that any generation to follow can pray the same way, and they too will see God answer their prayers. If there is evidence that God sent deliverance to those of the first generation of Christians, then other Christians living in different ages can be assured that he will answer their prayers also. My prayer is that someday the hopeless fear that pervades the modern church will be transformed into a kingdom-building hope.

3
COMING WITH THE CLOUDS

"BEHOLD, HE IS COMING WITH THE CLOUDS, and every eye will see Him, even those who pierced Him; and all the tribes of the earth will mourn over Him. So it is to be. Amen." (Rev. 1:7)

Introduction

If you have read the entirety of chapter 1 of Revelation, you may have a number of questions. You may think that Pastor Ball has put forth a good argument for the concept of historical limitation and has applied it well to the first few verses of chapter 1 (and then again you may not!). However, an additional challenge comes now. As you look ahead in chapter 1, you will read about Jesus coming again with the clouds. You will read about how all the tribes of the earth will mourn. You may ask how this could be anything but the Second Advent of Christ. You may ask what trick Pastor Ball will pull out of his magic hat this time. Well, as I hope you will see, there is no magic hat.

The first question is, how do I handle "he is coming with the clouds" in Revelation 1:7 as cited above? Does not "he is coming with the clouds" refer to the Second Advent? The second question is how can I limit the events to the apostolic period and to the land of Israel when John speaks in Revelation 1:7 of "all the tribes of the earth"? Does not "all the tribes of the earth" have a global reference rather than being restricted to the land of Israel in the apostolic age? These are excellent questions. My goal in this chapter is to answer them.

Answering the Two Questions

To answer the two questions above about the meaning of Jesus' coming on the clouds and the global reference to the earth, it is important to look at two more principles of interpretation. I believe these will help answer our questions. They will also be used as a basis to interpret the remainder of Revelation. It is important to consider methods and rules of interpretation prior to interpreting books of the Bible (or any book for that matter). Theologians call the study of these rules and methods of interpretations *hermeneutics*, which is the science of how to interpret texts of the Bible. It's a little like discussing the rule book before you play the game. I have already looked at the principle of historical limitation in chapter 1. I will now look at the *principle of literalism* and the *principle of comparing Scripture with Scripture*. Once I review these two principles of how we interpret the Bible, then I will return to answer the questions that I just posed to the reader. Since I have already considered the principle of historical limitation (principle number 1), I will call these principles numbers 2 and 3.

Principle No. 2:
Literalism

I am known as a conservative, Bible-believing Christian. Bible-believing Christians hold the view that the Bible is the infallible, inerrant Word of God. However, they are also known as those who take the Bible literally. This has almost become a badge of fidelity to God. I believe that God created the world in six literal twenty-four hour days. I believe that Adam was a real man and not just a character in an allegorical story. I believe the Flood was real. I believe it covered the whole earth, and that Noah, his family, and the animals were rescued by an ark, which Noah built. Some folks would consider me naive for believing such things, but actually, it is much easier to believe that a personal God created the world in six literal days than it is to believe that the world came into existence from a large explosion and evolved into its present state over millions (or billions) of years. Faith is necessary for both views. It is not a question of science versus faith, but a question of faith versus faith. The question is, whose faith is true faith? I also believe that Jesus performed the miracles recorded in the Gospels. I believe Jesus died and was raised from the dead and now lives at the right hand of God the Father "from thence he will come to judge the quick [living] and the dead" (as the Apostle's Creed states it). I say these things not only as a minister of the Gospel, but also as a college-trained mathematician and scientist.

However, as I matured in the Christian faith, I began to reconsider the position that I must always interpret the Bible literally. I concluded that even though I do take most of the Bible texts literally (for example, Jesus turning the water into wine), yet there are texts I cannot take literally. It would be contrary to the teaching of the Bible itself to interpret all Scriptures literally. Actually, Jesus teaches that it would be a major mistake to interpret all of his words literally. For example, in John 2:18–21, when Jesus was cleansing the temple, we read: "The Jews then said to Him, 'What sign do You show us as your authority for doing these things?' Jesus answered them, 'Destroy this temple, and in three days I will raise it up.' The Jews then said, 'It took forty-six years to build this temple, and will you raise it up in three days?' But He was speaking of the temple of His body." The Jews thought Jesus was speaking of the literal Jewish Temple, but he was speaking of his physical body. There was a meaning behind the meaning of the literal image. Jesus must not be taken literally here. Not everything written in the Bible should be taken literally.

In John 3:3, Jesus said to Nicodemus, "Truly, truly, I say to you, unless one is born again he cannot see the kingdom of God." Nicodemus responded by asking if a man could enter a second time into his mother's womb. This was a response of a man who took the words of Jesus literally. However, there was a meaning behind the literal image. Jesus was speaking of the new birth in the hearts of men by the power of the Holy Spirit. Not everything in the Bible should be taken literally.

Jesus said, "I am the vine, you are the branches." (John 15:5). He said, "I am the Light of the world." (John 8:12). He said, "I am the good shepherd." (John 10:11). All of these have meanings behind the obvious literal ones. We never take them literally or at face value. As I approach the Bible, I must confess that I cannot and should not interpret all the texts literally. I certainly cannot do this in Revelation. For example, there I find "a great red dragon having seven heads and ten horns, and on his heads were seven diadems. And his tail swept away a third of the stars of heaven and threw them to the earth" (12:3–4). It is a real challenge to take this literally. I also find in Revelation "the woman drunk with the blood of the saints, and with the blood of the witnesses of Jesus" (17:6). I don't think a person can get drunk by drinking blood. I would imagine they would become very sick or die.

Another passage in Revelation that cannot be taken literally is as follows: "The city is laid out as a square, and its length is as great as the width; and he measured the city with the rod, fifteen hundred miles; its length and width and height are equal" (21:16). This is a reference to the New Jerusalem, and I contend that we cannot take it literally. Space shuttles go about 300 miles high above the earth. Fifteen hundred miles is five times higher than the height a space shuttle reaches. These pictures are metaphors. Once again, they should not be taken literally. We will apply the principle of literalism (or maybe more properly it could be called the principle of non-literalism) as we move through the book.

When I was a young Christian, I read the Bible literally. For example, in Matthew 17: 20, Jesus said: "For truly I say to you, if you have faith the size of a mustard seed, you will say to this mountain,

'Move from here to there,' and it will move; and nothing will be impossible to you." I remember sitting on the front porch of my home in West Virginia, looking at two large mountains in front of me, thinking that if I had enough faith, I would see those mountains move. I tried! I was serious about it. I believed the mountains would move. I believed as much I could, but they never moved. So much for literalism!

Davy Crockett was a childhood hero of mine. Who can forget Fess Parker playing that rugged role? Davy in real life became a folk hero of the American pioneer frontier. He once described himself as "half horse, half alligator, and a little attached snapping turtle." Even as a child I did not take this literally. Likewise, in reading Revelation, the principle of literalism must be kept in mind.

Principle No. 3:
Comparing Scripture with Scripture

Another important approach to the Bible is to compare Scripture with Scripture. This principle will also help to answer the two preceding questions. When some particular meaning of a text is difficult to understand, Bible interpreters usually follow certain procedures. First, they may study the original languages of the text. Secondly, they may study its context. What thoughts precede and follow the text? And lastly, they may compare the text with others in the Bible. For example, they may compare a text in the book of Ephesians with a text in the book of Romans. This latter procedure is what I am calling the principle of *comparing Scripture with Scripture*.

One main tenet of this principle is that the more obscure or difficult texts should always be interpreted in light of the less difficult (or clearer) texts. No doubt, Revelation generally will be the more difficult text. Since the book contains a great deal of content from the Old Testament, it will be helpful to compare passages in

Revelation with similar passages in the Old Testament, as well as with other passages in the New Testament. It has been estimated that of the 404 verses in Revelation, 278 of them contain allusions to the Old Testament.

As a general example of interpreting the more obscure text in light of the clearer text, consider the following example. In regard to Jesus' teaching as related to the legitimacy of divorce, he said in the Gospel of Mark: "Whoever divorces his wife and marries another woman commits adultery against her" (10:11). Mark does not mention any exception here. His concern was the abuse of divorce, not the exceptions. However, if we compare what Matthew said about the same issue, we find Jesus actually spoke about an exception. "Whoever sends his wife away, let him give her a certificate of divorce; but I say to you that everyone who divorces his wife, except for the reason of unchastity [fornication], makes her commit adultery; and whoever marries a divorced woman commits adultery" (Mat. 5:31–32). Matthew records the full statement by Christ. By comparing Scripture with Scripture, I get a better picture of when divorce might be legitimate. My point is simply that I must always be careful to compare various Scriptures before I decide what a particular text teaches. Now, I will take the principles of both literalism and that of comparing Scripture with Scripture, and use them to answer the preceding two questions.

Question No. 1:
Coming with the Clouds

The first question I mentioned above relates to the language previously cited which describes Jesus as COMING WITH THE CLOUDS (Rev. 1:7). As we shall see, this image of God in the clouds appears in the Old Testament as well, so indicated by the capitalized words here in verse 7.

As I traditionally understood this verse, it appeared to contradict my previous point that Jesus was coming soon. Surely, this is about some future time when Jesus will return to judge the whole earth. Surely, this is a description of the Second Advent. How can I reconcile this with the teaching that Jesus came in the apostolic age? If the teaching of a passage in the Bible is unclear, then we need to compare that passage with other biblical passages that use the same language. As I understand how language is used in other texts, then I can compare the other usages with the text before me. This is what I intend to do here. I will throw in a few Greek words (to impress the reader of my Greek repertoire).

First, let me state that I believe there will be a visible Second Advent of Christ. At least two passages in the New Testament make this clear. The first speaks of Jesus descending from heaven with a shout, and the second speaks of Jesus returning again on the clouds as he left this earth on the clouds:

> "For the Lord Himself will descend from heaven with a shout, with the voice of *the* archangel and with the trumpet of God, and the dead in Christ will rise first" (1Thes. 4:16).

> "And after He had said these things, He was lifted up while they were looking on, and a cloud received Him out of their sight ...This Jesus, who has been taken up from you into heaven, will come in just the same way as you have watched Him go into Heaven" (Acts. 1:9,11).

These texts do provide a basis for the hope of the Second Advent of Christ which will be visible and personal. Thus, I hold firmly to the traditional Christian belief in the Second Advent.

However, some comings of Christ are used in the Scriptures to refer to Christ coming in judgment, not personally and visibly. I call this an invisible coming of Christ. Christ comes to bring forth his anger against his enemies (sometimes his own people), and he often does this by using another nation as the instrument to carry out his wrath. This is another type of coming. This is certainly true of God in the Old Testament where we see not a visible return but a return nevertheless — in time and space before the Second Advent of Christ. The point I am making here is simply that this image of God or Christ coming with the clouds, or riding on the clouds, is used in two different ways in the Bible. Sometimes it refers to the Second Advent of Christ, and sometimes it refers to an invisible and intermediate coming in judgment before the Second Advent.

The question in Revelation is which of the two options reflects the language here? Remember, the context tells the reader that the events spoken of in Revelation chapter 1 were to happen soon. Since Jesus did not come personally and visibly at anytime that could be considered "soon," then the only other option is that he came invisibly in judgment. This fits well with the interpretation that the events in Revelation correspond with the destruction of Jerusalem in A.D. 70, and that Christ came on the clouds to bring judgment on Jerusalem using the instrument of the Roman armies. Again, not all biblical texts should be interpreted literally.

Biblical Examples of Judgment by Other Nations

The precedent of God using a pagan nation to judge his own people is a pattern in the Old Testament. In the book of Habakkuk, God used the Chaldeans to bring judgment on his people. He punished Judah using the instrument of another nation. "Look among the nations! Observe! Be astonished! Wonder! Because I am doing something in your days — you would not believe if you were told. For behold, I am raising up the Chaldeans, that fierce and impetuous people who march throughout the earth to seize dwelling places which are not theirs" (Hab.1:5–6).

Notice in Matthew 23:37–38, Jesus speaks of the coming judgment of Jerusalem during the generation of the apostles.

"Jerusalem, Jerusalem, who kills the prophets and stones those who are sent to her! How often I wanted to gather your children together, the way a hen gathers her chicks under her wings, and you were unwilling. Behold, your house is being left to you desolate!" Then finally, Jesus says in verse 39: "For I say to you, from now on you will not see Me until you say, BLESSED IS HE WHO COMES IN THE NAME OF THE LORD!" In this text, Jesus was associating his coming with the destruction of Jerusalem, and speaking to the Jews who lived there. He was referring to his coming in judgment on the city of Jerusalem using the Roman armies.

God's Coming On the Clouds

In Matthew 26:63–64 there is a heated conversation between Jesus and the high priest. After the high priest demanded that Jesus "tell us whether You are the Christ, the Son of God" (v. 63), Jesus responded to the high priest: "You have said it yourself; nevertheless I tell you, hereafter you will see THE SON OF MAN SITTING AT THE RIGHT HAND OF POWER and COMING ON THE CLOUDS OF HEAVEN" (v. 64).

The point I wish to make is that Jesus was talking to the high priest, a particular individual living during the year of Christ's death. These words are historically limited. Jesus did not speak these words to me or to any of us living in the present time. He was telling the high priest that soon, before the high priest died, he would see the results of Jesus' ascension to the throne of God. This coming of Jesus on the clouds would be evident when the high priest witnessed the armies of Rome coming over the walls of Jerusalem.

The image of coming on the clouds in judgment is also common in the Old Testament. In Isaiah 19:1–2, Isaiah speaks of judgment against Egypt in the imagery of God coming on the clouds. "The oracle concerning Egypt. Behold, *the Lord is riding on a swift cloud* [emphasis added] and is about to come to Egypt; the idols of Egypt will tremble at His presence, and the heart of the Egyptians will melt within them. So I will incite Egyptians against Egyptians; and they will fight against his brother and each against his neighbor, city against city and kingdom against kingdom" (vs. 1–2). Notice that Isaiah speaks of the Lord "coming to Egypt" riding on a swift cloud, and how Egypt "will tremble at His presence." This obviously was not a visible coming of God. God is a spirit and has not a body like men. God did not ride clouds literally in the Old Testament, but the Bible uses such language for effect. It symbolizes the greatness of God. God did not judge Egypt by making a personal and visible appearance. He did it by creating tension between their tribes and kingdoms, whereby they fought and destroyed each other. This is how he came riding on the clouds.

In Psalm 104:1–3 we read: "Bless the Lord, O my soul! O Lord my God, You are very great; You are clothed with splendor and majesty, covering Yourself with light as with a cloak, stretching out heaven like a tent curtain. He lays the beams of His upper chambers in the waters; *He makes the clouds His chariot* [emphasis added]; He walks upon the wings of the wind; He makes the winds His messengers, flaming fire His ministers." Here, the language is obviously not to be taken literally.

In summary, the picture of God or Christ coming with the clouds or riding on the clouds is used in two different ways in the Bible. Sometimes it refers to the Second Advent of Christ, and sometimes to an intermediate coming in judgment using an instrument on earth to accomplish God's purposes. The question in Revelation 1:7 is which of the two options is meant by the language here? Remember, the context tells us that the events spoken of in Revelation chapter 1 were to happen soon. Since Jesus did not come personally and visibly soon, the only other option is that he came invisibly in judgment. This fits very well with my thesis that the events in Revelation correspond with the destruction of Jerusalem in A.D. 70, and that Christ came on the clouds to bring judgment on Jerusalem through the instrument of the Roman armies. This answers the first question.

Question No. 2:
The Meaning of the Word "Earth" in Revelation

I will answer the second question by using the principle of *comparing Scripture with Scripture* and speaking to the issue of what is meant by the word "earth" in verse 7. This too is critical in interpreting Revelation as a whole. How should we treat the use of the word earth in this verse? At first glance it would appear that earth means the whole earth in a global sense (as seen from the moon). This is how I have been taught to read the word earth. However, it is interesting that the Greek word translated earth can also be translated "land."

The same Greek word translated in Rev.1:7 as earth (*ge* in the Greek) is translated in other places in the New Testament and Revelation as land (*ge* in the Greek). For example, the same Greek word for earth in verse 7 is also used in the translation of the following passage: "Get up, take the Child and His mother, and go into the *land* [emphasis added] of Israel; for those who sought the Child's life are dead. So Joseph got up, took the Child and His mother, and came into the *land* [emphasis added] of Israel" (Matt. 2:20–21). Joseph had been in Egypt to deliver Jesus from death. It would be confusing if the Bible used the word earth here rather than the word land.

Note a further demonstration of this double use of the Greek word *ge*. Later in Revelation, *ge* is translated as the word land. "He placed his right foot on the sea and his left on the *land* [emphasis added] …Then the angel whom I saw standing on the sea and on the *land* [emphasis added] lifted up his right hand to heaven . . ." (Rev. 10:2, 5).

It is similar to the English word "geography." The word geography can be used in two separate ways. The word geography comes from two Greek words: *ge,* which as just noted, means earth or land, and *graphikos* which means to write (graphics) or to describe. The word geography can be defined as either a study of the earth (as seen from the moon) or a study of a portion of the earth — the land (for example, the land of the country in which you live), depending on the context.

"All of the tribes of the earth will mourn over Him. So it is to be. Amen" (1:7). There were twelve tribes in the land of Israel. Israel was divided into twelve parts, one for each tribe. It is only natural when we see the word "tribes" that we should think of the land of Israel rather than the global land of the whole earth. The Old Testament is mostly an account about the twelve tribes of Israel. Jerusalem was the religious center of the tribes of Israel. The tribes of Israel did mourn as a result of the judgment of Christ as they saw the Roman Army coming to destroy Jerusalem.

In Revelation 1:7b, we also read "and every eye will see him, even those who pierced Him." If I interpret this to mean that every eye on the global earth will see him, then it contradicts the identification of *those who pierced him.* If I interpret "every eye" to mean the eyes of the Jews then present in Jerusalem during the death of Christ, then this makes more sense. Remember what Peter preached to the Jews on the day of Pentecost: "this *Man,* delivered over by the predetermined plan and foreknowledge of God, you nailed to a cross by the hands of godless men and put *Him* to death" (Acts 2:23). The eyes of those who pierced him were the eyes of the Jews still living in Jerusalem, who were responsible for the death of Christ. These were the eyes of those living in the apostolic period.

If I take this literally, then it seems reasonable to interpret the words of John to mean that those unbelieving Jews in Jerusalem, who actually put Jesus to death, using the Romans leaders as instruments, would see him coming with the clouds. Indeed, they did! Those who crucified Jesus saw the destruction of Jerusalem. They saw Jesus riding on the clouds. In this catastrophe, the testimony of Christ that he was the Son of God, was demonstrated to be true. The tribes now mourned over Christ (v. 7). Christ was vindicated!

Thus, if I translate the word earth as land in Rev. 1:7, it fits in well with the context of chapter 1, and especially with the principle of historical limitation. The principle of comparing Scripture with Scripture allows me to do this. Revelation 1:7 would thus read: "BEHOLD, HE IS COMING WITH THE CLOUDS, and every eye will see Him, even those who pierced Him; and all the tribes of the *land* [emphasis added] will mourn over Him, So it is to be. Amen." This answers the second question above.

Principle, No. 4: The Literary Device of a Metaphor

Before I move on to some of the more difficult texts in Revelation, there is one more principle that needs to be understood. I call it the *literary device of a metaphor*. Thus far I have referred on occasion to the word "metaphor." The English dictionary defines a metaphor as "a figure of speech in which a word or phrase is applied to an object or action to which it is not literally applicable." A metaphor is an image, and it represents or symbolizes something that could be said in a simple statement. A metaphor has two parts, the basic truth to be communicated and the illustration or image that helps us understand the basic truth.

The word metaphor comes from two Greek words: *meta* which means "alongside of" and *pherein* which means to "transport" or "carry." Literally, a metaphor is an image that has been transported from a basic truth. For example, I recently heard one of my granddaughters (three years old) say to her younger sister (one year old), "hold your horses," when she was trying to encourage her sister to be patient. No doubt she had heard this from her mother and father. "Hold your horses" cannot be taken literally because my one-year-old granddaughter has no literal horses to hold. The basic truth was, be patient. The illustration or metaphor was "hold your horses."

A metaphor is a more exciting and imaginative way to say something simple. Remember with a metaphor, the reader generally must not take the image literally as a substitute for the simple truth. The image may be true, but it should not nullify or become a substitute for the basic truth to be communicated. This negates the whole purpose of a metaphor. As we shall see in Revelation, sometimes metaphors can be difficult to understand. To what is John referring when he uses such strange language? This will be a question I will ask throughout this book.

God has chosen in most of Revelation to use metaphors. In the latter part of the opening chapter of the book, God used a metaphor which I will examine shortly. Here in chapter 1, not only does he use this device, but happily, he interprets it for us so that we understand its meaning. This is almost like a trial run. It would seem that God thinks I need an example of a metaphor before I move into the main body of the book. It is a template for me to follow as I move through Revelation. Once I see how this is used here, then I will have some idea of how to interpret the metaphors I will meet later where, sadly, God does not give me the interpretation. I will be left on my own to search out the meaning of the images using my four principles of interpretation to help me understand the meaning of the metaphor or the illustration used to communicate a simple truth.

In Revelation 1:12–20 seven lampstands are introduced, and in the middle of the lampstands there is "one like a son of man." He holds seven stars, and "out of His mouth came a sharp two-edged sword; and His face was like the sun shining in it strength" (v. 16). This is the metaphor. Later in this passage I am given the meaning of the image. "As for the mystery of the seven stars which you saw in my right hand, and the seven golden lampstands; the seven stars are the angels of the seven churches, and the seven lampstands are the seven churches" (v. 20). There is here both a metaphor and the interpretation of the metaphor. The image of the seven stars points me to the seven angels (ministers or readers) of the seven lampstands. The seven lampstands are the seven churches.

Another important point here that needs to be made is that we should pay attention to the words in Revelation 1:20, "As for the mystery . . . ." This is a way of introducing the metaphor's explanation which tells me that God himself uses metaphors, and these metaphors need interpretation, which here, God himself interprets. There is no better interpreter of a metaphor than God.

This is a fourth principle of interpretation needed to understand Revelation. The reader must understand the literary device of a metaphor, and here in chapter 1, not only does God give a metaphor but he interprets its meaning as well. It is as if God were saying, "Look — this is the way to interpret Revelation." Don't use literalism when the language is metaphorical. Look for the meaning behind the meaning.

Conclusion

My principle of historical limitation has been put to the test. In chapter 2 of my book, I concluded that the events in Revelation happened in the apostolic age. However, Revelation 1:7 seemed to present some problems with that interpretation since it speaks of Christ coming on the clouds and uses the language of all the tribes of the earth. These appeared to negate my position. Yet, they do not pose a problem if we understand a few other principles of interpretation. I presented to you the fact that we cannot interpret everything in the Bible literally. Also, we must always compare Scripture with Scripture. By applying these two principles to the two questions, I believe these principles of interpretation adequately helped to answer them.

Finally, I looked at one more principle of interpretation that will be useful as we move on into the body of Revelation. This principle deals with the use of a metaphor. Revelation is written in mostly metaphorical language. We saw in the concluding part of chapter 1 that Jesus used the metaphors of the stars and the lampstands. Not only did he use a metaphor, but he interpreted it for us as well. As we move further into the mysterious language of Revelation, we will seldom have Jesus' explanation of various metaphors. We will have to interpret them on our own, and this poses a challenge. However, I think by using the metaphor of the stars and lampstands here and interpreting it for us, Jesus is preparing us to deal with the many future metaphors in Revelation. On a few occasions in future chapters, Jesus will again interpret a metaphor for the reader, but on the whole, the interpretation will be left to the reader.

Thus, I am finished with examining chapter 1 of Revelation. There are a number of texts in this chapter I have not covered, but remember, this book is not a verse-by-verse commentary. It is a primer to introduce you to Revelation. The four principles I have presented thus far are tools that I have learned after spending over forty years in the ministry and studying the Bible almost every week in order to preach and teach on the Lord's Day. I have used the first three principles here in chapters 1 of Revelation — historical limitation, literalism, and comparing Scripture with Scripture. We also examined the fourth principle relating to the use of the literary device of a metaphor. The character of a metaphor will become extremely helpful as we proceed into the more mysterious language of Revelation after chapters 2 and 3. But first things first! In chapters 2 and 3 of Revelation, I will examine the letters to the seven churches.

4
THE LETTERS TO THE SEVEN CHURCHES

"To the angel of the church in Ephesus write . . . ." (Rev 2:1)

Introduction

Chapters 2 and 3 of Revelation include the letters of John to the seven churches. A great deal has been written on this material over the centuries by godly Christian men. Therefore, my coverage will be limited. You can find many superb commentaries that deal with these letters.

Chapters 2–3 are not written in metaphorical language, although they do contain some metaphors. The language is not highly mysterious as are other parts of Revelation. The points that John makes are fairly straight-forward. God included these letters in Revelation for a reason, and I think I should cover not only some of their content but should also ask what function these letters have as part of the book as a whole. In what follows, I will state the relationship of the letters to the overall theme of Revelation, and then I will look to some degree at the content of the letters. One problem of interpreting Scripture is taking texts out of context. To consider the seven letters apart from the context of Revelation as a whole does an injustice to them. Keep this in mind as I look at the letters individually.

These seven letters share a common structure. Each contains a salutation or greeting. Following that, some attribute of Christ is mentioned that pertains to the issues in each particular church. For example, the church at Pergamum was tolerating false doctrine. The letter to this church begins by presenting an image of Christ as "The

One who has the sharp two-edged sword says" (Rev. 2:12a). Probably this is referring to the Word of God as a way to deal with false doctrine in the church. After Christ's attributes are applied to each church, Jesus then points out the positive qualities of each. Next, he reminds the churches of their serious problems. A warning is given to each church with the exception of Smyrna and Philadelphia; of these churches nothing negative is said. On the other hand, there is nothing good to say about the church at Laodicea. Jesus concludes with words of encouragement to each church, reminding them of God's blessing that await those who repent. Finally, he ends each letter with the words, "He who has an ear, let him hear what the Spirit says to the churches."

Theme of Revelation

It is evident that the seven churches were suffering persecution. This came from both Rome and the unbelieving Jews. It would seem that both Jerusalem and Rome were actually in charge of what happened in the world of the seven churches. The Jews had a major presence in the area of Asia Minor where the churches were located. Unbelief and paganism were the twin gods ruling over their world.

However, John reminds the saints there that things are different than what they appear. Jesus is on his throne. "And from Jesus Christ, the faithful witness, and the firstborn of the dead, and the ruler of the kings of the earth. To Him who loves us and released us from our sins by His blood" (Rev. 1:5a). This was a bold statement to the churches living in the midst of the hubris of Jerusalem and the arrogance of Rome. Actually, Jesus ruled both Rome and Jerusalem. They were pawns in his hands. Jesus is the Ruler of all the kings of the earth! "The king's heart is *like* channels of water in the hand of the Lord; he turns it wherever he wishes" (Proverbs 21:1).

As we have just read, Jesus is the "faithful witness." His words are always true. He is the "firstborn from the dead." This is a reference to his resurrection and assumes his ascension to the throne of God. Thus, John is telling the seven churches, that according to the words of Jesus and contrary to all other evidence, he is alive and sitting on his throne. He rules all the nations on the earth. Christians in every age must never lose faith in this fact, no less than those of the apostolic age who needed to be comforted by this truth.

God's people were experiencing persecution, especially at the hands of the apostate Jews. Some were to be cast into prison and some had died. John spoke to the churches about their persecution by those apostate Jews, referring to himself as "your brother and fellow partaker in the tribulation and kingdom and perseverance *which are* in Jesus" (1:9a). Examples of the persecution of the churches are mentioned in the seven letters. John speaks of enduring perseverance (2:3), suffering in prison (2:10), the death of Antipas (2:13), and holding fast (2:25). He does not mention Rome at all, but twice mentions persecution by the Jews.

This persecution is a major theme of Revelation. John's letter was to comfort the suffering people of God by reminding them of the Kingship of Christ. Contrary to what they saw on earth and contrary to the claims of both Rome and Jerusalem, John affirms that Jesus is King, and that all kings on earth will bow before him. Even the apostate Jews "will bow down at your feet" (3:9). Contrary to what they thought about the persecution they faced, nothing happened apart from the hand of a loving God who was and is in control of all things. God was concerned about their suffering, and he came to bring vengeance on their enemies. They are the people of God. His words gave comfort: "and He has made us *to be* a kingdom, priests to His God and Father — to Him *be* the glory and the dominion forever and ever. Amen" (1:6). As the King of kings, unto Jesus belongs glory and dominion forever and ever. Eternal glory did not belong to Caesar or to the powers in Jerusalem.

Regardless of what they saw and heard, John assured them that all power and all authority was and is in the hands of Jesus. No one can rule on earth apart from his permission, and no one can remain a ruler on earth apart from His consent. There is no king greater than Christ Jesus, and he is truly the reigning King. This is no less true now than it was when Revelation was written. What comforting words!

In chapter 1 John told them that Jesus was "coming with the clouds," meaning that they should be comforted because relief from the persecution of the apostate Jews was on the way. Revelation is a book of comfort for God's people in the midst of their suffering and tribulation. It is in this context that the letters to the seven churches should be read.

The Calling to Suffer

It also should be noticed that even though relief was on the way, Christians in the seven churches were reminded that they must endure suffering in this world. Peter spoke of the suffering that came to the churches of the early Christians in 1 Peter 4:12–13. "Beloved, do not be surprised at the fiery ordeal among you, which comes upon you for your testing, as though some strange thing were happening to you, but to the degree that you share the sufferings of Christ, keep on rejoicing, so that also at the revelation of His glory you may rejoice with exaltation." Hope in the future does not negate suffering in the present. Christians must not only prepare for deliverance, but for suffering as well.

Judgment Begins with the Household of God

The seven churches needed to know something else important. Peter also warned in his first epistle: "For it is time for judgment to begin with the household of God; and if *it begins* with us first, what *will be* the outcome for those who do not obey the gospel of God?" (4:17). Note that judgment begins with the household of God. As John spoke to the churches about Christ's coming in judgment upon Jerusalem, he first reminded them of what Peter had already said. They needed to get their own house in order. God expects faithfulness from his church. If the church (in this case the seven churches) is not remaining faithful to Christ, then they need to shape up or face discipline by God. John admonished the churches concerning what they must do; the churches must return to holiness. They claimed they were not of the world, but sometimes they acted very worldly. It should not have been this way.

The Church:
Sometimes Pitiful

In my forty years in the ministry, I found the most delightful and wonderful people on earth in God's church. The churches where I served as pastor were full of godly people who loved the Lord Jesus Christ and were full of good deeds in their lives. They were indeed a special people. I could tell they were God's handiwork.

However, there were also problems in those churches. In addition to the particular church I pastored, I also had partial oversight of a number of churches in my denomination, and I can testify that in all of them there were difficulties. I have seen false teaching, adultery, addiction to pornography, lying, drunkenness, suicide, homosexuality, and numerous other sins. I have seen churches divided, and I have seen churches split. If I were to concentrate on what was wrong with the church, I might say that it is a pitiful place. Indeed, many churches today are like salt that has lost its savor. They are good for nothing but to be thrown out and trampled under the feet of men. Most of the seven churches had serious problems. As we shall see, John went as far as calling the church at Sardis a dead church.

The church down through the ages has varied in her commitment to Christ. It varies even from individual church to individual church. Sometimes the church can become so corrupt that it can hardly even be called a church. The Westminster Confession of Faith was written in the seventeenth century in London, England, at Westminster Abbey by godly men from all over Great Britain. In chapter 25, Section 5, they wrote:

> "The purest churches under heaven are subject both to mixture and error; and some have so degenerated, as to become no churches of Christ, but synagogues of Satan. Nevertheless, there shall always be a church on earth, to worship God according to his will."

However, even today if a church still believes in the Bible as the final authority, it may be irrelevant to the culture. The modern church has a pitiful influence on the world. As there has been an explosion of mega-churches and contemporary worship, there has been no corresponding influence on the culture. Where true reformation comes, there will be a godly change in the culture. When I think about the modern church scene, I can only conclude — except for the shining lights that do exist in some places — the church as a whole is most pitiful.

The same things I have said above could be said about the seven churches to whom John writes. They were a mixture of the good, the bad, and the ugly. John first pointed out the good he observed, and then the bad and the ugly. This is a good approach for all of us as we deal with others in personal relationships. A wise man points out the positive qualities of others first, and then notes their problems.

Lastly, where it was needed, John called them to repentance. Repentance was their hope. Judgment begins with the household of God, and it had to begin with its members. The seven churches had to root out what was sinful, and then they would be ready for both persecution and the blessings that Christ would bring with his coming on the clouds. The fact that God is sovereign was a great comfort to those early believers. Even their suffering did not happen apart from his holy and good will. Following are a few pastoral comments about the seven churches looking at their positive and negative qualities. Also, I will note the warnings and encouragements given by Christ in Revelation.

The Letter to the Church at Ephesus

> "I know your deeds and your toil and perseverance, and that you cannot tolerate evil men, and you put to the test those who call themselves apostles, and they are not, and you found them *to be* false; and you have perseverance and have endured for My name's sake, and have not grown weary" (Rev. 2:2–3).

> "Yet this you do have, that you hate the deeds of the Nicolaitans, which I also hate" (Rev. 2:6).

The Ephesus church was known for good works and resilience. They would hang in there when others would have quit. They were also known for church discipline. They did not tolerate false prophets, especially a cult leader whose followers were called Nicolaitans. As I identify the various problems of the churches, I will establish the fact that the most common problem was some type of idolatry that led to sexuality immorality. The latter may be just a metaphor for spiritual immorality, but I am inclined to think that spiritual idolatry leads to physical immorality. This was probably true of the Nicolaitans. Apostasy starts with substituting an idol for God, and then ends in fornication, adultery, and homosexuality. There is nothing new under the sun! "But I have *this* against you, that you have left your first love" (2:4).

It may seem strange that Christians can have good works and practice church discipline and yet leave their first love, which is the love of Jesus Christ. However, according to this letter, it can happen. The church can do many good deeds and practice church discipline for the sake of the name of Christ and yet not love him as she once did. Sometimes, our Christian duties become perfunctory, and we do not focus on the person of Christ as the great love of our life. "Therefore remember from where you have fallen, and repent and do the deeds you did at first; or else I am coming to you and will remove your lampstand out of its place — unless you repent" (2:5).

These are strong words. The church had fallen. The church was not doing the deeds she had done when she first loved Christ. The church needed to repent. If she failed to change, she would be removed from the city of Ephesus. The Kingdom of God sometimes would be much better served if some churches were removed from this earth. I have known some like this. "He who has an ear, let him hear what the Spirit says to the churches. To him who overcomes, I will grant to eat of the tree of life which is in the Paradise of God" (2:7).

Only God can give the church ears to hear, yet the church bears the responsibility to repent. If the church repents of her sins, she will be ready to enjoy the promises of God. The tree of life image was taken from the Garden of Eden, but undoubtedly it was a reference to the person of Christ himself. After the church heard this indictment, she should not have been discouraged. Then as now, if the church will turn from her sins, God will forgive and bless her. Any church can fully participate in the blessings of Christ. There is always hope as long as there is life.

The Letter to the Church at Smyrna

> "And to the angel of the church in Smyrna write: The first and the last, who was dead, and has come to life, says this: I know your tribulation and your poverty (but you are rich), and the blasphemy by those who say they are Jews, and are not, but are a synagogue of Satan." (Rev. 2:8–9).

This church was willing to accept poverty for the sake of Christ. Accepting the condition of poverty for the faith is also mentioned in the book of Hebrews. "For you showed sympathy to the prisoners and accepted joyfully the seizure of your property, knowing that you have for yourselves a better possession and a lasting one" (10:34). It takes committed faith to give up wealth in this life for Christ. Sometimes being poor in this world because of persecution is really being rich in the blessings of God. Some in the church would be called to die for the faith. They would pay the ultimate price for Christ. It is interesting to note that Polycarp, who had been a disciple of the Apostle John, was martyred at Smyrna. "Be faithful until death, and I will give you the crown of life" (2:10).

There are no indictments or warnings against the church at Smyrna. This is a wonderful testimony for any church. When I preached through Revelation at the church where I was called as an overseer for thirty-one years, I told them before I retired that I had no indictments against them. That does not mean they were sinless, but, in my view, they fulfilled all the requirements to be called a biblical church with no need of rebuke. It spoke well of the church that I loved for so many years.

The Letter to the Church at Pergamum

"I know where you dwell, where Satan's throne is; and you hold fast My name, and did not deny My faith even in the days of Antipas, My witness, My faithful one, who was killed among you, where Satan dwells" (2:13).

This church was in the midst of Satan's dwelling, which means many unbelieving Jews were present and ready to kill them. As I mentioned before, Asia Minor was filled with unbelieving Jews. One of the Pergamum church's members, Antipas, had been killed. Yet the church held fast to the faith, even in the midst of the threat of death.

"But I have a few things against you, because you have there some who hold the teaching of Balaam, who kept teaching Balak to put a stumbling block before the sons of Israel, to eat things sacrificed to idols and to commit acts of immorality. So you also have some who in the same way hold the teaching of the Nicolaitans" (2:14–15). Again, the church tolerated heretics among them. Remember, the final stage of heresy is always immorality, which results from some type of idolatry. Balaam is an Old Testament character who learned to defeat the Israelites by tempting them with prostitutes. The Israelites could not resist. Today, modern man has made an idol of himself, and the final end of such idolatry is sexual immorality, the ultimate form being homosexuality. Sexual immorality is becoming a normal and accepted part of our present culture, and sadly it is becoming an accepted part of the modern church.

"Therefore repent; or else I am coming to you quickly, and I will make war against them with the sword of My mouth" (2:16). Repentance is always the way of hope. Things may be bad, and we may have made a big mess of things in our lives, but repentance and faith is the way back to a good standing with God.

Notice that Jesus said he was coming "quickly" if the church did not repent. Here, I will remind you of one of my main points of this book. Did quickly mean 2000 years in the future? If that is what Jesus meant, then the warning is an empty warning. No, it was something the church expected to happen soon.

"He who has an ear, let him hear what the Spirit says to the churches. To him who overcomes, to him I will give *some* of the hidden manna, and I will give him a white stone, and a new name written on the stone which no one knows but he who receives it" (2:17). The hidden manna is a reference to the manna in the Old Testament that was a gracious gift to Israel in the wilderness. This hidden manna was now new manna, and it was much more delicious. If they ate this manna, they would never need to eat again (John 4:14). This is a reference to Christ as the manna (or bread) of life. Remember that Jesus told the woman at the well in Samaria that if she drank of living water (which was Christ himself) she would never thirst again (John 4:14).

The stone is an allusion to the dress of the high priest who entered the Holy of Holies of the temple once a year. The stones had the names of the twelve tribes of Israel on them. They symbolized election in Christ and the intimate relationship God has with Christians through their high priest, Jesus Christ. Every Christian has a name, and by a personal name every Christian is known by Christ.

The Letter to the Church at Thyatira

> "I know your deeds, and your love and faith and service and perseverance, and that your deeds of late are greater than at first" (Rev. 2:19).

These qualities are certainly positive in the life of any church. There was progress being made. Theologians call this progress sanctification. At Thyatira, the Christians were growing in righteousness. Peter shows us what this looks like: "Now for this very reason also, applying all diligence, in your faith supply moral excellence, and in *your* moral excellence, knowledge, and in *your* knowledge, self-control, and in *your* self-control, perseverance, and in your perseverance, godliness, and in *your* godliness, brotherly kindness, and in *your* brotherly kindness, love. For if these qualities are yours *and are increasing* [emphasis added], they render you neither useless nor unfruitful in the knowledge of our Lord Jesus Christ" (2 Pet. 1:5–8).

John goes on to say to the church at Thyatira: "But I have this against you, that you tolerate the woman Jezebel… I gave her time to repent, and she does not want to repent of her immorality" (Rev. 2:20–21). Notice, first of all, that the church at Thyatira was divided into two groups. There were those who tolerated the false prophetess, a woman John called Jezebel (from the Old Testament Jezebel, who was a wicked woman). Notice also the goal of this woman: "She teaches and leads My bond-servants astray so that they commit acts of immorality and eat things sacrificed to idols (2:20)." Again, remember that immorality is always the end of idolatry.

However, there was a second group in the church: "But I say to you, the rest who are in Thyatira, who do not hold this teaching, who have not known the deep things of Satan, as they call them — I place no other burden on you" (2:24). There was a division in this Church. Some followed heresy and others did not. Many churches have suffered under division, and the Thyatira church was no exception. Even in bad churches there are good people. We should not stereotype everyone by their official associations.

"Behold, I will throw her on a bed *of sickness*, and those who commit adultery with her into great tribulation, unless they repent of her deeds. I will kill her children with pestilence, and all the churches will know that I am He who searches the minds and hearts; and I will give to each one of you according to your deeds" (2:22–23). Remember I intimated previously that the churches would read each other's letters. John said here that "all the churches will know" (2:23a). Hopefully, Christians learn from the judgment of others. As Paul wrote to Timothy: "Those who continue in sin, rebuke in the presence of all, so that the rest also will be fearful of *sinning*" (1 Tim. 5:20).

Secondly, one sees here the nature of a covenant. Often, children receive either blessing or curse as a result of their parent's actions. "And I will kill her children with pestilence" (2:23a). I would suggest that her children here are a reference to her followers.

"He who overcomes, and keeps My deeds until the end, TO HIM I WILL GIVE AUTHORITY OVER THE NATIONS; AND HE SHALL RULE THEM WITH A ROD OF IRON, AS THE VESSELS OF THE POTTER ARE BROKEN TO PIECES, as I also have received authority from my Father; I will give him, the morning star. He who has an ear, let him hear what the Spirit says to the churches" (2:26–29). Part of this quote is from Psalm 2 where God claims Kingship over all the nations. If Christians overcome, then they too shall rule with Christ. Eventually Christianity, through the preaching of Christ as Lord and Savior, will be the prominent religion of all nations. God would also give the Christians in Thyatira the morning star which symbolized the beginning of the day and the beginning of new life. It symbolized Christ, who is the bright and morning star.

The Letter to the Church at Sardis

"But you have a few people in Sardis who have not soiled their garments; and they will walk with Me in white, for they are worthy" (Rev. 3:4).

Here, there was not an equal division in the church, but a majority and a minority. Most of the Christians were spiritually dead, but there were a few who had not followed the majority. They had remained faithful. In regard to some churches today, about all we can say is they have a few fine Christians.

John writes: "He who has the seven Spirits of God and the seven stars, says this: 'I know your deeds, that you have a name that you are alive, but you are dead. Wake up, and strengthen the things that remain, which were about to die; for I have not found your deeds completed in the sight of My God'" (3:2). Notice again that a dead church does not mean everyone in it is dead. There are many dead churches with members who have not followed the majority. Even though it is biblically legitimate to say, "That church is dead," we must remember there can be life in some of those who are a part of that church. The church is not the same as the individuals in the church. A church has a life similar to a corporation. When a director of a corporation dies, the corporation continues to exist. When a person leaves a church, the church continues. The church is not defined by the individual Christian.

The issue here too was nominal Christianity. Some churches are Christian in name only. There is nothing else. There is no union with Christ, and thus, there is no life. There is no holiness. There is nothing but a name.

> "So remember what you have received and heard; and keep *it*, and repent. Therefore if you do not wake up, I will come like a thief, and you will not know at what hour I will come to you" (Rev. 3:3).

> "He who overcomes will thus be clothed in white garments; and I will not erase his name from the book of life, and I will confess his name before My Father and before His angels. He who has an ear, let him hear what the Spirit says to the churches" (Rev. 3:5–6).

Repentance (3:3) is always the hope the Christian has. If a Christian repents, then he overcomes. The promises here include white garments which are a sign of the imputed righteousness of

Christ: "And there was given to each of them a white robe" (6:11). He who overcomes by the grace of God, and is clothed in white garments, can be assured that his name is written in the Book of Life (3:5).

The Letter to the Church at Philadelphia

The church at Philadelphia was weak, and they knew they were weak. This is a good quality of any church or any Christian — to know you are weak and not strong. When we recognize our weakness, then we are strong. The Apostle Paul understood this about himself, writing in 2 Corinthians 12:10, he said: "Therefore I am well content with weaknesses, with insults, with distresses, with persecutions, with difficulties, for Christ's sake; for when I am weak, then I am strong." What the weak need to hear is the message of Christ's strength. They do not need to hear that they can pull themselves up by their own bootstraps.

Christ opens and closes the door to his kingdom, and no one can interfere with this because he is almighty. Our strength does not depend on our own ability. He gives us strength through the ministry of the church. The visible church on earth has power derived from Christ himself. "I will give you the keys of the kingdom of heaven; and whatever you bind on earth shall have been bound in heaven, and whatever you loose on earth shall have been loosed in heaven" (Matthew 16:19). This text is often restricted to the area of church discipline, but I believe the principle is broader than that. For the Philadelphian church there was no indictment or warning. Like the church at Smyrna, there was nothing that Christ could lay charge against them at their feet. There have always been churches like this.

However, even the best churches need encouragement. Notice that the unbelieving Jews will bow at the feet of the church. "Behold, I will cause *those* of the synagogue of Satan, who say that they are Jews and are not, but lie — I will *make them* come and bow down at your feet, and make them know that I have loved you" (Rev. 3:9). These apostate Jews believed God loved them, but God really loved the church at Philadelphia. Those who persecuted this church would bow before her in humiliation. This would happen after the city of Jerusalem and the temple had been destroyed. The tide would be changed.

Testing was coming for Christians everywhere, but the Philadelphian Christians would be exempt because they had already proved their faith. This was their reward. "Because you have kept the word of My perseverance, I also will keep you from the hour of testing, that hour which is about to come upon the whole world, to test those who dwell on the earth (v.10). I am coming quickly; hold fast what you have, so that no one will take your crown" (3:10–11). Again, notice this is the same issue that I dealt with in chapter 2 of this book. Jesus was not speaking here of his visible Second Coming, but yet he did come quickly in judgment. They would be threatened by persecution and death soon, but Jesus would deliver them.

Lastly, the saints were promised they would be made pillars in the temple of God. Pillars are stable and secure. The saints would be stable and secure in the midst of their persecution. The name of the City of God, the New Jerusalem, would be written on them. The New Jerusalem comes down out of heaven from God (3:12). We shall consider this language about the New Jerusalem later.

The Letter to the Church at Laodicea

There was nothing positive to say about the church at Laodicea. However, as we shall see, this did not mean the church was without hope. John makes an assessment of the church in the following words: "I know your deeds, that you are neither cold nor hot; I wish that you were cold or hot. So because you are lukewarm, and neither hot nor cold, I will spit you out of My mouth" (3:15–16).

This may be one of the most well-known texts of the letters to the seven churches. As a church grows older, and as the previous love for Christ often wanes, a church risks the danger of becoming lukewarm to the things of God. This can happen to an individual Christian as well as to a church.

Materialism had deadened the zeal they first had for Christ. They thought they were rich, but they were really poor. "Because you say 'I am rich, and have become wealthy, and have need of nothing,' and you do not know that you are wretched and miserable and poor and blind and naked" (3:17). They did not need to pursue the rich garments of this world, but they should have pursued the rich garments of God. They did not need to buy more of the gold of this world, but they needed the gift of gold from God. They needed to be reminded of the words of Peter: "your faith, *being* more precious than gold which is perishable, even though tested by fire, may be found to result in praise and glory and honor at the revelation of Jesus Christ" (1 Peter 1:7).

Jesus can spit them out of his mouth. They risked the shame of their nakedness being revealed (Rev.3:18). They were blind to their condition, and yet Jesus was their friend in that he was willing to tell them the truth. The emperor has no clothes! The Bible is clear about the need of loving correction, as the following verses indicate:

> "I advise you to buy from Me gold refined by fire so that you may become rich, and white garments so that you may clothe yourself, and *that* the shame of your nakedness will not be revealed; and eye salve to anoint your eyes so that you may see" (3:18).

> "Those whom I love, I reprove and discipline; therefore be zealous and repent" (Rev. 3:19).

"Faithful are the wounds of a friend, but deceitful are the kisses of an enemy" (Prov. 27:6).

If a church or individual Christian answers the call of Christ, then he shall be restored to fellowship with Christ — even if there is nothing good Jesus can say about him. This is an invitation directed to lukewarm Christians and affirmed in the famous verse as follows: "Behold, I stand at the door and knock; if anyone hears My voice and opens the door, I will come in to him and will dine with him, and he with Me" (Rev. 3:20).

The result of restoration with Christ is to enjoy the blessings of Christ. This is made clear in the following: "He who overcomes, I will grant to him to sit down with Me on My throne, as I also overcame and sat down with My Father on His throne. He who has an ear, let him hear what the Spirit says to the churches" (Rev. 3:21–22).

Christians will sit down with Christ on his throne. This is indeed a great mystery. Paul also makes reference to Christians reigning with Christ. "It is a trustworthy statement: for if we died with Him, we will also live with Him; if we endure, we will we shall also reign with Him; if we deny Him, He also will deny us; if we are faithless, He remains faithful, for He cannot deny Himself" (2 Timothy 2:11–13).

Although Christians will reign with Christ in heaven, it is interesting to note that John intimates that this reign with Christ will begin soon — when the unbelieving Jews are made to bow at the feet of the church (Rev. 3:9). Matthew Henry interprets this bowing by the Jews as follows:

"They shall worship at thy feet; not pay a religious and divine honour to the church itself, not to the ministry of it, but shall be convinced that they have been in the wrong, that this church is in the right and is beloved of Christ, and they shall desire to be taken into communion with her and that they may worship the same God after the same manner."[1]

Conclusion

My goal in this chapter has not been to do a thorough study of the letters to the seven churches. Others have already done this. I have simply made a few pastoral comments about each church.

However, remember my focus in this book is to help unlock the mystery of Revelation as a whole. The seven churches (except for Smyrna and Philadelphia) had their problems. Jesus had nothing good to say about Laodicea. The encouragement for the churches was that God was ready and willing to forgive if the churches repented and trusted in the blood of Christ. As the seven churches received the good news that relief was coming from the persecution of the unbelieving Jews, they first needed to get their own house in order, for indeed judgment begins with the household of God (I Pet. 4:17).

---

[1] Matthew Henry, *Matthew Henry's Commentary on the Whole Bible* (Old Tappan, N.J.: Revell), 6:1133.

5
THE SEALED BOOK

"Then I began to weep greatly because no one was found worthy to open the book or to look into it." (Rev. 5:4)

Introduction

Chapter 4 of Revelation has caused scant controversy in the history of interpretation. For this reason, I will spend only a limited amount of time on it. My coverage is limited not because it is unimportant — actually it may be the most important chapter in Revelation because it gives a picture of the holiness and power of God as he sits on his throne. However, in keeping with the notion that my book is a primer, I would remind you that I cannot cover everything in Revelation in detail. The purpose of my book is to introduce the reader to a basic framework on how to interpret the book. I will spend only a small amount of time with non-controversial texts. Other, more controversial texts such as chapter 5, I will cover in more detail.

The Throne of God

Chapter 4 shows a picture of God on his throne in imagery form. Revelation moves from John's vision of Christ on earth in chapter 1 to John's vision of God on his throne in heaven in chapter 4. Through John's writing, the reader gets a glimpse into heaven itself. This is important because it demonstrates at the beginning of Revelation that God is in charge of all things from his throne in heaven, including all history. He is sovereign. We are reminded that all the events following this chapter will happen because God is in total control. This is true for both individuals and nations. John is told: "Come up here, and I will show you what must take place after these things" (4:1). Not only does God know what is going to happen in the future, but he also ordains everything that happens. John will be amazed by what he sees in heaven, but his first priority here is to understand the things that will soon come to pass on earth, the things that are at hand.

God is a Spirit and does not have a body like men. He dwells in unapproachable light (1 Timothy 4:16). Thus, to describe the throne of God, John must use metaphors and images. There is no other way to describe him. Plain and ordinary words simply will not do. He has to rely upon images. John combines a number of Old Testament images to do this. I have often said that before a person begins to study Revelation, he first should be quite familiar with the Old Testament because John takes much of his material from those sources. Sadly, too many people who study the Bible begin with the last book of the Bible — Revelation. This would be similar to studying the last chapter in an algebra book before studying all the previous chapters. It is not a wise way to approach the discipline of algebra or the Word of God.

John alludes to precious stones in chapter 4 in order to give some insight into the nature of God. These are costly stones with brilliance and beauty that reflect something of the nature of God himself. What physical things on earth are considered beautiful and precious? Jewels, including diamonds! In the Old Testament temple, the breastplate of the high priest had on it twelve precious stones to represent the twelve tribes. The high priest wore these as he entered God's presence in the Holy of Holies. These stones remind the reader of the beauty and splendor of the great omnipotent God of the universe who is holy and pure.

In the presence of the throne are flashes of lightning and sounds with peals of thunder (4:5), just as Moses saw and heard on Mt. Sinai. There is a sea of glass or crystal sea (4:6), which is a reference to the laver in the Old Testament temple. It symbolizes the need of washing and cleansing of sin by those who served God. There is the candelabra or menorah (4:5), similar to the one in the Old Testament temple with seven candles, that symbolizes the Holy Spirit. Note again how each of these images is taken from the Old Testament.

Two Other Groups before the Throne

Along with God sitting on his throne, two other groups in heaven are worshiping him and singing. In fact, there is a lot of singing in heaven. There always has been and always will be. The first group consists of 24 elders sitting on 24 thrones (vv.4,10). They are clothed in white garments (covered by the righteousness of Christ), and they wear golden crowns on their heads. They are reigning with God. The number 24 is a reference both to God's people in the Old Testament and to the church in the New. The *twelve* tribes constituted God's chosen people in the Old Testament. The *twelve* apostles founded the church in the New Testament. Thus, these 24 elders represent God's chosen people under two covenants, the old and the new.

The second group consists of four living creatures. This is similar to the picture in Ezekiel 1: "As for the form of their faces, *each* had the face of a man; all four had the face of a lion on the right and the face of a bull on the left, and all four had the face of an eagle. Such were their faces. Their wings were spread out above; each had two touching another *being*, and two covering their bodies" (v.10–11). The creatures here in Revelation chapter 4 resemble a lion (strength), a calf (vitality), a man (intelligence), and a flying eagle (swiftness). Angels carry out God's will by means of strength, vigor, intelligence, and swiftness. They also have six wings and are full of eyes. They had the ability to maneuver quickly, and they see everything in all directions.

Let me give a word of caution here. Be careful and don't dwell on the mental picture that comes into your mind. These are symbols describing attributes of angels who do God's bidding in carrying out his will on earth. We should not carry these literal pictures (and other pictures in Revelation) to bed with us. They may give us nightmares. Actually, the book of Hebrews tells us that angels, as they appear on earth, may look like mere men. "Do not neglect to show hospitality to strangers, for by this some have entertained angels without knowing it" (13:2). However, this metaphorical image tells us that they run "to and fro" doing God's work "like bolts of lightning" (Ezekiel 1:14). Isaiah had a vision of heaven and he relates that in heaven there were "Seraphim who stood above Him, each having six wings; with two he covered his face, and with two he covered his feet, and with two he flew" (Isa. 6:2). Seraphim are angels. Four wings are used to cover themselves in the presence of a holy God, and the other two wings are used to move and do the work they are given to do.

Both groups are singing praises to God. Remember again that there is constant singing in heaven. The elders and the living creatures sing praises about the holiness of God, the eternal nature of God, and the wonder of God as Creator. They have seen what God has done in the past, and they look forward to seeing God's plans for the immediate future. The 24 elders fall down before him and cast their crowns before the throne (4:10). Ultimately, they realize that even the crowns they wear are nothing compared to God's crown, and they realize that all praise and glory belong to God alone.

A Preview of the Seals, Trumpets, and Bowls

In chapter 5, John introduced a book in the midst of this heavenly scene. This is a unique book. As John shows, it is a book with seven seals. Looking ahead, after the seven seals are opened, seven trumpets will blow. Following this, there will be an introduction to the pouring out of seven bowls. I call these the *three sevens*. As I follow the events associated with the three sevens (seals, trumpets, and bowls), I will take the reader through a large portion of Revelation (into chapter 16). So, before I move on, remember: *Three Sevens!* Seven seals followed by seven trumpets followed by seven bowls. Understanding the nature of this seven-sealed book in chapter 5 is important to understanding the meaning of the other two sets of sevens, and thus a great portion of the book of Revelation.

I majored in mathematics in college and was trained to think in terms of discrete, logical steps. I always wanted difficult things reduced to short, concise outlines. Logic is my game, not feelings, even though I have feelings too. Maybe it is just my personality. Revelation is a long and complex book, and I need some short, overarching outline to hang onto while I am wading through it. The *three sevens* provide that outline for me, and I think it will for you the reader. Hold on to the three sevens like review notes or a catchphrase before taking an examination.

Many interpreters believe that the three seven's structure was a recapitulation of one single event. The writer was describing the same event three times. They believe that John basically said the same thing in three different ways. I am not persuaded of this. I believe there was a chronology to the three sevens, which I will list as (1) the declaration, (2) the warning, and (3) the execution. These actually described three separate stages in the battle that led to the final destruction of Jerusalem and the temple. It is my position that we have three stages of judgment over a three and one-half year period (the time period of the battle) in chronological order.

It is a common pattern in the Scriptures that God carries out his judgment by first declaring judgment through his prophets. Secondly, he gives a warning to the people through the blowing of a trumpet. If the declaration and warning are rejected, God carries out or executes his judgment. The following examples demonstrate this process.

First, God often used his prophets to declare to his people the judgment that was to come. Isaiah answered God's call, and his duty was to go and declare judgment to the people of Israel. For example, God told Isaiah the following: "He said, 'Go, and tell this people: Keep on listening, but do not perceive; keep on looking, but do not understand'" (Isa. 6:9).

God told Jeremiah: "But the LORD said to me, do not say, 'I am a youth, because everywhere I send you, you shall go, and all that I command you, you shall speak'" (Jer. 1:7).

Also, God told Ezekiel: "Then He said to me, 'Son of man, I am sending you to the sons of Israel, to a rebellious people who have rebelled against Me; they and their fathers have transgressed against Me to this very day. I am sending you to them who are stubborn and obstinate children, and you shall say to them, Thus says the Lord GOD'" (Ezek. 2:3–4).

The opening of the seven seals was the first of the three sevens. It was a declaration of war. A taste of that judgment would accompany the declaration. Actually, by the time God declares judgment upon a people, a partial judgment has already come. Men and nations that transgress God's law are already experiencing his judgment. We see this in a decline of their culture. Partial judgment was present upon Jerusalem at the time of the declaration of judgment. With that declaration, a partial judgment had already begun with a fourth of the land being decimated (Rev. 6:8).

Secondly, before the final execution of judgment, God gave a warning. The blowing of the seven trumpets introduced that warning. This showed God's mercy and is rooted in the military law in Deuteronomy, which required an offer of surrender before an engagement in war. "When you approach a city to fight against it, you shall offer it terms of peace" (Deut. 20:10). God keeps his own law. He always desires to see people repent.

The blowing of trumpets was commonly used in the Old Testament to warn the people of impending judgment. When the walls of the city of Jericho fell to the ground, it was partially a result of the blowing of trumpets. "Also seven priests shall carry seven trumpets of rams' horns before the ark; then on the seventh day you shall march around the city seven times, and the priests shall blow the trumpets. It shall be that when they make a long blast with the ram's horn, and when you hear the sound of the trumpet, all the people shall shout with a great shout; and the wall of the city will fall down flat, and the people will go up every man straight ahead" (Josh. 6:4–5).

The irony of this is that in Revelation, it was not the walls of Jericho that would fall; on the contrary, it was the walls of Jerusalem. Notice also that the number of trumpets that blow before the fall of both Jericho and Jerusalem is seven. Again, John picks his imagery from the Old Testament.

Isaiah warned Israel of judgment with his voice, and his voice sounded like the blowing of a trumpet. "Cry loudly, do not hold back; raise your voice like a trumpet, and declare to My people their transgression and to the house of Jacob their sins" (Isa.58:1).

Jeremiah also spoke of warning to the people with the sound of a trumpet. "Thus says the LORD, 'Stand by the ways and see and ask for the ancient paths, where the good way is, and walk in it; and you will find rest for your souls. But they said, we will not walk *in it*. And I set watchmen over you, *saying*, listen to the sound of the trumpet! But they said, we will not listen. Therefore hear, O nations, and know, O congregation, what is among them. Hear, O earth: behold, I am bringing disaster on this people, the fruit of their plans, because they have not listened to My words, and as for My law, they have rejected it also'" (Jer. 6: 16–19).

It is clear in the book of Joel that the blowing of trumpets was associated with a warning of God's judgment. "Blow a trumpet in Zion, and sound an alarm on My holy mountain! Let all the inhabitants of the land tremble, for the day of the LORD is coming; surely it is near" (Joel 2:1). Similar to the words in Revelation, Joel said the time is near. God always gives warning following the declaration of judgment and before its execution. God is patient, "not wishing for any to perish but for all to come to repentance" (2 Pet. 3:9). The destruction in Revelation that followed the warning covered a third of the land (Rev. 8:7), in contrast to a fourth of the land in the declaration (6:8). Judgment had already begun in part.

Finally, there would be the execution of judgment after the declaration and the warning. "Then the seventh angel poured out his bowl upon the air, and a loud voice came out of the temple from the throne, saying, 'It is done'" (Rev. 16:17).

The Purpose of the Seven-Sealed Book

What was the purpose of John introducing the seven-sealed book? I will spend more time on this because it is very important and sets the stage for the rest of Revelation.

But first we should recognize an important distinction. A New Testament book was not the same as we think of a book today. The books in the apostolic times were more like scrolls. A scroll is a paper made of papyrus with a wooden spool on each end so the scroll can be rolled up for storage and transportation. This is probably why John referred to the book with seven seals as "written inside and on the back" (Rev.5:1). This is not critical to understanding Revelation, but it is noteworthy. The same type of book written on the front and the back existed also in the Old Testament (Ezek. 2:10).

Weeping John

The Apostle John gave a short description of the seven-sealed book in verse 1 where he said: "I saw in the right hand of Him who sat on the throne a book written inside and on the back, sealed up with seven seals." Notice in verse 4 that John wept as he saw this book with seven seals unopened. "Then I began to weep greatly because no one was found worthy to open the book or to look into it."

Of course, only Jesus Christ was worthy to open the sealed book. He is the Son of God who was faithful to the Father even unto death. He perfectly completed God's will in his life and death. God the Father was well-pleased with him. But why was John weeping? Why would a man weep as he stood in the midst of this wonderful view of the greatness and holiness of God in heaven? That ought to have been an opportunity for singing, not weeping. John gives the answer in verse 3. "And no one in heaven or on the earth or under the earth was able to open the book or to look into it." It is frustrating when there is a sealed book in heaven and there is no one to open it.

However, I think the reason for John's tears goes further than this. Remember Revelation 1:1, where John pointed out that the purpose of Revelation is "to show to his bond-servants the things which must soon take place..." As I alluded to earlier, the context of Revelation in the early church was the suffering saints who were being persecuted by the unbelieving Jews. Jerusalem was the hub or center of this persecution. John referred to himself in Revelation 1:9, as a "fellow partaker in the tribulation." Like other Christians, John was suffering persecution at the hands of both unbelieving Jews and Romans. Remember too my reference to Revelation 6:10, another key verse. The martyrs in heaven were asking God: "How long, O Lord, holy and true, will You refrain from judging and avenging our blood on those who dwell on the earth?"

This seven-sealed book would give John the answer as to how God intended to avenge the enemies of his people, and how long it would be before he would rescue his people, especially those Christians in the seven churches. John would learn that the answer was coming quickly (Rev. 1:1), but the seven-sealed book also would tell him how it would come. It would give John the reassurance that judgment was certain. Opening the book would activate its coming. John's tears were those of frustration because it appeared that no one was worthy to open the book that would show and activate the process of God's vengeance against the enemies of Christians. Opening the book would actually initiate the process of announcement, warning, and execution of the judgment of God against the unbelieving Jews. It would hasten the beginning of that process. John needed to see this, but the seven-sealed book appeared to be permanently closed.

The Nature of the Seven-Sealed Book

The book had seven seals. These, no doubt, were put there by God himself. Seals symbolize authority. The seven-sealed book had been closed by God, and no one had authority to open it apart from God's approval. There is no inherent power in a seal. It is easy to break. The power comes from the fear of the authority that puts the seal on the book. It's a little like the yellow tape you see at a crime scene.

Again, this concept of seals is found in the Old Testament. King Ahasuerus decreed liberty for the Jews in the book of Esther and guaranteed its authority with a seal. "Now you write to the Jews as you see fit, in the king's name, and seal it with the king's signet ring; for a decree which is written in the name of the king and sealed with the king's signet ring may not be revoked" (8:8). Even though a seal is easily broken physically, men are afraid to break seals because the existence of the seal carries the power of some authority behind it. If we open the seal without permission or authority, we will be in deep trouble. It tells us that even though we can easily break the seal physically, if we do so without the permission of the king, then the king may break us.

Also, it verifies that the king is the source of the document. For example, if you need your high school or college transcripts in applying for a job, you will need the official seal of the school on the transcripts. Otherwise, it could be a forgery. Thus, the seal symbolized the importance of the document's contents, the integrity of the content, and the authority of the one who stood behind the content. This seven-sealed book was God's book. Only someone with permission from God would be allowed to open the book. The number seven is used to symbolize completeness. Once the seventh seal was broken, it would initiate visions about the warnings and execution of God's judgment.

The Content of the Seven-Sealed Book

One of the most important questions that can be asked is what was in this seven-sealed book? I believe the contents of this book cover most of the events described in the remainder of Revelation. It determines how we deal with the next eleven chapters of Revelation. Some have speculated that it was the Lamb's Book of Life referred to in Revelation 21:27. The Book of Life was a list of the names of God's elect written from before the foundation of the world. This book, however, does not appear to be simply a list of names.

Another suggestion is that the sealed book was God's last will and testament. Proponents of this view compare it to the reference in Hebrews where the writer refers to the concept of testament (Hebrews 9). Again, this seems to carry no weight because Christians have the New Testament and there is no need for another. Then, too, there are those who believe it was a history of the major events of the world before the Second Advent (historicist view), but if this is true, it only drags us into the realm of speculation as to what events in church history correspond to the events in Revelation. Also, it destroys the comfort to the suffering saints in the early church.

Similar Language in Old Testament Books

The best source book to understand the nature and content of this sealed book is the Old Testament itself. Remember my basic principle — when in doubt, go to the Old Testament. The Old Testament speaks of a sealed book in at least three places. In Isaiah 29:9–16, there is a sealed book which reveals Isaiah's vision. Similar to the seven-sealed book in Revelation, it appeared there was no one to open the book. In Isaiah it also appeared that there was no one able to read the book. The potential reader was illiterate. "Then the book will be given to the one who is illiterate, saying, 'Please read this.' And he will say, 'I cannot read'" (v.12). Even though this parallel is not an exact duplicate, as is often the case with parallel passages, there is a great similarity.

For our purpose, notice the content of the book in Isaiah. It predicted the judgment of God on the unbelieving Jews or apostate Israel. "Then the Lord said, 'Because this people draw near with their words and honor Me with their lip service, but they remove their hearts far from Me, and their reverence for Me consists of tradition learned *by rote*"(v. 13). Then, in verse 14, God pronounced judgment upon this people. "Therefore behold, I will once again deal marvelously with this people, wondrously marvelous; and the wisdom of their wise men will perish, and the discernment of their discerning men will be concealed." Thus, if I consider the parallel passage in Isaiah, then I conclude that such books sealed by God were books that revealed his judgment upon a rebellious people.

This is further supported by a similar book found in Ezekiel 2:9–10. "Then I looked, and behold, a hand was extended to me; and lo, a scroll *was* in it. When He spread it out before me, it was written on the front and back, and written on it were lamentations, mourning and woe." Notice how the book was handed to Ezekiel as the sealed book was to Jesus, and that it was written on the front and back. This is an exact parallel to Revelation chapter 5. Also, notice that the content of the book was described as "lamentations, mourning and woe."

Daniel also spoke of a sealed book. In Daniel 12:4, and in 12:9, he wrote:

> "But as for you, Daniel, conceal these words and seal up the book until the end of time; many will go back and forth, and knowledge will increase."

> "He said, '*Go your way*, Daniel, for *these* words are concealed and sealed up until the end time.'"

Could this sealed book in the book of Daniel be the same one that we have here in Revelation? I think this is a good possibility because it spoke of the end time for the national Jews as God's people (the closing of the Old Covenant). As with the other sealed books in the Old Testament, this book in Daniel spoke of judgment to come. "Many will be purged, purified and refined, but the wicked will act wickedly; and none of the wicked will understand, but those who have insight will understand" (Dan 12:10). The seven churches will be saved. The wicked Jews will perish. He who has ears to hear, let him hear.

Thus, at least from these examples in the Old Testament, the reader should expect the seven-sealed book in Revelation to contain something to do with judgment. The reader should expect that it has something to do with lamentations, mourning, and woe. This aligns with what I have set forth as the theme of Revelation — the description of God's judgment on the unbelieving Jews who were persecuting the Christians. This judgment would come quickly in the destruction of Jerusalem in A.D. 70. The seven-sealed book described in more detail how that judgment would happen. After the seven seals were broken, seven trumpets would blow, and then seven bowls of wrath would be poured out on Jerusalem. Keep in mind that as John described the seven seals, he was not watching a blow-by-blow description of that judgment, but rather, he was getting a preview of what would happen a few years later in Jerusalem's destruction.

An Edict of Judgment

My view is that the seven-sealed book was an edict of God's judgment on the Old Covenant Jews of Jerusalem who were living in the generation of the apostles. I lean heavily on the language in the books of Esther and of Daniel for this view. In the book of Esther, because Queen Vashti refused to appear before the King, he (King Ahasuerus) issued an edict (or a decree) to replace her and to prevent Queen Vashti's contempt from spreading to other women throughout the empire. In Esther 1:19–21 we read: "If it pleases the king, let a royal edict be issued by him and let it be written in the laws of Persia and Media so that it cannot be repealed, that Vashti may no longer come into the presence of King Ahasuerus, and let the king give her royal position to another who is more worthy than she. When the king's edict which he will make is heard throughout all his kingdom, great as it is, then all women will give honor to their husbands, great and small. This word pleased the king and the princes, and the king did as Memucan proposed."

The same language was used in the book of Daniel when Daniel's enemies were trying to remove him from his position of power. They convinced King Darius to sign an edict that forbade prayer to any god except to the king himself. In Daniel 6:8–9, the petition of Daniel's enemies is described, as well as the king's response: "Now, O king, establish the injunction and sign the document so that it may not be changed, according to the law of the Medes and Persians, which may not be revoked. Therefore King Darius signed the document, that is, the injunction."

Most people have heard of the laws of the Medes and Persians. The most important element of those laws to know is that they were irrevocable. They could not be changed or altered even by the king himself. It would be good advice that when an edict was to be delivered, that the king had given much thought and contemplation before signing it. Once the edict was signed, the matter was settled.

I believe that the seven-sealed book was an edict of judgment by God. Judgment would come upon unrepentant Jerusalem. The matter was closed. It was irrevocable. The edict of the seven-sealed book could not be reversed apart from repentance on the part of the apostate Jews. Once the seven-sealed book was opened, a preview of the judgment process would begin. Following the declaration (opening of the seven seals), there would be a preview of a warning by the blowing of the seven trumpets (which gave them time to repent), and then a preview of the executions of judgment itself symbolized by the pouring out of wrath from the seven bowls.

The Target of Vengeance

It is clear from other texts in the Bible that the target of God's vengeance was Jerusalem and the apostate Jews. This will prove helpful later when I will deal with the identity of the great harlot (Rev. 17). Luke speaks of Jerusalem as the object of God's vengeance where we read: "When He approached *Jerusalem*, He saw the city and wept over it, saying, if you had known in this day, even you, the things which make for peace! But now they have been hidden from your eyes. For the days will come upon you when your enemies will throw up a barricade against you, and surround you and hem you in on every side, and they will level you on top of the ground and your children within you, and they will not leave in you one stone upon another, because you did not recognize the time of your visitation" (Luke 19:41–44).

In Luke 21:20–22 Jesus said: "But when you see Jerusalem surrounded by armies, then recognize that her desolation is near. Then those who are in Judea must flee to the mountains, and those who are in the midst of the city must leave, and those who are in the country must not enter the city; because these are days of vengeance, so that all things which are written will be fulfilled."

When Jesus was led away to the cross, a large crowd of the people, including a number of women, was weeping for him. Luke reports for us Jesus' response to the women where he says: "But Jesus turning to them said, 'Daughters of Jerusalem, stop weeping for Me, but weep for yourselves and for your children. For behold, the days are coming when they will say, Blessed are the barren, and the wombs that never bore, and the breasts that never nursed. Then they will begin TO SAY TO THE MOUNTAINS, FALL ON US, AND TO THE HILLS, COVER US'" (Luke 23:28–30).

Conclusion

Thus, this seven-sealed book was an edict of judgment by God upon Jerusalem that accomplished a divorce. Later in Revelation, Jesus would take a new wife — the church of the New Covenant. Gentry develops this divorce motif in more detail in his writings. He argues that the edict is actually a writ of divorce by God against Israel.

Woes were pronounced on Old Testament Israel because she had become a harlot. God's vengeance was against the harlot who persecuted Christians. The seven-sealed book would give the saints a preview of this. The seven seals must be opened to preview God's judgment and to activate that judgment. There would follow also a preview of seven warnings followed by a preview of the pouring out of seven bowls — which was the final execution following both the initial declaration and the last warnings. John wept because no one appeared to be worthy to break the seals of the book — that is until he saw Jesus Christ.

"And I saw between the throne (with the four living creatures) and the elders a Lamb standing.... And He came and took the book out of the right hand of Him who sat on the throne" (5:6–7). Once Jesus took the heavenly book from the hand of God the Father, the four living creatures and the twenty-four elders fell down before the Lamb and "they sang a new song" (v. 9). The fact that Jesus was worthy and that he was present to open the seven-sealed book gave the Christians a reason to sing a new song. In the Bible, new songs were often written when some major event happened (see Psalm 40).

John's tears were turned into shouts of joy. We can almost hear God saying, "Don't cry, John. Rejoice! Jesus is here. He is worthy to open the heavenly book because he has given his life as a sacrifice for the sins of his people. He has pleased the Father. He has risen from the dead and has ascended into the very presence of God. He is here. Do not cry!"

Indeed, God had heard the prayers of his people in their suffering. Soon the suffering from the unbelieving Jews would come to an end. "Behold, I will cause those of the synagogue of Satan, who say that they are Jews and are not, but lie — I will make them come and bow down at your feet, and make them know that I have loved you" (Rev. 3:9).

Both Jerusalem and the temple would be destroyed. This was predicted in 1 Kings 9: 6–9 where we read:

> "But if you or your sons indeed turn away from following Me, and do not keep My commandments and My statutes which I have set before you, and go and serve other gods and worship them, then I will cut off Israel from the land which I have given them, and the house which I have consecrated for My name, I will cast out of My

sight. So Israel will become a proverb and a byword among all peoples. And this house will become a heap of ruins; everyone who passes by will be astonished and hiss and say, 'Why has the LORD done thus to this land and to this house?' And they will say, 'Because they forsook the LORD their God, who brought their fathers out of the land of Egypt, and adopted other gods and worshiped them and served them, therefore the LORD has brought all this adversity on them.'"

As I alluded to previously, God had issued an edict that accomplished a divorce. God's edict declared a rejection of the harlot, and he would take a new wife. That new wife would include both Jews and Gentiles. Today, we call her the church. Jesus spoke clearly to this event:

"I say to you that many will come from the east and west, and recline *at the table* with Abraham, Isaac and Jacob in the kingdom of heaven; but the sons of the kingdom will be cast out into the outer darkness; in that place there will be weeping and gnashing of teeth" (Matt. 8:11).

"Therefore I say to you, the kingdom of God will be taken away from you and given to a people, producing the fruit of it" (Matt. 21:43).

Don't weep anymore. Rejoice! Once Jesus took the heavenly book from the hand of God the Father, John would know the details of how this transformation was to happen. Action would begin. The time of judgment would be hastened. He could be assured that it will happen soon. As a result of all of this, there was much more singing in heaven (4:8–11).

An Important Point about the Jews

The Bible makes a harsh judgment on the unbelieving Jews who killed Christ. The greater blessing that a nation enjoys, the greater will be their judgment if they reject God. Paul said in Romans: *There will* be tribulation and distress for every soul of man who does evil, of the Jew first and also of the Greek" (2:9). Peter, speaking to the men of Israel, said as he preached on the Day of Pentecost: "this Man, delivered over by the predetermined plan and foreknowledge of God, you nailed to a cross by the hands of godless men and put Him to death" (Acts 2:23). It is quite clear that Peter held the Jews guilty of Christ's death. Rome was only the instrument they used in this horrendous murder. Revelation is the story of God's judgment upon the Israel who crucified Christ. It is a story about the judgment against "those who pierced Him" (Rev. 1:7).

When Pilate referred to Jesus as their King, the apostate Jews replied: "Away with *Him*, away with *Him*, crucify Him! Pilate said to them, 'Shall I crucify your King?' The chief priests answered, 'We have no king but Caesar'" (John 19:15). Peter clearly held the apostate Jews guilty for the death of Christ when he said before the Jewish Council: "The God of our fathers raised up Jesus, whom you had put to death by hanging Him on a cross" (Acts 5:30). Stephen told the apostate Jews that they were "betrayers and murderers" of the Righteous One (Acts 7:52). The Apostle Paul spoke of the Jews as those "who killed the Lord Jesus and the prophets, and drove us out" (1 Thess. 2:15).

However, it is good to remember as I proceed with this book that God has yet a special blessing for the descendants of the same Israel who crucified Christ. In Romans Paul said of the Jews "that a partial hardening has happened to Israel until the fullness of the Gentiles has come in, and so all Israel will be saved, just as it is written…" (Rom 11:25–26).

> "For just as you once were disobedient to God, but now have been shown mercy because of their disobedience, so these also now have been disobedient, that because of the mercy shown to you they also may now be shown mercy. For God has shut up all in disobedience so that He may show mercy to all." (Rom 11:30–32)

Again, I cannot cover in detail the text here in Romans. Suffice it to say that many interpreters believe that this refers to a general conversion of the Jewish people before the Second Advent. Thus, even though Revelation is harsh toward the unbelieving Jews who killed Christ and persecuted Christians, yet there remains a great hope for that nation. Before the end of time, they will turn to faith in Christ.

6
SEVEN SEALS BROKEN

"Then I saw when the Lamb broke one of the seven seals, and I heard one of the four living creatures saying with a voice of thunder, "Come." I looked, and behold a white horse, and he who sat on it had a bow; and a crown was given to him and he went out conquering and to conquer." (Rev. 6:1)

Introduction

In this chapter I will cover several chapters of Revelation. In the previous chapter, I considered what was in the seven-sealed book. Here, I will explain what happened as the seven seals were actually opened. This will be the first group of seven in the *three sevens*. Hold on, as I move from Revelation chapter 6 through Revelation chapter 8, verse 5. Following Revelation 8:5, 8:6 speaks of the beginning of the blowing of the seven trumpets, the second group in the *three sevens*. "And the seven angels who had the seven trumpets prepared themselves to sound them" (8:6). This will lead to chapter 16, where the seven bowls of wrath will be poured out — the third group of the *three sevens*.

Remember, the opening of the seals of the seven-sealed book was God's way of declaring judgment on the Jews of the Old Covenant who rejected Christ, and also it was God's answer to persecuted Christians who were crying out for vengeance. Remember too, that John was given a preview of what was to happen as the city of Jerusalem fell in A.D. 70. These are descriptions of what *will happen* in the apostolic age after John writes Revelation.

I will quickly summarize the function of each seal. The opening of the *first four* seals triggered the appearance of four horsemen on the land who had the authority to declare the judgment to come. The opening of the *fifth* seal moved the theater of action from earth to heaven, where the martyred saints were crying out for vengeance. The *sixth* seal described the fear of men in Jerusalem as they were confronted with the declaration of God's judgment. The *seventh* seal predicted an increase in prayer for vengeance, as well as the initiation of the blowing of the seven trumpets. Between the opening of the *sixth* and the *seventh* seals, there was what has been called an interlude. Its purpose was to identify the Christians who would still be in Jerusalem before the final destruction. They needed to escape from Jerusalem. God would not let them die in this catastrophe. The elect Christians in Jerusalem would be identified by a seal on their forehead.

God's judgment on the land of Israel and Jerusalem would come in steps or increments rather than all at once. Actually, it would come over a period of three and one-half years. This was the reason John said in chapter 6 that, at first, only a portion of the land (a fourth) would be affected. "Authority was given to them over a fourth of the earth, to kill with sword and with famine and with pestilence and by the wild beasts of the earth" (Rev. 6:8).

The declaration of judgment would come with signs. Signs always point to something else that is greater than the sign itself. These signs were partial judgments on the land. They would come as destructive forces. They pointed to the final and complete destruction of Jerusalem that would come later.

The Four Horsemen

The first *four* seals were identified with four horses and four horsemen. This has come to be one of the more popular images of Revelation. Most likely, you have heard of the "four horsemen," at least if you are a football fan and remember the name being coined to describe the University of Notre Dame running backs many years ago.

These four horsemen on four separate horses would reveal to apostate Israel, by means of signs, that God had declared judgment against them. There were four different horses, and each was identified with a different color. The "first horse was white" and the rider wore a crown. He went out upon the earth "conquering and to conquer" (6:2). White symbolizes purity, but it also symbolizes victory. As I recall, the Lone Ranger rode a white horse, and he was always successful! Some interpreters identify the rider with Jesus Christ; however, I don't think this is the case here. This was only one rider of four. Jesus Christ will come later riding a white horse in much greater power and glory (chapter 19). This rider announced with signs what would shortly come to pass, as would the three other horsemen. Gentry suggests that the horseman on the white horse here represented the approach of the Roman army in March of A.D. 67, which was the first formal engagement of the Roman army with Jerusalem.

With the breaking of the second seal there appeared a *red horse* whose rider went out to "take peace from the earth, and that men would slay one another" (6:4b). In the Bible, the color red typically symbolizes blood. With the signs that accompanied the declaration of judgment, there would be blood. The peace that Israel had under Rome would be taken away. The *Pax Romana* (the peace that Rome brought to her empire by sheer fear and force) would be removed from the land of Israel. Notice that the mitigation of the Pax Romana in Israel was carried out simply by God removing his grace that provided for peace. When God's common grace (as opposed to God's saving grace) is removed from this world, then men begin to fight and war with one another. During this time, civil war occurred within the city of Jerusalem among a number of factions of Jewish leaders.

With the breaking of the third seal, the third rider came forth on a *black horse* (6:5). Black symbolizes famine or the shortage of food. In Lamentations 4:8, those affected by famine are described in terms of the color black. "Their appearance is blacker than soot. They are not recognized in the streets; their skin is shriveled on their bones, it is withered, it has become like wood." Here in Revelation the third rider carried a pair of scales in his hand that symbolized the inflated price of the food. "A quart of wheat for a denarius, and three quarts of barley for a denarius, and do not damage the oil and the wine" (v. 6). A denarius was a day's wage; this demonstrated the high cost of food. Think of a day's wage buying a loaf of bread! It's what today is called runaway inflation.

Josephus describes what was happening in Jerusalem prior to the final destruction of the city. He explains that one of the militant factions, lead by a man named Simon, "set on fire those houses that were full of corn, and of all other provisions" (*The Wars of the Jews* 5.1.4). This was done by one faction to keep the food out of the hands of the other factions. John tells us that the wheat and barley were scarce. Evidently, the oil and wine were not touched. This was a famine caused by the Jews themselves.

During the famine, there were reports of cannibalism. Cannibalism was mentioned as part of the covenant curses that God brings upon his rebellious people. These terrifying curses are listed in Deuteronomy:

> "Then you shall eat the offspring of your own body, the flesh of your sons and of your daughters whom the Lord you God has given you, during the siege and the distress by which your enemy will oppress you." (Deut. 28:53)

> "The refined and delicate woman among you, who would not venture to set the sole of her foot on the ground for delicateness and refinement, shall be hostile toward the husband she cherishes and toward her son and daughter, and toward her afterbirth

which issues from between her legs and toward her children who she bears; for she will eat them secretly for lack of anything *else*, during the siege and the distress by which your enemy will oppress you in your towns." (Deut. 28:56–57)

This is awful! However, cannibalism happened in Jerusalem before the Romans reached the city. It was a sign of the declaration of God's judgment. It appears that the worst enemies of the Jews were not the Romans, but rather the Jews themselves. They had more to fear from their own people than they did from the Romans. Some Jews considered the Romans as possible saviors from the evil of their own people.

Then, finally with the opening of the fourth seal an *ashen* (gray, green, or pale) *horse* came forth, and the name of the rider was Death (6:8). He was given "authority over a fourth of the earth to kill with sword and with famine and with pestilence and by the wild beasts of the earth" (6:8). Gray or pale is the color of death. Some people would die during this time. This is another sign of the declaration of God's judgment.

Four Horsemen in the Old Testament

What is the meaning of the four horsemen? Remember that I interpret Revelation by searching other Scriptures. In other parts of the Word of God, I always hope to find the meaning of the metaphors. To understand the metaphors of the four horsemen, I will be comparing Scripture with Scripture.

Notice a parallel passage in the Old Testament where there were four horses and various colors. Zechariah the prophet had a similar vision in chapter 1:8 as follows: "I saw at night, and behold a man was riding on a red horse, and he was standing among the myrtle trees which were in the ravine, with red, sorrel and white horses behind him." In verse 10 of Zechariah chapter 1, we are told that the task of the horseman was "to patrol the earth." The concept of the four horsemen in Revelation is not new. Four horses have already appeared once in Zechariah. Their mission in that book was to prepare the land for final judgment. The four horses in Revelation had the same mission.

As the actual events transpired, and as the Roman armies approached Jerusalem, the Jews would see the signs of God's final judgment in dead bodies resulting from famine, and dead bodies eaten by the beasts of the earth. The covenant curses in Deuteronomy predicted this in the following: "your carcasses will be food to all birds of the sky and to the beasts of the earth, and there will be no one to frighten them away" (28:26). Not all of the Israelites would die, but nearly a fourth of them would before the Romans even approached the walls of Jerusalem.

Opening of the Fifth Seal

The opening of the *fifth* seal returned the theater of action back to heaven. In heaven, we find the response of the martyrs as they saw the seven-sealed book being opened. They were anxious to see the judgment of God on those who had put them to death for their faith in Christ. "When the Lamb broke the fifth seal, I saw underneath the altar the souls of those who had been slain because of the word of God, and because of the testimony which they had maintained" (6:9).

> "And they cried out with a loud voice, saying, 'How long, O Lord, holy and true, will You refrain from judging and avenging our blood on those who dwell on the earth?'" (6:10).

> "And there was given to each of them a white robe; and they were told that they should rest for a little while longer, until *the number of* their fellow servants and their brethren who were to be killed even as they had been, would be completed also" (6:11).

As I have previously noted, the phrase "for a little while longer" reaffirms my position as to the timing of these events in Revelation. The time was near. God would avenge in just a little while longer. "A little while longer" surely does not mean 2000 years into the future. If there was to be no relief shortly, then either God was mistaken, or God was not telling the truth. Therefore, I conclude that the events of Revelation must have occurred during the apostolic age. I've said this before, and I will probably say it again because it is so important.

Vengeance Targeted against Israel

Notice also how this text (Rev. 6:9–11) limits the word "earth" to the "land" of Israel, a point I made in chapter 3 of this book. The martyrs were calling for the death of those who persecuted them "on the earth" (v. 10}. The word earth cannot mean the whole entire earth (as seen from the moon), or the earth as defined by the extent of the Roman Empire. The earth was the location of the persecution which had taken place. It is not the earth in some global sense. Those Christians in heaven who were slain for the faith before John wrote the book were praying for vengeance for their own blood. The vengeance was directed against "those who pierced Him" (Rev. 1:7). Those who pierced him lived in the land of Israel. Stephen is considered the first martyr of the church (Acts 7). These prayers were fully answered later when the seven bowls of wrath were poured out.

This vengeance was predicted by Jesus himself in Matthew 23:34–36. After Jesus pronounced woe on the scribes and Pharisees he went on to say: "I am sending you prophets and wise men and scribes; some of them you will kill and crucify, and some of them you will scourge in your synagogues, and persecute from city to city, so that upon you may fall *the guilt of* all the righteous blood shed on earth, from the blood of righteous Abel to the blood of Zechariah, the son of Berechiah, who you murdered between the temple and the altar. Truly I say to you, all these things will come upon this generation." I ask you, the reader — is it not obvious here that Revelation is speaking of the same judgment that Jesus pronounced in the book of Matthew against the Scribes and Pharisees? Again, this limited the recipients of God's judgment in Revelation to the Scribes and Pharisees of the New Testament era and also to their followers.

Jesus spoke of the destruction of the temple in Matthew 24:2. "And he said to them, 'Do you not see all these things? Truly I say to you, not one stone here will be left upon another, which will not be torn down.'" The disciples had just asked Christ about the temple in Matthew 24:1. "Jesus came out from the temple and was going away when His disciples came up to point out the temple buildings to Him." I have mentioned this before, but I think it is important to quote the text again. The exact timing of this judgment was revealed by Christ in Matthew 24:34. "Truly I say to you, this generation will not pass away until all these things take place." Thus, the generation of Jesus and the apostles watched these events occur in Jerusalem.

Heaven is Watching Us

It is tempting to speculate about how those in heaven are aware of what is happening on the earth. The martyrs prayed that God might bring judgment on those who had killed them and were still alive on the earth. There is a hint here that those saints who have gone on before us are well aware of our struggles as we live here on earth. They watch God's plan unfold in history and pray for justice for God's persecuted saints. I think it is fair to deduce the possibility that those beloved Christians who have died before us and gone to heaven are very aware of our trials here on earth.

Notice also that these martyrs were slain because of the Word of God. "When the Lamb broke the fifth seal, I saw underneath the altar the souls of those who had been slain because of the word of God and because of the testimony which they had maintained" (6:9). They not only believed in the Word of God, but they maintained that belief unto death. They had been tortured, jailed, and beaten, but they never denied the authority or the testimony of the Lord Jesus Christ.

The testimony of the Word of God is that Jesus is the Son of God who came and died for our sins. He rose again the third day and sits at the right hand of God the Father. He will come to judge the quick and the dead. Jesus has left his written Word in the Holy Scriptures for all mankind. Christians today must stand for the Word of God, regardless of the consequences. Christians must be faithful even unto death. May God give Christians the grace to do so, even as the saints in heaven may very well be praying for them.

The Breaking of the Sixth Seal

With the breaking of the *sixth* seal we are given an image of how much men in the land would fear God's judgment. This fear would be so great that men would hide themselves in caves and among the rocks of the mountains, and they would say to the mountains and to the rocks: "Fall on us and hide us from the presence of Him who sits on the throne and from the wrath of the Lamb; for the great day of their wrath has come, and who is able to stand" (v.16–17). This was a fulfillment of Jesus' prophecy in Luke 23:30. "Then they will begin to SAY TO THE MOUNTAINS, 'FALL ON US,' AND TO THE HILLS, 'COVER US.'" Also, this judgment would be so horrible that everyone would hide from the wrath of God. Futurists, as opposed to other views, put this judgment sometime into the future beyond our present age; however, I believe it pertains to the destruction of Jerusalem in the apostolic age. Once the horrific devastation of Jerusalem is comprehended, we can better understand the anxious apprehension of the inhabitants of the city. The caves surrounding Jerusalem have always given the Jewish people a place to hide from foreign intruders.

To the Old Testament Again

I hold the position that the language used with the opening of the sixth seal is also metaphorical and is not to be taken literally. Take note of the prophecy that follows: "I looked when He broke the sixth seal, and there was a great earthquake; and the sun became black as sackcloth made of hair, and the whole moon became like blood; and the stars of the sky fell to earth, as a fig tree casts its unripe figs when shaken by a great wind. The sky was split apart like a scroll when it is rolled up, and every mountain and island were moved out of their places" (Rev. 6:12–13). If I search both the Old and New Testaments for similar language, I find that this is common language to describe major events of destruction in Israel's history.

In our own day, think of events such as the atomic bomb being dropped on Japan or the destruction of the twin towers by Muslim terrorists. The world changed in a day! I could metaphorically say the sun became dark, and the moon turned into blood. Too, one could say the skies were literally darkened on those days, and the sun became as dark as sackcloth made of hair. Think of the smoke that covered New York City as the towers fell to the ground. The smoke was dark and black. It prevented the sun from shining. The same was to happen in the skies over Jerusalem.

This metaphorical language of a darkened world is common language in other parts of the Bible. The most common example is in the word of the prophet Joel, when he said: "The sun will be turned into darkness and the moon into blood before the great and awesome day of the LORD comes" (Joel 2:31). This is not to be taken literally. Peter tells us Joel's prophecy was fulfilled on the Day of Pentecost as many were converted to Christ. In Acts 2:20, Peter said specifically that what they were seeing was the fulfillment of the words of the prophet Joel: "but this is what was spoken of through the prophet Joel…The sun will be turned into darkness and the moon into blood." This passage did not have a literal fulfillment here with dark skies, etc. It was clearly metaphorical.

Another common example of this dark metaphorical language is found in Isaiah chapter 13, where the prophet spoke specifically about the Old Testament city of Babylon. In verse 1, Isaiah said: "The oracle of Babylon which Isaiah the son of Amoz saw." Then, in verse 10, Isaiah described the judgment against Babylon in the following terms: "For the stars of heaven and their constellations will not flash forth their light; the sun will be dark when it rises and the moon will not shed its light."

The point of these images about darkness was that the judgment of God would be so catastrophic that only such figurative language could be used to describe it. To interpret these prophecies as if these things were to happen only literally is to miss the point. The same can be said of the language here in Revelation chapter 6. The events would be so catastrophic that only metaphorical language could be used to describe them. The world would be changed. It would never be the same. Again, using a modern example, when Pearl Harbor was attacked, it was a day that changed the whole world. President Roosevelt called it "a day that will live in infamy." Indeed one could easily say it was a day when the sun became dark, and the moon turned into blood. Darkness and blood! This is common metaphorical language used to describe catastrophic events as they have occurred in the history of the world. Actually here, it lends itself to both a metaphorical and a literal image.

The Interlude

Remember that chapters 6 through 8:5 deal with the opening of the seals of the seven-sealed book. Chapter 6 begins with the opening of the first of the seven seals. In 8:5, the seventh seal was opened. The blowing of the seven trumpets would begin in 8:6. However, chapter 7 of Revelation is an interlude. You know what an interlude is. If you have ever watched the movie *The Ten Commandments*, you may remember that it was so long there was an interlude in the middle. There was a break for getting popcorn and going to the restroom. John seemed to be building up to a crescendo, and then all of sudden there is this break (interlude) in order to say something else of equal importance.

There is a clear purpose for this interlude. In chapter 7, the declaration of judgment against Jerusalem was put on hold until God had put a mark on the Christians and allowed them to escape from the city.

> "After this I saw four angels standing at the four corners of the earth, holding back the four winds of the earth, so that no wind would blow on the earth or on the sea or on any tree. And I saw another angel ascending from the rising of the sun, having the seal of the living God; and he cried out with a loud voice to the four angels to whom it was granted to harm the earth and the sea, saying, 'Do not harm the earth or the sea or the trees until we have sealed the bond-servants of our God on their foreheads.'" (Rev. 7:1–3)

Winds are used in the Bible to describe the power and force of God. Here, John said that God would hold back the winds of judgment until the Christians had their foreheads marked and had escaped from the city. During the destruction of Jerusalem, God provided a way out of the city for the Christians before it was decimated. This is referred to in Matthew where God warns those who are in the city to flee to the mountains: "then those who are in Judea must flee to the mountains. Whoever is on the housetop must not go down to get the things out that are in his house. Whoever is in the field must not turn back to get his cloak" (Matt 24:16–18).

The Christians in Jerusalem must flee. If they do flee, they will be saved from the destruction that would come at the hands of the Romans. In A.D. 68, Nero, the Caesar of Rome, committed suicide. The Roman army had surrounded Jerusalem just when they received news that Nero was dead. However, because Nero had committed suicide, the Roman General, Vespasian, returned to Rome to help transition Rome to a new Caesar. The Roman soldiers retreated from their positions. There was a pause in the battle against Jerusalem, and this facilitated the Christians' escape from the city.

A Mark on the Forehead

The point of the interlude in chapter 7 was that before the Christians escaped, they needed a mark to identify them. God would set them apart so that they might be preserved. They would not die in that terrible fire that would engulf Jerusalem and blacken the sky. In biblical terms, God knows his elect, and here, he declared that he would deliver his elect from the city's destruction. These Christians were described in verse 14 as follows: "These are the ones who come out of the great tribulation and they have washed their robes and made them white in the blood of the Lamb." These Christians were cleansed through the blood of Christ. The great tribulation was the process of Jerusalem's destruction.

These Jewish Christians were also described in terms of the twelve tribes of Israel by the number 144,000 (Rev. 7:4). This probably was a reference to the Jewish Christians living in Jerusalem, those who came from the twelve tribes. Remember the early Christians were Jewish. This is something we tend to forget. The number is symbolic. The number can easily be associated with the arithmetic product of 12 tribes times 12 apostles times 1,000. The number 1,000 is symbolic of completeness. The number 1000 is not meant to be an exact number. For example: "God owns the cattle on a thousand hills" (Psalm 50:10). He really owns the cattle on more than a thousand hills, but the number 1,000 symbolizes all the hills of the earth. The number 144,000 was the symbolic number of Christians from the *twelve tribes* of Israel, converted to Christ through the work of the *twelve apostles*, who would be delivered at that particular point in the battle before Jerusalem fell.

They would be known by a seal on their forehead. One of the angels of heaven said: "Do not harm the earth or the sea or the trees until we have sealed the bond-servants of our God on their foreheads" (7:3). Destruction would be delayed until the Jewish Christians from the twelve tribes were delivered out of the city. I will explain in the next two sections the nature of a seal, and why they were put on the foreheads of Christians.

The Meaning of Seals

What do seals mean in the Bible? Seals are symbolic. Generally, they are not to be taken literally. Signs and seals are found throughout the Bible. Again, when in doubt, go elsewhere in the Bible. Seals appeared in Revelation 5, on the seven-sealed book. They define ownership. The heavenly book belonged only to God, and only Jesus Christ had the right to break the seals. Likewise, the mark or seal of God on the forehead of Christians meant they belonged to God.

Think of the brand "T" put on cows in the western movies. The mark defined ownership. Many a war was fought over cattle. The branding iron was a way to identify those to whom the cattle belonged. Also, if you work for a large corporation, you probably have a badge with the company logo on it along with your name. Years ago, when I worked for the state of West Virginia as a highway construction inspector, I wore a white construction hat with my name on it to identify me as an official state inspector of work being done by private contractors as they built interstate highways. The white hat said to the construction workers that I had the power to approve or disapprove what they were doing. I had the authority of the state of West Virginia behind me.

Seals, marks, and badges tell who owns you and from whom you derive your power, at least during the hours you are at work. I remember once that Barney Fife from the *Andy Griffith Show* used his badge to let a person know from where he derived his authority. He did not have much physical presence as a man. He did have his bullet, which he carried in his shirt pocket, and an empty gun. However, his authority was derived from the badge he wore which represented the power of the civil government behind the badge.

In Romans 4:11, circumcision administered in the Old Testament was called a seal: "and he received the sign of circumcision, a seal of the righteousness of faith which he had while uncircumcised…" In the New Testament, baptism is a seal that unites us to Christ. In the sacraments, the seals represent the authority of God acting in the sacrament. Thus, the concept of a seal is not new. Christians are identified in the book of Ephesians as those who have been sealed with the mark (seal) of God. "In Him, you also, after listening to the message of truth, the gospel of your salvation — having also believed, you were sealed in Him with the Holy Spirit of promise, who is given as a pledge of our inheritance, with a view to the redemption of *God's own* possession, to the praise of His glory" (Eph. 1:13–14). A seal identifies Christians as belonging to God. God owns Christians.

What Does the Mark on the Forehead Mean?

The next question is what was meant by this mark or seal being put on the forehead? What does the Bible say about marks on the forehead? Later in Revelation 22:3–4, there is another reference to this mark. "There will no longer be any curse; and the throne of God and of the Lamb will be in it, and His bond-servants will serve Him; they will see His face, and His name will be on their foreheads."

Here again, when in doubt go to the Old Testament to look for help. In Exodus 28: 36–38 we read: "You shall also make a plate of pure gold and shall engrave on it, like the engravings of a seal, 'Holy to the Lord.' You shall fasten it on a blue cord, and it shall be on the turban; it shall be at the front of the turban. It shall be on Aaron's forehead, and Aaron shall take away the iniquity of the holy things which the sons of Israel consecrate, with regard to all their holy gifts; and it shall always *be on his forehead* [emphasis added] that they may be accepted before the Lord."

Notice, this is a seal on Aaron's forehead, and the seal says "Holy to the Lord." The seal on the forehead symbolized that Aaron was separated unto God. In this case there was a literal seal, but more importantly, there was a spiritual seal. Likewise, Christians are separated unto God because they know God and because God knows them. The people of Israel were reminded by the Spirit of God that they belonged to God, and that they must love the Lord their God with all their heart, and with all their soul, and with all their mind.

Deuteronomy 6:6 speaks of wearing the words of God "as a sign on your hand and they shall be as frontals on your forehead." This refers to the commandments of God being the source of all their thinking (foreheads) and all their actions (hands). These were literal boxes (phylacteries) on the forehead of Jews. Under the New Covenant, we are not required to wear phylacteries. If I look to the spiritual meaning behind this command, I believe the forehead represents the mind. God owns the mind, the eye, the ear, and the heart of every Christian. He also owns the hands. God owns the thoughts and the actions of his people. God's holiness, God's Law, and God's glory are so impressed in the minds and actions of his children that he speaks of his influence as seals on their foreheads.

The seal of God on Christians can be identified by how they think and live.

In Revelation 13, we will be introduced to the mark of the beast, and that particular mark will be signified by those who worship the image of the beast. This mark is therefore the seal of those who worship the beast with their minds and their actions. Thus, a mark tells who your God is. Where you see people who love the Lord Jesus Christ, and who worship and obey Him, you see the mark of God upon them. Thus here in Revelation, God has marked out His children by capturing their minds and their hearts as worshipers of him. From the destruction of Jerusalem they shall be saved.

More Singing

In Revelation 7:9–17, we find singing again. "Salvation to our God who sits on the throne and to the Lamb" *(v. 10)*. Here, John makes it clear that those who sing are the elect of God "from every nation and all tribes and peoples and tongues" (v. 9a). This was not a Jewish church here, but a church made up of both Gentiles and Jews. This church was the result of the evangelism of Gentiles by the Jewish Christians as recorded in the book of Acts.

The elders and the four living creatures continue to sing (v. 11). Included are the elect martyrs who died. "They have washed their robes and made them white in the blood of the lamb" (v. 14). They endured suffering on earth, but God would provide their every need in heaven. They would no longer suffer on earth. "They will hunger no longer; nor thirst anymore; nor will the sun beat down on them, nor any heat; for the Lamb in the center of the throne will be their shepherd, and will guide them to springs of the water of life; and God will wipe every tear from their eyes" (v. 16–17). This awaits the people of God. This concludes the interlude of chapter 7.

The Opening of the Seventh Seal

The opening of the *seventh* seal served two purposes. It again described the response of those in heaven, and it was to introduce the blowing of the seven trumpets. "When the Lamb broke the seventh seal, there was *silence* [emphasis added] in heaven for about half an hour. And I saw the seven angels who stand before God, and seven trumpets were given to them" (Rev. 8:1).

This silence was not an interlude. This silence was astonishment! The astonishment was so great in heaven that when the content of the seven-sealed book was revealed there was silence for about half an hour. If this is interpreted literally here, it would not be a typical moment of silence as is known today at a public event, but something much greater. Think what it would be like to be in silence for half an hour. A major task in our own day!

Another angel came forth and stood at the altar in heaven, and he too added to the prayers of the saints as were prayed in heaven by the martyrs. More prayer was offered for the hastening of the coming judgment against apostate Israel. "Another angel came and stood at the altar, holding a golden censer; and much incense was given to him, so that he might add it to the prayers of all the saints on the golden altar which was before the throne" (Rev. 8:3). This was symbolized by the smoke of a golden censer (remember the incense in the Old Testament temple). "Then the angel took the censer and filled it with the fire of the altar, and threw it to the earth; and there followed peals of thunder and sounds and flashes of lightning and an earthquake" (Rev. 8:5). Prayer has power! Again, this was to show the awesome power and the great degree of the vengeance of God against the unbelieving Jews who rejected Christ and shed the blood of Christians.

Conclusion

I have shown the opening of the first four seals with the releasing of the four horses and horsemen. This was followed by the opening of the fifth seal where the martyred saints in heaven were crying out for vengeance (theologians refer to this type of prayer as *imprecatory* prayers). The sixth seal showed the fear of men in Jerusalem as they saw judgment coming. Between the sixth and seventh seal was an interlude wherein the saints of God were identified with a mark on their foreheads. Those still in Jerusalem would be given time to escape before the city's destruction.

We get a glimpse of heaven again with its picture of the church-at-large including "a number no man can count" (v.9) praising God. The twenty-four elders and the four living creatures are again singing. Lastly, the seventh seal was broken, and the prayers for judgment against apostate Israel were multiplied. This concludes the first set of the three sevens. The seven seals have been opened and judgment has been declared upon Jerusalem. This declaration is accompanied with signs of a partial destruction. This leads to the second set of the three sevens — the blowing of seven trumpets that will act as a gracious warning of God to the people of apostate Israel.

7
SEVEN TRUMPETS AND THREE WOES

"And I saw the seven angels who stand before God, and seven trumpets were given to them." (Rev. 8:2)

Introduction

In this chapter I will move from the opening of the seven seals to the blowing of the seven trumpets in chapters 9–11 of Revelation. Later we shall deal with the pouring out of the seven bowls in Revelation chapter 16. Keep in mind my catchphrase of *three sevens*.

An Outline of the Seven Trumpets

In order to help the reader follow the texts dealing with the seven trumpets, I have developed the following outline. Note that, just as there was an interlude between the opening of the sixth and seventh seals, there also will be an interlude between the blowing of the sixth and seventh trumpet. The outline is as follows:

The Blowing of the first Four Trumpets – Rev. 8:1–13.
The Blowing of the Fifth Trumpet – Rev. 9:1–12. Internal Conflict in Jerusalem.
Blowing of the Sixth Trumpet – Rev. 9:13–21. The Armies Approach Jerusalem.
Interlude
The Drama Witness – Rev. 10
A Modern Day Drama Witness
Two More Witnesses – Rev. 11:1–14

The Blowing of the Seventh Trumpet – Rev. 11:15–19. Another scene in Heaven.

Trumpets in the Old Testament

First however, I will deal with the use of trumpets in the Old Testament. The blowing of trumpets was not something new. As you might expect, it finds its roots in the Old Testament. The blowing of trumpets was heard on the Day of Atonement and at the beginning of the Year of Jubilee. Often it was used to call an assembly, similar to the church bells that used to ring in small-town America years ago — and still do in some places.

The most familiar event in the Old Testament involving the blowing of seven trumpets was the fall of the city Jericho in Joshua 6. The city of Jericho was the enemy of God's people, and its walls came tumbling down just like the walls would soon come falling down around the city of Jerusalem. As I alluded to earlier, there is irony here. In the Old Testament the destruction of Jericho was accompanied by the blowing of seven trumpets. Here in Revelation, the tables are turned, and the destruction of the walls of Jerusalem will be accompanied with the blowing of seven trumpets. In the Old Testament, Israel was the victor. Now she will be the victim.

There is another reason in this chapter to believe that the blowing of the seven trumpets should be associated with a warning to the city of Jerusalem. Again, I call your attention to the fact that the war against Jerusalem was carried out over a three and one-half year period (from A. D. April 67 to A. D. August 70). One of the reasons for this long time period was to give opportunity for the repentance of Israel. Thus, the use of fractional numbers is prevalent in describing the period of the blowing of the seven trumpets. A fractional number tells me the judgment will happen in increments.

Notice the use of the fractional number one-third. I shall only list the verses, and leave it up to you to proof-text them. Look at chapter 8, verses: 7, 8, 9, 10, 11, and 12. Also, look at chapter 9, verses: 15 and 18. The fractional number one-third is mentioned in each verse. I think most interpreters overlook the important point here. The fractional number one-third is not particularly the salient point. What is important is that the judgment of God comes in increments in order to give time for repentance.

Was the City Jerusalem?

I believe it is obvious in Revelation that the city to be destroyed was Jerusalem. In Rev. 11:8, we are told that the city was mystically called Sodom and Egypt; but, in actuality, it was the city where Christ was crucified. "And their dead bodies will lie in the street of the great city which is mystically called Sodom and Egypt, where also their Lord was crucified" (11:8). Jesus Christ was condemned and died upon a cross just outside the city limits, but Jerusalem is where it all happened. Thus, John tells us clearly that the events described in Revelation were about the city of Jerusalem. Morally, the city had become like the pagan places of Sodom and Egypt. The blowing of the seven trumpets would be a warning to the city.

The First Four Trumpets

Again, I will not get into the details of the descriptions of the various destructive powers of God associated with the blowing of the trumpets. I believe they are generally metaphorical, and therefore, there is a need to refrain from reading too much into the metaphors. The language used to describe the results of the blowing of the first four trumpets is common in the Old Testament. Remember, the theme surrounding the blowing of the seven trumpets is to demonstrate the terrible destructive forces of the Roman Army as they will approach Jerusalem.

Trumpet No. 1 — There will be "hail and fire, mixed with blood" (Rev. 8:7).

Trumpet No. 2 — "A great mountain burning with fire will be thrown into the sea," and a third of the sea will become blood causing the sea creatures to die (v. 8). A third of the ships will be destroyed (v. 9).

Trumpet No. 3 — "A great star fell from heaven, burning like a torch. The name of the star is called Wormwood [bitterness]; and a third of the waters became wormwood and many men died from the waters, because they were made bitter" (vv. 10 and 11).

Trumpet No. 4 — "A third of the sun and a third of the moon and a third of the stars were struck, so that a third of them would be darkened and the day would not shine for a third of it, and the night in the same way" (v. 12).

This descriptive language is similar to the presence of God on Mt. Sinai when the trumpet blew to warn the people that God was near. "So it came about on the third day, when it was morning, that there were thunder and lightning flashes and a thick cloud upon the mountain and a very loud trumpet sound, so that all the people who were in the camp trembled" (Exodus 19:16). Also, both the water turning into blood and the curse of darkness remind me of the plagues on Egypt. A star falling from heaven in the Old Testament was a metaphor for a nation that was collapsing.

The Fifth Trumpet or the First Woe

The blowing of each of the last three trumpets was also called a woe (Rev. 8:13). With the blowing of the *fifth trumpet,* John described both a key and a bottomless pit. This language shall be seen again in chapter 20. The bottomless pit (abyss) was the dwelling place of Satan and his demons. When Jesus cast out the demons from the man in Gerasenes, there was recorded the demon's response to Jesus: "They were imploring Him not to command them to go away into the abyss" (Luke 8:31). Satan and his demons hate the abyss because they cannot do any damage there. They want to be on earth bringing sickness and death to all of God's creation.

When Christ was physically on earth, the demons were afraid of him. Their ability to do damage was limited. Jesus warned the Jews that if they did not repent, then the demons of Satan, who were limited in the presence of Christ, would come back to overpower them. "Now when the unclean spirit goes out of a man, it passes through waterless places seeking rest, and does not find it. Then, it says, I will return to my house from which I came; and when it comes, it finds it unoccupied, swept, and put in order. Then it goes and takes along with it seven other spirits more wicked than itself, and they go in and live there; and the last state of that man becomes worse than the first. That is the way it will also be with this evil generation" (Matthew 12:43–45). The Jews did not repent, and God let the demons out of the abyss to do their work in the destruction of Jerusalem.

The demons have a king over them. He is the angel of the abyss; his name in Hebrew is "Abaddon," and in Greek he has the name "Apollyon" (9:11). The words Abaddon and Apollyon mean "destruction" in the respective languages of Hebrew and Greek. No doubt, these two words were a reference to Satan.

With the opening of the abyss, the demons came out to do their damage. The metaphor of locusts (from the plagues of Egypt) was used to describe them. Power was given to them like the scorpions of the earth, but again that power was limited. They could only harm those who did not have the mark of God on their foreheads. We are told they could not "hurt the grass of the earth, nor any green thing, nor any tree, but only the men who do not have the seal of God on their foreheads" (Rev. 9: 4). They were not allowed to kill but only to torment, and that torment could last for only five months. "And they were not permitted to kill anyone, but their torment was like the torment of a scorpion when it stings a man" (Rev. 9:5).

Gentry makes an interesting observation here. First, he notes that the five- month period from A.D. April 70 to A.D. August 70 was the last five months of the final siege of Jerusalem. The entire war lasted for three and one-half years. In chapter 11 verse 2, as the temple was measured, there was a time frame given for the destruction of the holy city: "…and they will tread underfoot the holy city for forty-two months." Forty-two months equals three and one-half years. In chapter 11 verse 3, this quantity of time was restated using the number "twelve hundred and sixty days" which is the same as 42 months or three and one-half years, counting each month as 30 days ($30 \times 42 = 1260$).

Internal Conflict in Jerusalem

The five months inside the city of Jerusalem before the final siege was a time of internal conflict. During the five-month period, John was predicting what would occur inside the city prior to the final day of destruction. Josephus in his *The Wars of the Jews* described the torment that occurred in the city before the Romans scaled the walls.

Quotes from Josephus

The awful state of the inhabitants of the city of Jerusalem before being conquered by the Roman Army is often unknown to most readers of Revelation. As I have mentioned before, first it was Jew against Jew. Pillage and torment were rampant among the various sects of the Jews. Many of the Jews saw the Romans as possible saviors from their own people.

The following are quotes from Josephus in order that you might understand just how bad it was in the city. Also, I think it is important to get a flavor of the style of Josephus as he writes about these events:

> "And now, as the city was engaged in a war on all sides, from these treacherous crowds of wicked men, the people of the city, between them, were like a great body torn in pieces. The aged men and the women were in such distress by their internal calamities that they wished for the Romans, and earnestly hoped for an external war, in order to their delivery from their domestic miseries…The noise also of those that were fighting was incessant, both by day and by night; but the lamentation of those that mourned exceeded the other, nor was there ever any occasion for them to leave off their lamentations, because their calamities came perpetually one upon another, although the deep consternation they were in prevented their outward wailing; but, being constrained by their fear to conceal their inward passions, they were inwardly tormented, without daring to open their lips in groans … and when they had resolved upon anything, they executed it without mercy, and omitted no method of torment or barbarity." (*Wars* 5.1.5)

Josephus continues to tell us just how terrible were the conditions in Jerusalem during this time of torment:

"It is therefore impossible to go distinctly over every instance of these men's iniquity. I shall therefore speak my mind here at once briefly; neither did any other city ever suffer such miseries, nor did any age ever breed a generation more fruitful in wickedness that [sic] this was, from the beginning of the world. (*The Wars of the Jews* 5.10.5)

Josephus continues:

"So those that were thus distressed by the famine were very desirous to die; and those already dead were esteemed happy, because they had not lived long enough either to hear or to see such miseries… That, however, this action of eating one's own child ought to be covered with the overthrown of their very country itself; and men ought not to leave such a city upon the habitable earth to be seen by the sun, wherein mothers are thus fed, although such food be fitter for the fathers than for the mothers to eat of, since it is they that continue still in a state of war against us, after they have undergone such miseries as these." (*Wars* 6.3.4–5)

Thus, we have a description by Josephus of the torment that Revelation speaks about in chapter 9. The Jews failed to repent. They rejected Christ. The demons had been defeated and were being sent to the bottomless pit while Christ was physically present on earth, but now the warning was that the demons would be let out of the pit to carry out this torment. John summarized it rightly when he said: "And in those days men will seek death and will not find it; they will long to die, and death flees from them" (Rev. 9:6). This was the end of the first woe (the blowing of the fifth trumpet). We have here the fulfillment of the words of Christ: "For then there will be a great tribulation, such as has not occurred since the beginning of the world until now, nor ever will be" (Matt. 24:21). Josephus certainly recognized this. This ended the preview of torment that would follow the blowing of the fifth trumpet (or the first woe). "The first woe is past; behold, two woes are still coming after these things" (Rev. 9:12).

The Blowing of the Sixth Trumpet or the Second Woe

Whereas the blowing of the fifth trumpet dealt with the internal condition of the city of Jerusalem before the Romans captured it, the blowing of the *sixth trumpet* (second woe), mentioned in Rev. 9:13, takes the action back outside the city where the Jews witnessed the approach of the Roman Armies. After the blowing of the sixth trumpet, four angels were released, which I believe directed the Roman Army to move toward Jerusalem.

The movements of armies upon the earth are controlled by God's angels as God gives his commands. God is sovereign in all things, even in war, even "to the hour, and day and month and year" (Rev. 9:15). John writes that a great army will be released. "The number of the armies of the horsemen was two hundred million. I heard the number of them" (9:16).

Josephus tells us that four legions of Roman Armies were stationed at the Euphrates River. The Euphrates was the northeastern border of the Promised Land. Most of the enemies of Israel came from the north. These armies were directed by Rome to move toward Israel to lead in the destruction of Jerusalem. The number of them was two hundred million (in the Greek language *myriads of myriads*). Again, this is a metaphor. This is the same as the modern use of the word "gazillion" — a number beyond counting.

In chapter 9, some of the most fearful things on earth were used to describe the armies of Rome. Again, this was all dreadful:

> "and the heads of the horses are like the heads of lions; and out of their mouths proceed fire and smoke and brimstone" (v. 17b).

"For the power of the horses is in their mouths and in their tails; for their tails are like serpents and have heads, and with them they do harm" (v. 19).

Imagine standing on the walls of Jerusalem and watching a gazillion soldiers dressed in red with brilliant helmets, bright breastplates and shining swords reflecting in the sun as they marched toward the city. Imagine seeing death and destruction behind the soldiers with the knowledge that they were coming for you. Is there any better metaphorical way to describe the fear of those left in the city of Jerusalem than by John's description of the soldiers? "The second woe is past; behold, the third woe is coming quickly" (Rev. 11:14).

Another Interlude

Chapters 10 and 11 of Revelation are typically described as an interlude between the blowing of the sixth and seventh trumpets. These two chapters serve a very important purpose at this juncture. The necessity of the interlude between the second and third woes becomes clear if the importance of the concept of witnesses, a theme that runs through the Bible, is understood. There must be witnesses before a final verdict can be carried out against the accused. This principle is applied here in Revelation.

The Importance of Two or Three Witnesses

Jesus said about Himself in John 5:31–32: "If I *alone* testify about Myself, My testimony is not true. There is another who testifies of Me, and I know that the testimony which He gives about Me is true." Jesus was not denying his own integrity, but only recognizing that without witnesses, *judicially*, a man's statement should not be accepted as true. He goes on to include the Scriptures as a witness to his divine Sonship. "You search the Scriptures because you think that in them you have eternal life; it is these that testify about Me; and you are unwilling to come to me so that you may have life" (John 5:39–40). My point is that witnesses are critical in a judicial trial. It would be improper for God to condemn apostate Israel without first calling witnesses to appear before the judgment seat of God.

Revelation is the story of God's indictment against Israel, and God must keep his own law in regard to the necessity of witnesses. We find this principle taught clearly in the Old Testament Law. In Deuteronomy 19:15 we read: "A single witness shall not rise up against a man on account of any iniquity or any sin which he has committed; on the evidence of two or three witnesses a matter shall be confirmed." In regard to church discipline, Jesus said: "If your brother sins, go and show him his fault in private; if he listens to you, you have won your brother. But if he does not listen to you, take one or two more with you, so that BY THE MOUTH OF TWO OR THREE WITNESSES EVERY FACT MAY BE CONFIRMED" (Matt.18:15–16).

Not only are witnesses required in the discipline of members of the church, but also they are required in the discipline of the elders of the church. "Do not receive an accusation against an elder except on the basis of two or three witnesses" (I Timothy 5:19). In the mind of the Apostle Paul, it was important that he make two trips to the Corinthian church as he said in 2 Corinthians 13:1: "This is the third time I am coming to you. EVERY FACT IS TO BE CONFIRMED BY THE MOUTH OF TWO OR THREE WITNESSES." Paul commanded the Corinthian Church to discipline some members before he described what would hopefully be his next trip there. He reminded the Church that if he had to carry out the discipline, he would "not spare *anyone*" (13:2). He reminded them that his multiple visits for the purpose of discipline were rooted in the biblical law concerning witnesses.

The point is that the Law of God demanded two or three witnesses before a verdict of judgment could be carried out against the accused. These witnesses need not be a witness to the sin itself, but they may be witnesses to the failure of the accused to repent. Thus in regard to the witnesses here in Revelation, it should not surprise us that they appear here in chapter 11. Witnesses must appear at this point. Before God carried out His discipline against the city of Jerusalem, there had to be two or three witnesses. Actually, there were three witnesses. In the next several sections, I shall present a drama witness (one who testifies in the form of acting out a drama), and then in a following section I shall present two further witnesses.

A Little Book for the Drama Witness

In Revelation chapter 10, the interlude opens in directing our attention to a small book. "I saw another strong angel coming down out of heaven, clothed with a cloud; and the rainbow was upon his head, and his face was like the sun, and his feet like pillars of fire; and he had in his hand a little book which was open" (Rev. 10:1–2).

Chapter 10 does not reveal what was in the little book. This is left to speculation. It is plausible that nothing was written in the little book (a scroll). It would appear that John was ready to write what he heard from a booming voice from heaven, and then he was told not to write anything, but to seal the little book. "When the seven peals of thunder had spoken, I was about to write; and I heard a voice from heaven saying, 'Seal up the things which the seven peals of thunder have spoken and do not write them'" (Rev. 10:4). In other words, don't write what you heard from the voice of the strong angel.

A Drama Witness

In Rev. 10:9–10, John was told: "Take it and eat it; it will make your stomach bitter, but in your mouth it will be sweet as honey. I took the little book out of the angel's hand and ate it, and in my mouth it was sweet as honey; and when I had eaten it, my stomach was made bitter." It's the sickness that really counts! Eat the book and digest it. It will be sweet as honey in the mouth but it will be bitter in the stomach. This sounds like some food I have eaten on occasion! Once, while traveling and waiting on a plane at an airport, I had a cinnamon bun before I got on the plane. It tasted great. However, when I got home, I was vomiting for hours. I was really sick. I know now what John was asked to experience.

Old Testament Drama Witnesses

The Old Testament helps in the understanding of chapter 10 of Revelation. In Ezekiel 2:8–3:4, the same instructions were given to Ezekiel where God was revealing the plans for the destruction of Jerusalem. The book given to Ezekiel was a book of judgment which was written on the front and back, and written on it were lamentations, mourning, and woe. Ezekiel was told to eat the book. "Then He said to me, 'Son of man, eat what you find; eat this scroll, and go, speak to the house of Israel.' So I opened my mouth, and He fed me this scroll. He said to me, 'Son of man, feed your stomach and fill your body with this scroll which I am giving you.' Then I ate it, and it was sweet as honey in my mouth" (3:1–3).

In Ezekiel 3:14 we read: "So the Spirit lifted me up and took me away; and I went embittered in the rage of my spirit, and the hand of the LORD was strong on me." Sweetness was followed by bitterness, probably the bitterness of rejection felt by Ezekiel. I think the point here is simply that before God sent his judgment upon Jerusalem, both in the Old Testament and now in the New

Testament, he called his prophets to perform a drama which in this passage happens to be eating a book, sweet as honey, but which becomes bitterness in the stomach. The drama predicted the future of Jerusalem. Sweetness would become bitterness.

Other examples of drama exist in the Old Testament. In the Old Testament Ezekiel was told to act out the siege of Jerusalem. "Now you son of man, get yourself a brick, place it before you and inscribe a city on it, Jerusalem. Then lay siege against it, build a siege wall, raise up a ramp, pitch camps and place battering rams against it all around. Then get yourself an iron plate and set it up as an iron wall between you and the city, and set your face toward it so that it is under siege, and besiege it. This is a sign to the house of Israel" (4:1–3). Ezekiel was to lie on his left side for 390 days and on his right side for 40 days. God would put ropes on Ezekiel so he could not move. Then Ezekiel would prophesy against Israel. Imagine Ezekiel lying bound by ropes in front of a brick with the name Jerusalem inscribed on it; lying on his left side for 390 days and his right side for 40 days. Imagine what the people thought as they passed by him and saw this unusual sight. This was Ezekiel acting out what God had told him to do, in order that the people of the city of Jerusalem might repent. Ezekiel's drama was a judicial witness against Jerusalem.

Also, in chapter 12 of Ezekiel, the prophet was told to pack his bags and escape the city in the sight of everyone for the purpose of symbolizing that God was going to remove them from the city. "I did so, as had been commanded. By day I brought out my baggage like the baggage of an exile. Then in the evening I dug through the wall with my hands; I went out in the dark and carried *the baggage* on *my* shoulder in their sight" (12:7). He was to dig a hole in the wall and go through the hole with his luggage in the sight of the people. This drama of Ezekiel leaving with his baggage was a witness against Israel. If they did not repent, they would be taken into exile.

A New Testament Drama Witness

In the book of Acts, Agabus was told to act out or perform theatrics to warn Paul of the danger of going to Jerusalem. "As we were staying there for some days, a prophet named Agabus came down from Judea. And coming to us, he took Paul's belt and bound his own feet and hands, and said, 'This is what the Holy Spirit says: in this way the Jews at Jerusalem will bind the man who owns this belt and deliver him into the hands of the Gentiles'" (Acts 21:10–11). It is difficult to understand this in our own day. Modern preachers do not act out theatrics in order to witness to the people about judgment. However, God used drama as a witness against the people of Jerusalem who refused to repent. This was exactly what was happening here in chapter 10 of Revelation. As I mentioned previously, the identity of the little book is subservient to the drama itself.

A Modern Day Drama Witness

As a side note, I once thought of doing something like this myself. For example, inflation of the dollar in America is rampant. The Federal Reserve Bank controls the printing of money (or the digitizing of money), and there is no limit on the amount that is printed. The more dollars that are printed, the less they are worth. I believe this is theft. Few people understand the nature of inflation. To warn the public about this deceit, I once thought of going to the steps of one of the banks in our local town and setting fire to one-dollar bills all day long. I thought this would get the attention of the public. It may have resulted in me being put in jail, too! It certainly would have made me poorer. And then too, I had to think how this might affect my local congregation. I decided not to do it, but I thought at least I had precedence in the Bible of putting on an act of drama as a man of God. It was one way to witness to the people that judgment is coming.

Two More Witnesses

In the second chapter of the interlude, Chapter 11, the central characters were two witnesses. For more information on the two olive trees and the two lampstands that stand before the Lord, see Zechariah chapter 4. Like Elijah, these witnesses "have the power to shut up the sky, so that rain will not fall during the days of their prophesying" (Rev. 11:6a). Their testimony was to be in the form of doing harm to their enemies: "and they have power over the waters to turn them into blood, and to strike the earth with every plague, as often as they desire" (Rev. 11:6b). This was reminiscent of Elijah, and also the plagues on Egypt. These powers were given to the two witnesses in chapter 11, to give testimony to the truth which they spoke. This is quite common in the Bible. The miracles of Christ attested to His authority as the Son of God.

After their testimony was finished, the witnesses would be put to death temporarily by the beast that came up out of the abyss (Satan), and their dead bodies would lie in the street of Jerusalem. Their enemies would rejoice with each other over their deaths. "And those who dwell on the earth will rejoice over them and celebrate; and they will send gifts to one another, because these two prophets tormented those who dwell on the earth" (Rev. 11:10). There would be the exchange of gifts like Christians do at Christmas. However, the two witnesses would rise from the dead and be taken up into heaven (like Elijah). There would be an earthquake in which 7,000 people would be killed. This 7,000 is identified as a tenth of the city. This tenth of the city could be taken literally, if the population of the city were about 70,000. It is not stretching it at all — to believe that literally the population of Jerusalem at that time was about 70,000 people.

Remember the process of incrementalism which means the city was destroyed over time. In the breaking of the seven seals, the fraction one-fourth demonstrated a partial judgment. In the blowing of the seven trumpets, the fraction one-third also demonstrated a partial judgment. Here, the fraction one-tenth indicates a partial judgment of the city. At the time of the two witnesses, about 7,000 people of the city would die. More would die later. Jerusalem would die a slow death.

The Blowing of the Seventh Trumpet or the Third Woe

Remember the *three sevens*: the seven seals, the seven trumpets, and the seven bowls. The last five verses of Chapter 11 present the blowing of the *seventh trumpet*. John takes the reader back into heaven again, as he often did before. The pouring out of the wrath of God in the seven bowls had not started yet, but the celebration in heaven had already begun. "Then the seventh angel sounded; and there were loud voices in heaven saying, 'The kingdom of the world has become the kingdom of our Lord and of His Christ, and He will reign forever and ever'" (Rev. 11:15). Anyone who appreciates music will recognize the words here as part of the hallelujah chorus of Handel's *Messiah*. What glorious sounds are uttered in this music to celebrate the ultimate victory of Christ over the kingdoms of this world, and to know that he will reign forever and ever. Revelation is a story about victory. What Christian can listen to the hallelujah chorus without tears of joy flowing down his cheeks!

"And the nations were enraged, and Your wrath came, and the time came for the dead to be judged, and *the time* to reward Your bond-servants the prophets and the saints and those who fear Your name, the small and the great, and to destroy those who destroy the earth [land]" (Rev. 11:18). This was the third woe. This is also a reiteration of Psalm 2.

Finally, in the last verse of chapter 11, "the temple of God which is in heaven was opened; and the ark of His covenant appeared in His temple, and there were flashes of lightning and sounds and peals of thunder and an earthquake and a great hailstorm." Here again, notice the irony. As the temple on earth was destroyed, we are given a glimpse into the temple of God in heaven. The first temple was temporary, and the second heavenly temple was eternal.

Conclusion

In this chapter of my book, the reason is given for the blowing of the seven trumpets, the second set of the *three sevens*. They were to give warning of the final execution of judgment. The blowing of each of the last three trumpets was also called a woe. In the interlude, between the sixth and seventh trumpet, the city of Jerusalem was identified as "the place where also their Lord was crucified" (11:8). This was not the end of Israel because only a portion of the land (one-third) would be judged. John gave a view of what was happening both inside the city and outside the city. The final blow was yet to come.

Before the final judgment, one more biblical law must be fulfilled. According to biblical law there must be two or three witnesses before the accused (Jerusalem) could be condemned. Here in these two chapters there were three witnesses. There was the witness of a drama performed by John, and there were two other witnesses that followed him. The pouring out of the seven bowls, the last set of the three sevens, would begin in Chapter 16 of Revelation. However, in Chapters 12 through 14, John first will identify in more detail the three enemies of the persecuted church. Also, in chapter 15, John will return to the scene in heaven to observe the worship of God. I will cover these in my next chapter.

8
THREE ENEMIES OF THE EARLY CHURCH

"Here is wisdom. Let him who has understanding calculate the number of the beast, for the number is that of a man; and his number is six hundred and sixty-six." (Rev. 13:18)

Introduction

Where am I in Revelation? Remember the *three sevens*? God told the seven churches that relief from persecution from the apostate Jews would be coming soon. His edict of judgment was made manifest in the opening of the seven-sealed book. Following that, God sent forth warnings to Jerusalem in the form of seven trumpets. He would soon follow this with the pouring out of his wrath from seven bowls. I called these series of events the *three sevens*. Before John shows the wrath from the seven bowls in chapter 16 of Revelation, he first identified the three major enemies of the church. He did this in chapters 12–14.

The Three Enemies

The three prominent enemies of the saints identified in Revelation chapters 12–14 were: 1) Satan, 2) the Roman Empire, and 3) The Jewish priesthood. In preparation for the pouring out of the wrath of God in the seven bowls, a pause was needed to identify the three enemies who would be working together to destroy the early church. The first two enemies seem rather obvious to me from the text. They were Satan and Rome. There is some disagreement in regard to the identity of the third enemy. In what follows, I will identify the third enemy as the Jewish priesthood. After holding various other views myself for many years in regard to the identity of this third enemy, I finally concluded that the Jewish priesthood is the choice that best fits the description in the text.

The First Enemy: Satan

In chapter 12 of Revelation, there was the introduction of a woman who was giving birth to a child, and also of a red dragon who sought the life of the child. Notice the description of this red dragon: "Then another sign appeared in heaven; and behold, a great red dragon having seven heads and ten horns, and on his heads were seven diadems" (Rev. 12:3). John clearly identified who this red dragon was. "And the great dragon was thrown down, the serpent of old who is called the devil and Satan, who deceives the whole world" (12:9a).

Later, John would also identify the second enemy (Rome) by the similar description as one who had seven heads, ten horns, and ten diadems. Both the Devil and Rome were so united in purpose, that the two enemies could be described interchangeably. This analogous description revealed the alliance between the two.

Notice the fractional number again limiting the power of what the red dragon could do. "And his tail swept away a third of the stars of heaven and threw them to the earth" (Rev. 12:4a). I cannot emphasize this fractional number limitation enough. Fractions describe increments or small steps. The war against Jerusalem happened in increments. It happened over time, step by step. John was making sure that his readers did not forget this important point.

Observe that Satan acted in two realms in chapter 12. First, he appeared in heaven, and then he was cast out of heaven to the earth (v.10). On earth he was unable to destroy the child of the woman (v. 13–14), and after this failure he would go off to make war with the rest of her children (v.17).

Satan in Heaven

It is very interesting that Satan was in heaven first. Even though the text first presented him on earth ready to kill the child to be born (v. 4), yet it was revealed later in the text that chronologically he appeared first in heaven; then he was thrown down to earth. "And when the dragon saw that he was thrown down to the earth, he persecuted the woman who gave birth to the male *child*" (v. 13).

It is curious to me that Satan was even in heaven. However, the resolution to my quandary is not really as difficult as one might expect. Look at it this way — remember that God was on his throne as a Judge. There was the venue of a courtroom in Revelation. Satan was there pleading his case before Almighty God. He was bringing accusations against the saints of God. "Then I heard a loud voice in heaven, saying, Now the salvation, and the power, and the kingdom of our God and the authority of His Christ have come, for the accuser of our brethren has been thrown down, he who accuses them before our God day and night" (Rev. 12:10).

Notice that Satan was (and still is) the accuser of the brethren. A good example of Satan as the accuser of the brethren is presented in the Book of Job where Satan accused Job of having an empty or false love of God, only fearing him because he was materially wealthy. Notice that Satan appeared before God, just as he did here in Revelation. "Now there was a day when the sons of God came to present themselves before the Lord, and Satan also came among them" (Job 1:6). Satan was looking to cause trouble, and this was implied in his response to God's question in regard to why he was present before him. "The Lord said to Satan: "From where do you come?' Then Satan answered the Lord and said: 'From roaming about on the earth and walking around on it'" (Job 1:7). Satan was looking for some way to cause havoc on the earth. Remember that Satan is not happy unless he is bringing sickness and death to anything that belongs to God. He was looking to bring temptation into the life of someone so that he might cause some faithful man of God to fall into sin.

The Lord then presents Satan with a challenge. "The Lord said to Satan, 'Have you considered my servant Job? For there is no one like him on the earth, a blameless and upright man, fearing God and turning away from evil.' Then Satan answered the Lord, 'Does Job fear God for nothing? Have you not made a hedge about him and his house and all that he has, on every side? You have blessed the work of his hands, and his possessions have increased in the land. But put forth Your hand now and touch all that he has; he will surely curse You to your face'" (Job 1: 8–11).

This illustration of Job is a perfect example of Satan standing before God accusing faithful believers. Likewise, we are told in Revelation that Satan went before the throne of God and accused Christians (Rev. 12:10). He did this "before our God day and night" (v. 10). This was why Satan was in heaven in this text. He did not live there. He did not like it there. His place was in the abyss, but he often appeared before God accusing the brethren of being empty hypocrites.

Satan Back on Earth

Also, in chapter 12 of Revelation there was a woman on earth who was about to give birth to a child. "A great sign appeared in heaven: a woman clothed with the sun, and the moon under her feet, and on her head a crown of twelve stars; and she was with child, and she cried out, being in labor and in pain to give birth" (Rev. 12:1–2). The woman giving birth to a child might first appear to be a description of Mary giving birth to the baby Jesus; however, in the context of the story here, I think this was a reference to the faithful Jews who believed in Jesus Christ, and who gave birth to the early Christian Church (which first consisted of Jews who believed in Jesus Christ and then later included Gentiles). I take this position for several reasons.

First, when James addressed the early Christian church, he called them "the twelve tribes" (James 1:1). The description of the woman reminds me of the elect Jews of the Old Covenant. The twelve stars on her crown remind me of the twelve tribes of Israel. Secondly, the context of Revelation was the destruction of Jerusalem. Jesus had already been born and there was no point in dealing with that here. The person of Mary as being persecuted by the Devil is not a prominent theme in the apostolic church, or thereafter.

Thirdly, just like the woman in the text, the Jewish church in Jerusalem did flee the city into the wilderness. Jesus spoke of this to his disciples in Matthew 24, warning them of the coming destruction and their need to flee from the threat of death.

> "Therefore when you see the ABOMINATION OF DESOLATION which was spoken of through Daniel the prophet, standing in the holy place (let the reader understand), then those who are in Judea must flee to the mountains. Whoever is on the housetop must not go down to get the things out that are in his house. Whoever is in the field must not turn back to get his cloak. But woe to those who are pregnant and those who are nursing babies in those days! But pray that your flight will not be in the winter, or on a Sabbath. For then there will be a great tribulation, such as has not occurred since the beginning of the world until now, nor ever will. Unless those days had been cut short, no life would have been saved, but for the sake of the elect those days will be cut short." (Matt. 24:15–22)

The elect of God (the Jewish church) were told they must flee Jerusalem or be killed.

Fourthly, another reason to interpret this child as the Jewish church is that the number of 1260 days appears again here in Rev. 12:6. Remember, this was the time period of the destruction of

Jerusalem (three and one-half years). The Devil was told in verse 12 that he only had "a short time." Rome was going to destroy Jerusalem, and the Jewish Christians had a short time to escape. In addition to these reasons, verse 17 of this same chapter spoke about the rest of her children. "So the dragon was enraged with the woman, and went off to make war with the rest of her children, who keep the commandments of God and hold to the testimony of Jesus." This does not sound like Mary and the rest of her children. The rest of the children probably refer to the Gentile church, those not presently in Jerusalem, but those Gentiles who were converted to Christ. Satan would turn his attention toward them.

God's Deliverance

Ultimately, the Devil always loses. God used his great powers to deliver the woman and her male child from Satan. "But the two wings of the great eagle were given to the woman, so that she could fly into the wilderness to her place, where she was nourished for a time and times and half a time, from the presence of the serpent. And the serpent poured water like a river out of his mouth after the woman, so that he might cause her to be swept away with the flood. But the earth helped the woman, and the earth opened its mouth and drank up the river which the dragon poured out of his mouth" (Rev. 12:14–16).

Old Testament Israel was carried on the wings of eagles as she escaped from Egypt into the wilderness. "You yourselves have seen what I did to the Egyptians, and how I bore you on eagles' wings, and brought you to Myself" (Exodus 19:4). God promises grace to all of his people who grow weary. He gives strength to the weary, and to him who lacks might He increases power as Isaiah says: "Though youths grow weary and tired, and vigorous young men stumble badly, yet those who wait for the Lord will gain new strength; they will mount up with wings like eagles, they will run and not get tired, they will walk and not become weary" (Isa. 40: 30–31).

The book of Daniel (12:7) refers to time, times, and a half time which can be interpreted as a year, two years, and half a year which is three and one-half years, the time for the destruction of Israel. God would be with His people during the destruction of Jerusalem. In the book of Exodus the sea opened its mouth to gush forth water in killing the Egyptian soldiers. Here in Revelation, the earth opens its mouth to drink up the water of the serpent so that the woman and her child might be saved (12:16). Also, the earth drank up the water of the great flood after Noah, and his family was saved. Again, notice how the Old Testament is the source book for understanding Revelation.

The Second Enemy: The Roman Empire

There are two other additional enemies to identify. First, there was the "beast from the sea." He is generally recognized as the prominent beast in Revelation, although as we will see, there was also a beast of the land. The number of the beast is six hundred and sixty-six (Rev. 13:18). This beast in Revelation has been identified with various persons down through history. During the reformation period, there was the tendency to identify him with the Pope. During World War II, the beast was identified as Hitler. I have found that during my lifetime that whoever is President of the United States will be the most popular candidate for the beast identified by the number 666. Ronald Wilson Reagan was once identified as the beast because he had six letters in each of his three names.

I believe the sea beast was the Roman Empire or more specifically the Caesar of Rome, or even more specifically, he was Caesar Nero. I will examine the evidence here for this conclusion.

First of all, notice that the source of power of the sea beast was Satan himself. In Rev. 13:1, we find "the dragon stood on the sand of the seashore" as if he were calling the sea beast to come over and do his destructive work against Jerusalem. In verse 4, we notice that the sea beast worshiped the dragon (Satan) "because he gave his authority to the beast." This was a beast under the power of Satan.

There are several hints in chapter 13 as to who this sea beast was. First, he came from the sea. If you remember your geography, you will know that Rome is across the Mediterranean Sea from Jerusalem. When Paul went to Rome, he went by way of a ship crossing the Mediterranean. The quickest route to Jerusalem from Rome was by sea, so it seems natural to identify the sea beast as Rome.

The sea beast had "ten horns and seven heads, and on his horns were ten diadems, and on his heads were blasphemous names" (v.1). Remember the similar description of Satan in the previous chapter. Again, this reveals an alliance between Rome and Satan.

John identified the seven heads explicitly later in 17:9–10. "Here is the mind which has wisdom. The seven heads are seven mountains on which the woman sits, and they are seven kings; five have fallen, one is, the other has not yet come; he must remain a little while." For those familiar with the Roman history of this period, they will know what the seven mountains signified. The seven mountains or hills signified the city of Rome. Rome was known as the city of seven hills, a city with seven mountains or hills surrounding it. As I mentioned before, each hill had a particular name.

History also tells us that Nero was the Emperor during A.D. 64–68, which was during the period I believe John wrote Revelation. The names of Rome and Nero were literally interchangeable as were Washington, D.C. and Lincoln in the American Civil War. Another example of the identification between a location and its leader was Nazi Germany and the name Hitler. The two names were interchangeable. The name Nero was synonymous with the city of Rome (or even the Roman Empire). Sometimes, when I refer to the beast,

I will be speaking of Rome, and at other times, I will be speaking of Nero.

Nero was the sixth Emperor of Rome. The first five were Julius Caesar, Augustus, Tiberius, Caligula, and Claudius. Nero followed Claudius and was therefore the sixth in order. When John speaks of the seven kings, he says: "five have fallen, one is, the other has not yet come" (v. 10). I have just named the five who were dead. The one "who is" should be identified as Nero. The seventh Emperor who followed Nero was Galba. Galba reigned seven months from A.D. June 68 to A.D. January 69, a very short time. Following him there was a civil war in Rome, and four emperors ruled Rome in one year. Thus John says: "and when he comes, he must remain a little while" (v10), referring to Galba.

In Rev. 17:11, we read: "The beast which was and is not, is himself also an eighth and is one of the seven, and he goes to destruction." The number eight is symbolic of "starting over." Sometimes, it is like getting another chance. The eighth day was the day of circumcision. The life of a covenant child in Israel began a second time as an official covenant child. Eight souls (Noah and his family) started a new life. The eighth day of the week starts a new week. After the civil war in Rome, a new stable king (the eighth) would reign. This initiated a new life for Rome. Rome almost perished during this time. The great Roman Empire had its own troubles. If you can imagine four emperors reigning in a period of one year, then you can understand the turmoil Rome faced. However, following this chaotic period, order was restored. In a symbolic sense, following the civil war, the eighth king ruled. Rome was starting over again. Stabilization had returned to Rome. Rome came back to be a vibrant kingdom after nearly dying.

Nero's death and Rome's civil war were further symbolized as follows: "I saw one of his heads as if it had been slain, and his fatal wound was healed" (Rev. 13:3). After the death of Nero, Rome was in disarray and the empire was on the verge of collapse. As I previously mentioned, after a short time, the empire was revived and order was restored. This corresponds with John's description of the fatal wound that was healed.

Thus, I believe the details of John's description matched very well the city of Rome, and particularly the head of that empire, Nero himself. Rome was the center of the Roman Empire. John's description also matched the history of the emperors in the days of the early church. The readers in the seven churches would have understood this clearly. They would have identified the beast from the sea as a reference to Nero himself, also because Nero was nothing less than a beast in his own right. He was the embodiment of evil. He murdered his own mother, brother, and wife. It is reported that he would tie slaves to stakes, dress himself in the skin of wild animals, and attack and sexually molest them. He had Christians killed in the great coliseum by vicious animals. This may be one reason John described the beast as one who "was like a leopard, and his feet were like those of a bear, and his mouth like the mouth of a lion" (Rev. 13:2). These were some of the animals used to put Christians to death. Today, in modern parlance, we would call him insane.

The Roman Emperor claimed to be god on earth. The people of the Roman Empire burned incense to the emperor. He thought of himself as a god. He was guilty of blasphemy. The word "blasphemy" was used by John to describe the Roman Caesar in verses 1, 5, and 6 of chapter 13. Thus, there was a reason for the blasphemous names on his horns. Rome and her emperors had set themselves up on earth in the place of the true and living God.

Another reference to Nero can be found in verse 10: "If anyone is destined for captivity, to captivity he goes; if anyone kills with the sword, with the sword he must be killed." Nero had become the enemy of his own people. He was the target of assassination. At the end of his life, his capture by his enemies was imminent. Rather than being dragged through the streets by his enemies, he preferred suicide. He died by intentionally falling on his own sword, the same sword that he had used to kill so many other people. Better to die falling on your own sword than to be tormented to death by your enemies. He lived by the sword and he died by the sword. He died at the age of 32.

Again, in verse 5, there is a reference to the period of forty-two months (A.D. April 67 – A.D. August 70). During this time period as the Romans attacked Jerusalem, their mouths were full of arrogant words and blasphemies. "There was given to him a mouth speaking arrogant words and blasphemies and authority to act for forty two months was given to him" (Rev. 13:5). Thus, I conclude that the sea beast was the Roman Empire, especially as the empire was identified with Nero himself. This is the second enemy of the church, Satan being the first.

The Land Beast

In chapter 13, after John spoke of the sea beast, he introduced the land beast. "Then I saw another beast coming up out of the earth, and he had two horns like a lamb and he spoke as a dragon" (v. 11). This land beast made those under his control worship the sea beast. "He exercises all the authority of the first beast in his presence. And he makes the earth [land] and those who dwell in it to worship the first beast, whose fatal wound was healed" (v. 12). The land beast induced the people to worship the sea beast (Rome) by performing great signs (v. 13), deceiving men (v. 14), and making an image of the sea beast (for the purpose of worship) (v. 15). The land beast led others to worship the sea beast. Those who did not worship the sea beast would be killed (v 15). He also put a mark on the right hand and on the forehead of those who worshiped the sea beast (v.16). Those without this mark, and who did not worship Rome or the Roman Emperor, would be economically punished: "and *he provides* that no one will be able to buy or to sell, except the one who has the mark, *either* the name of the beast or the number of the beast" (v. 17).

In any society where persecution prevails, one of the first acts of persecution is for people to suffer economically by losing their jobs and their businesses, that is, ultimately their livelihoods. The writer to the Hebrews mentions this as he described some of those in the early church. "But remember the former days, when after being enlightened, you endured a great conflict of suffering, partly by being made a public spectacle through reproaches and tribulations, and partly by becoming sharers with those who were so treated. For you showed sympathy to the prisoners and accepted joyfully the seizure of your property, knowing that you have for yourselves a better possession and a lasting one" (Heb. 10:32–34).

The Third Enemy: The Jewish Priesthood

Who then was the land beast? Who caused the people of the land (Israel) to worship Caesar rather than Christ? He was an evil beast, but he looked like a lamb (13:11). He had two horns, not ten like the sea beast, thus implying he had less power than the sea beast. "He exercises all the authority of the first beast in his presence" (Rev. 13:12a). He acted under the authority of the sea beast. I believe the Bible gives the answer to these two questions concerning the land beast in the Gospel of John. This is so important that I will quote the entire text from the relevant verses in John 19:

> "Jews cried out saying, 'If you release this Man, you are no friend of Caesar; everyone who makes himself out to be a king opposes Caesar.' Therefore when Pilate heard these words, he brought Jesus out, and sat down on the judgment seat at a place called The Pavement, but in Hebrew Gabbatha. Now it was the day of preparation for the Passover; it was about the sixth hour. And he

said to the Jews, 'Behold your King!' So they cried out, 'Away with Him, away with Him. Crucify Him!' Pilate said to them, 'Shall I crucify your King?' The chief priests answered, *'We have no king but Caesar.'"* (John 19:12–15; emph. added)

Notice that the Jewish crowd was a pawn in the hands of the chief priests. In this text in John, the Jews were being led by the chief priests. We see that the chief priests were inducing the people to worship Caesar. Caesar was their king. They taught that he alone was worthy of worship. They loved Caesar. They hated Christ. They wanted to see Christ dead. "Now the chief priests and the whole Council kept trying to obtain false testimony against Jesus, so that they might put Him to death" (Matthew 26:59). Thus, the chief priests of the Jews were the religious leaders who looked like lambs, but they led the people to worship the sea beast (Nero). "And it was given to him to give breath to the image of the beast, so that the image of the beast would even speak and cause as many as do not worship the image of the beast to be killed" (Rev. 13:15).

Out of dedication to the sea beast and all that he spoke, the land beast would kill Christians as a religious expression of his faith. This is exactly what happened to Christians as predicted by Christ. "They will make you outcasts from the synagogue, but an hour is coming for everyone who kills you to think that he is offering a service to God. These things they will do because they have not known the Father or me. But these things I have spoken to you, so that when their hour comes, you may remember that I told you of them. These things I did not say to you at the beginning, because I was with you" (John 16:2–4). The chief priests, who served Rome (and hated Christians), along with the Scribes and Pharisees, were not from across the sea. They were from the land of Israel. They dwelled in Jerusalem. The priesthood of Israel was the land beast, the third enemy of the church.

This worshipful attitude of the Jewish leadership toward Caesar is also found in the book of Acts. A Jewish mob gathered to bring Paul and Silas and other Christians before the city authorities. The charge was that "they all act contrary to the decrees of Caesar, saying that there is another king, Jesus" (Acts 17:7). This worship of Caesar by the Jewish leaders continued until the destruction of Jerusalem. The religious leaders of the Old Covenant Jews were teaching that Caesar was king rather than Jesus. They had become apostate. They were leading the people to worship Rome, the sea beast, rather than the Lord Jesus Christ. How very, very sad! In a sense they gave life to the worship of Rome. They enabled Rome to kill Christians. "And it was given to him to give breath to the image of the beast, so that the image of the beast would even speak and cause as many as do not worship the beast to be killed" (Rev. 13:16).

The Land Beast as a False Prophet

This beast from the land was known for his great powers. He performed great signs, so that he even made fire come down out of heaven to the earth in the presence of men. "And he deceives those who dwell on the earth because of the signs which it was given to him to perform in the presence of the beast, telling those who dwell on the earth to make an image to the beast who had the wound of the sword and has come to life" (Rev. 13:14). John later called the land beast the false prophet. "And I saw coming out of the mouth of the dragon and out of the mouth of the beast and out of the mouth of the false prophet, three unclean spirits like frogs" (Rev. 16:13).

Again, speaking of the final end of both the sea beast and land beast, John interchanged the identity of the land beast with the false prophet. In Revelation 19:20, John describes the final end of both the land beast and the sea beast, but he identifies the land beast with the false prophet. "And the beast [Nero] was seized, and with him the false prophet [the Jewish priesthood] who performed the signs in his presence, by which he deceived those who had received the mark of the beast and those who worshiped his image, these two were thrown alive into the lake of fire which burns with brimstone." The land beast was also the false prophet.

What were these miraculous powers of the Jewish priesthood that led the people into idolatry? This has been a common characteristic of false religious leaders down through the ages, and it must have been no less true of the Jewish priesthood. False prophets can perform miracles. Think of the sorcerers of Pharaoh. Think of Christian hypocrites. They were no doubt similar to those of whom Jesus warned when he said: "Many will say to Me on that day, 'Lord, Lord, did we not prophesy in Your name, and in Your name cast out demons, and in Your name perform many miracles?' And then I will declare to them, I never knew you; DEPART FROM ME, YOU WHO PRACTICE LAWLESSNESS" (Matthew 7:22–23).

The land beast was the false prophet (maybe more specifically the high priest of Israel) who led the people to worship in the synagogue of Satan (Rev. 2:9), the temple of Jerusalem. The leaders of the priesthood were in an alliance with Rome, and they would use that alliance to put Christ to death. They derived their right to exercise power from Rome, and yet Christ was a threat to that power. "Therefore the chief priest and the Pharisees convened a council and were saying 'What are we doing? For this man is performing many signs. If we let Him go on like this, all men will believe in Him, and the Romans will come and take away both our place and our nation'" (John 11:47–48). Thus, there is a great amount of evidence that the land beast could easily be identified with the Jewish priesthood.

The Mark of the Beast

What about the number 666 mentioned in Revelation 13:18? For generations, since the apostolic age, people have been identifying the mark of the beast with something in their own generation. A number of Christians in history have identified the number 666 with the end of the world. One thing for certain, as I alluded to before — they were all wrong! They lived and died, and the end of the world never came. However, each new generation thinks it is unique and has figured out the meaning of this mystery surrounding the number 666. They believed Jesus would return again in their generation. Soon, however, they all go to the grave and another generation follows. The next generation believes the same, but it has never happened. They were all wrong.

I was raised to be afraid of the number 666. I think most of us were, who believe in the authority of the Bible. I remember when I was the pastor of Bridwell Heights Presbyterian Church in Kingsport, Tennessee, I was just a little nervous about this. My telephone number for 31 years was 288-6664. Imagine the comments I received from callers about how I had the number of the beast. I lived off of exit 66 of the nearest interstate highway. Also, I lived on highway 126. The numbers in exit 66 and highway 126 include three digits of 6.

For years, I interpreted the number 666 by putting the emphasis on the digit 6. In the Bible the number 7 is symbolic of completion. The number 6 would then be symbolic of incompletion. Completion is associated with God and incompletion is associated with man or Satan. Three numbers of 6 in a row would symbolize the trinity of failure. I usually left the whole matter there with no other answer but that the number 666 was therefore a symbolic reference to fallen man or the Devil.

Notice that John said in verse 18: "Let him who has understanding calculate the number of the beast." Understanding or wisdom

Blessed Is He Who Reads 151

was needed to calculate the meaning of the number 666. Wisdom would take the reader behind the obvious words of the text to understand what John meant. The meaning was not beyond reach. Also, the number must be calculated. Calculation is a mathematical term. Some mathematical calculation must be performed to understand the reference of the number.

Calculating the Number of the Man

There was a method of calculation that was common during the writing of Revelation. This is why John said the following: "Here is wisdom. Let him who has understanding calculate the number of the beast, for the number is that of a man; and his number is six hundred and sixty-six" (Rev. 13:18). The Hebrew and Greek languages used letters as numbers. They did not have the system with which we are familiar today with the digits 1, 2, 3… This is called the Arabic number system. Counting in the Hebrew language was done with letters, and larger numbers were noted with a series of letters grouped together. Think of the Roman numeral system where the letter "I" equals the number 1, "V" equals 5, "X" equals 10, "L" equals 50, "C" equals 100, etc.

In the Hebrew system of the Bible period, the first letter of the alphabet was equivalent to our number 1. The second letter of the alphabet was equivalent to our number 2, and so on. Once the counter gets to the letter which symbolizes the number 9, the letters begin representing the numbers 10, 20, 30 through 100. Then the letters start representing the numbers 200, 300, through 900. To represent the numbers from 1,000 to 999,999, combinations of the same letters are reused to serve as thousands, tens of thousands, and hundreds of thousands. It may be a little more complicated than this, but again remember this is a primer.

To understand the Hebrew numbering system better, it would be similar in English to assigning the number 1 to the letter A, the number 2 to the letter B, the number 10 to the letter K, the number 20 to the letter L, etc. Using something similar to the Hebrew system, the counting for my name using the specific numbers for the letters in LARRY BALL would be L (30) plus A (1) plus R (200) plus R (200) plus Y (700) plus B (2) plus A (1) plus L (30) plus L (30). 30 + 1 +200 + 200 +700 +2 +1 +30 +30 = 1194.

Whew! It is nice to know that my number is not 666; otherwise, my friends who joked with me about my home phone number may have had a point. This Hebrew system of counting is completely foreign to those who learned to count with the Arabic numbers of 1, 2, 3… It seems like *hocus pocus* trying to count the number of the man. At least it seemed that way to me the first time I heard of it. Yet, it was very common to the Jews.

Greg Bahnsen mentions in one of his sermons on Revelation that there was a unique discovery at the unearthing of the old city of Pompeii. There was some graffiti on a wall that said "I love her whose name is 545." This was evidently very common in both the Greek and Roman cultures. Every name had a number. It sounds like code language, but it was not a code language to the Israelites. It was as common as tap water.

Different written languages have symbols for similar sounds. For example, the English letter (or symbol) we call "a" is equivalent to the Greek symbol we call "alpha," which is equivalent to the Hebrew symbol we call "aleph." The English letter (or symbol) we call "b" is equivalent to the Greek symbol we call "beta," which is equivalent to the Hebrew symbol we call "bet." A letter or word in one language can be represented in another language using corresponding symbols or letters. This is called transliteration. The English transliteration for the Hebrew term "Nero Caesar" would be "Nrwn Qsr." The Hebrew language is written in consonants only with vowels symbolized by markings over the consonants. The vowel markings are not included here. With the vowel markings the name would be pronounced "Neron Kaiser."

Now, what about the number 666? Someone familiar with calculating the number of names in biblical times could easily understand the meaning of the number "six-hundred and sixty-six." He could compare it with the Hebrew form for Nero Caesar (Nrwn Qsr); and conclude that the Emperor Nero was the man that corresponds with the number six hundred and sixty-six. If the numerical values of the consonants in the Hebrew name "Nrwn Qsr" are added together, then the total numerical value of the two words "Nrwn Qsr" equals six hundred and sixty six.

$$N+r+w+n+Q+s+r$$
$$=$$
$$50+200+6+50+100+60+200 = 666$$

Remember that John was a Jew, writing primarily to Christian Jews, and he was writing about the destruction of Jerusalem. His source book for his images was the Old Testament. It is not surprising that he would choose to identify the number of this man using the Hebrew mathematical system of calculation. It is important to know that the number was written in the Greek language (the New Testament language) as the phrase "six hundred and sixty-six." The three numerical digits in sequence "666" are short-hand (a mathematical symbol) and do not appear in the original text. Some people become fixated with the digit 6 because of the numerical symbol 666. It might be helpful if they understood that the number written in the original Greek was not simply three digits in a row (666), neither was it "six, six, six;" but rather the phrase "six hundred and sixty-six." "This is the number of a man and his number is six hundred and sixty-six" (v. 18). It does *not* say in the original language, "This is the number of a man and his number is 666." It does *not* say in the original language, "This is the number of a man and his number is six, six, six." There is a difference. Thus,

I believe that Nero was the man and his number was "six hundred and sixty-six."

Conclusion

With this chapter in my book I have identified the three enemies of the early Christian church. They included: 1) the Devil, 2) the sea beast (the Roman Empire or Nero), and 3) the land beast who was also called the false prophet (the Jewish priesthood). I calculated the number of Nero, and the calculation resulted in the number six hundred and sixty-six.

Revelation was written to the early Christians living in the apostolic age. Christians were being persecuted. Even though the destruction of Jerusalem would not end all their trials and tribulations (especially at the hands of the Romans), it would mitigate much of the persecution that arose from the hand of the Jews who rejected Jesus Christ. It would decimate the religion of the Jews and humiliate them before a watching world. The land beast (the Jewish priesthood) led the people to worship the sea beast (Rome) whose god Nero had a number of six hundred and sixty-six. Soon Jerusalem would be destroyed, and the Old Covenant would come to an end with the destruction of Jerusalem and the temple. Christians would rejoice. This is where I will end this chapter.

Don't lose sight of the picture of Revelation as a whole as I deal with so many details. As a reminder, I am in the midst of describing the *three sevens*. I have covered the opening of the seven-sealed book and the declaration of judgment. I also covered the warnings in the blowing of the seven trumpets. The Christians in Jerusalem have been identified and given the opportunity to escape. We have identified the three enemies of God's people. Now I shall move on to the pouring out of seven bowls of wrath.

9
THE SEVEN BOWLS OF WRATH

"Then one of the four living creatures gave to the seven angels seven golden bowls full of the wrath of God, who lives forever and ever." (Rev. 15:7)

Introduction

Don't forget the *three sevens*! In this chapter, I shall present the third set of the three sevens. John's vision of the outpouring of the wrath of God will come to the forefront. Remember "the time is near" (Rev. 1:3). The opening of the seven-sealed book was an edict of judgment delivered by God against Jerusalem. Following the opening of the seven seals, the seven trumpets sounded a warning against Jerusalem. I will now describe the seven bowls of wrath as they were to be poured out upon the city of Jerusalem and on the temple.

Preliminary Issues

Before John gives his vision of the outpouring of the seven bowls of wrath in Chapter 16, there are a few more preliminary events that deserve attention in chapters 14 and 15. First, John would protect the integrity of God. He does this in chapter 14. John would give a vision of Jesus on Mt. Zion with the 144,000 saints. John remembered that even in the midst of the destruction of Jerusalem, God was still in control. He is sovereign! Also in chapter 14, John spoke about the nature of hell itself. God is holy! In chapter 15, John would return to a vision of heaven. Then in Chapter 16, the reapers who carry out the will of God would appear, and one of the four living creatures would give to seven angels the seven bowls of wrath which would be poured out upon Jerusalem. Also, during the outpouring of the sixth bowl, John described the battle of Armageddon.

Notice also in Rev 14:8, there was another name given to Jerusalem. John called her "Babylon the Great." John makes reference to this new name only in passing in this verse. He will give more time to the meaning of this new name in a later chapter.

Jesus on Mt. Zion

As a preliminary to the pouring out of the seven bowls of wrath, John showed a picture of the lamb (Jesus) standing on Mount Zion with one hundred and forty-four thousand. "Then I looked, and behold, the Lamb was standing on Mount Zion, and with Him one hundred and forty-four thousand, having His name and the name of His father written on their foreheads" (Rev. 14:1).

I do not believe that Mt. Zion is to be taken literally here, any more than the number 144,000 should be taken literally. The lamb in this verse was obviously Jesus. The 144,000 had "His name and the name of His Father written on their foreheads" (Rev. 14:1). The number 144,000 represented the early Jewish church that came from the twelve tribes of Israel and from the twelve apostles. They worshiped Jesus, the Holy Spirit, and God the Father (the Holy Trinity) with their minds, hearts, and souls.

The important point to see here is the contrast of Jesus the Lamb of God with the other lamb (or one who had some appearance like a lamb) that was presented in the previous chapter of Revelation. "Then I saw another beast coming up out of the earth; and he had two horns like a lamb and he spoke as a dragon" (Rev. 13:11). As we saw in chapter 13, this lamb represented the land beast that

I identified as the Jewish priesthood (or the Jewish high priest). So there were two parallel references to a lamb in both chapter 13 and 14. The purpose of the parallel was to contrast the difference between them. The Jewish priesthood represented apostate Israel. Jesus represented the true Israel which is the church. Jesus, in reality, was in control of Mt. Zion, not the apostate Jewish high priest or the Jewish priesthood. Jesus was sovereign and would guarantee the safety of His elect (144,000) even as he brought judgment upon apostate Israel.

I would also suggest that the lamb here in chapter 14, was the same lamb that opened the seven-sealed book in Chapter 5. "When He had taken the book, the four living creatures and the twenty-four elders fell down before the Lamb, each one holding a harp and golden bowls full of incense, which are the prayers of the saints" (Rev. 5:8). In chapter 5, the bowls were full of incense. In chapter 14, the bowls are full of wrath. Jesus began the judgment of Israel by opening the seven-sealed book which released incense (prayers of the church) into the presence of heaven. Here he directed the final judgment which released wrath on apostate Israel.

Resting From their Labors

As John described the pouring out of the seven bowls of wrath, he reminded his readers again that "If anyone worships the beast and his image, and receives a mark on his forehead or on his hand, he also will drink of the wine of the wrath of God, which is mixed in full strength in the cup of His anger; and he will be tormented with fire and brimstone in the presence of holy angels and in the presence of the Lamb" (Rev. 14:9–10). There will be no rest, day and night, for the "smoke of their torment goes up forever and ever" (v.11a). This is certainly awful and fearful language. This is hell! It ought to cause everyone to seek Christ as his Lord and Savior. It ought to cause all men "to keep the commandments of God" because of their "faith in Jesus" (v. 12).

On the other hand, for those who are in Christ and have the mark of God on their forehead (who love God and think God's thoughts after Him), there is a wonderful promise here which is a favorite passage for Christian funerals and it ought to be. "And I heard a voice from heaven, saying, 'Write, Blessed are the dead who die in the Lord from now on! Yes, says the Spirit, so that they may rest from their labors, for their deeds follow with them'" (v.13).

The Reapers

Chapter 14 of Revelation concluded with the appearance of two separate reapers (v. 14 and v. 18). At first it might appear that both reapers had come to bring the final judgment on Jerusalem, but after some consideration, I believe the two separate reapers had two separate functions. Both were accompanied by a voice coming out of the temple (v.15 and v.17). The first reaper was sitting on the white cloud and "was one like a son of man, having a golden crown on his head and sharp sickle in his hand" (Rev. 14:14). This was a harvest reaper. The word "harvest" is usually associated with good fruit. This might be called a good harvest. In verse 4, these children of God were called the "first fruits to God and to the Lamb." Thus, the first reaper appeared to be Christ in the process of reaping the fruitful church for himself.

Notice the language that the "hour to reap has come" (v. 15). The time was not near anymore, but the hour actually had come. However, before judgment came upon apostate Israel, God would gather together his people.

The second reaper came with a sharp sickle (v. 17). This particular angel was associated with fire. He had come to reap the clusters of grapes (v. 18). The reaping of grapes is usually associated with wrath. Remember John Steinbeck's novel — *Grapes of Wrath*.

"So the angel swung his sickle to the earth and gathered *the clusters from the vine of earth*, and threw them into the great wine press of the wrath of God" (v. 19).

Notice too, the literary device of a metaphor. "And the wine press was trodden outside the city and the blood came out from the wine press up to the horses' bridles, for a distance of two hundred miles" (v. 20). As Christ suffered outside the camp in his crucifixion, so his enemies are pictured as suffering outside the camp. "For the bodies of those animals whose blood is brought into the holy place by the high priest as an offering for sin, and are burned outside the camp. Therefore Jesus also, that He might sanctify the people through His own blood, suffered outside the gate" (Hebrews 13:11–12).

Israelites died outside of Jerusalem as well as inside the city. According to the description of Josephus, dead bodies and blood were everywhere. Bodies were piled upon bodies. They were putrefied, decomposed, and rotten. Bodies were floating in the rivers and seas. The water was red with blood. John uses the hyperbole of blood being so deep that it came up to the horses' bridles. Again, this is metaphor, and it is intended to impress the reader with the reality of how bad this slaughter would be. It was a horrifying sight. It would be like a city totally destroyed by a tsunami. Think of the damage that myriads and myriads of soldiers could do (Rev. 9:16). Josephus describes the following scene:

> "And indeed the multitude of carcasses that lay in heaps one upon another, was a horrible sight, and produced a pestilential stench." (*Wars* 6.1.1)

This tragedy was the culmination of the sin of Israel. This is the way of God. Often, with patience, he waits until people are as bad as they can be, and then he brings horrendous judgment upon them. We find this in the Old Testament where Abram (Abraham) was told that his descendants would occupy the land of the Amorites, but not until the fourth generation. "Then in the fourth generation they will return here, for the iniquity of the Amorites is not yet complete" (Genesis 15:16). Wickedness usually must reach a pinnacle before God will bring judgment. The lamb has to be fattened before it is slaughtered. Paul predicted this about the Jews in his First Epistle to the Thessalonians as he spoke about the Jews hindering the preaching of the gospel to the Gentiles: "so that they [the Gentiles] may be saved; with the result that they [the apostate Jews] always fill up the measure of their sins. But the wrath has come upon them to the utmost" (1 Thessalonians 2:16).

The term 200 miles (Rev. 14:20) is a translation from the original language of 1600 stadia. A stadia was a unit of measurement for long distances like the measurement of a mile is today. It is interesting that the land of Israel was actually about two hundred miles long from north to south. Often in the midst of what appears to be a metaphor, we find something that can be interpreted very literally. This is the case here in this verse.

In chapter 16, the seven angels appear who will pour out the seven bowls of wrath. The contents of these bowls were called plagues, reminding the reader of the plagues sent against the Egyptians when Israel was delivered under the leadership of Moses. "Then I saw another sign in heaven, great and marvelous, seven angels who had seven plagues, *which* are the last, because in them the wrath of God is finished" (Rev. 15:1). Note the emphasis here in this verse that this will be the final blow. These plagues "are the last." Also, in them "the wrath of God is finished."

A Final Hymn

Prior to the pouring out of the seven bowls of wrath, there was singing in heaven (Chapter 15). "And they sang the song of Moses, the bond-servant of God, and the song of the Lamb" (v. 3a). There is both irony and parallelism here that came from the story of the exodus of Israel from Egypt. This may be the reason the Song of Moses was coming from the voices of those in heaven. The irony is that contrary to the exodus of Israel from Egypt, Israel is the victim now rather than the victor. The parallel here is presented to us in the use of plagues used both in Egypt and in Jerusalem. The theme of the song is that God is marvelous in all His works and righteous and true in all his ways. He is King of the nations! He is holy! As the nations watch the work of God, the day will come when all the nations "WILL COME AND WORSHIP BEFORE YOU, FOR YOUR RIGHTEOUS ACTS HAVE BEEN REVEALED" (Rev. 15:4). This, I believe, is a reference to the Gentile nations who became part of the church.

Transfer of the Bowls

Chapter 15 concludes with the transfer of the seven bowls from one of the four living creatures to the seven angels who were called to pour them out. "Then one of the four living creatures gave to the seven angels seven golden bowls full of the wrath of God, who lives forever and ever" (Rev. 15:7). The angels were dressed "in linen, clean and bright, and girded around their chests with golden sashes" (Rev. 15:6). They were dressed like priests. This was holy war. The angels were ready to bring judgment. A voice came from the temple: "Then I heard a loud voice from the temple, saying to the seven angels, 'Go and pour out on the earth [land] the seven bowls of the wrath of God'" (Rev. 16:1). Notice the similarity of these executioners with those in Ezekiel:

> "Then He cried out in my hearing with a loud voice saying, 'Draw near, O executioners of the city, each with his destroying weapon in his hand.' Behold six men came from the direction of the upper gate which faces north, each with his shattering weapon in his

hand; and among them was a certain man clothed in linen with a writing case at his loins. And they went in and stood beside the bronze altar. Then the glory of the God of Israel went up from the cherub on which it has been, to the threshold of the temple. And He called to the man clothed in linen at whose loins was the writing case." (Eze. 9:1–3)

Notice, that in this text, if the "certain man clothed in linen" is distinguished from the other six men, then, in actuality, there were seven men, as there were seven angels in Revelation 16.

Also, it is interesting to notice the similarity of the language of Ezekiel and Revelation in regard to the mark of God on the forehead of his elect. "The Lord said to him, 'Go through the midst of the city, even through the midst of Jerusalem, and put a mark on the foreheads of the men who sigh and groan over all the abominations which are being committed in its midst.' But to the others He said in my hearing, 'Go through the city after him and strike; do not let your eye have pity or do not spare. Utterly slay old men, young men, maidens, little children, and women, but do not touch any man on whom is the mark; and you shall start from My sanctuary.' So they started with the elders who were before the temple." (Ezekiel 9:4–6). It seems as if John borrowed his language directly from the words of Ezekiel.

Notice also in this text in Revelation that everything was at a standstill in heaven until this final act was complete: "and no one was able to enter the temple until the seven plagues of the seven angels were finished" (Rev. 15:8). It is the quiet before the storm.

The Seven Bowls of Wrath Poured Out

The time for the execution of the third part of the three sevens has come. Revelation chapter 16 contains the story of the outpouring of these seven bowls. Remember too, this was not a picture of the actual events in Jerusalem as they were happening. This was a vision of what would happen later. It is important to make this distinction. The seven seals and the seven trumpets have prepared the reader for the seven bowls. John was writing at least three and one-half years before the final destruction of Jerusalem in A.D. 70, encouraging the churches that God would come to their rescue. He was telling the churches how God would protect them and how He would bring vengeance against their great enemy — the apostate Jews. He would soon answer the prayers of the martyrs (Rev. 6:10). They would soon witness the last of the three sevens.

Seven Bowls – Seven Plagues

There were ten plagues that God inflicted upon Egypt. The last plague was the death of the first-born child. There certainly is some similarity between the seven bowls of wrath in Revelation and the ten plagues in Egypt. Some of those plagues that God used to deliver Israel from Egypt would now be used to bring judgment upon the city of Jerusalem.

The *first* plague that came from the first bowl was in the form of boils. "So the first angel went and poured out his bowl on the earth; and it became a loathsome and malignant sore on the people who had the mark of the beast and who worshiped the image" (v. 2). This corresponds to the sixth plague on Egypt. It also reminds us of Job: "Then Satan went out from the presence of the Lord and smote Job with sore boils from the sole of his foot to the crown of his head" (Job 2:7). It is awful to think of boils and cancer sores all over the body, but this was the description. For Job it was temporary, a time of testing. For those in Israel who did not repent of their sins, it would be continuous until death. It was the fulfillment of the curse promised to covenant breakers in Deuteronomy 28:27. "The Lord will smite you with the boils of Egypt and the tumors and with the scab and with the itch, from which you cannot be healed." With war came disease, and this physical condition also was probably a description of the physical ravages of what the Jews had to endure in their bodies before death.

The *second* and *third* plagues that came from the second and third bowls were described as a change of water into blood. In Egypt the water was turned into blood. Here Christ, through the instrument of the angels, came to curse Israel as Egypt was cursed in the Old Testament. Also, it is interesting to contrast this curse on Jerusalem with the work of Christ at the wedding in Cana. At Cana he changed water into wine. At Cana He came to bless. But here, Christ came to change water into blood. Here Christ came to curse.

The second plague was poured out into the sea, and "it became blood like that of a dead man" (v.3). The third bowl was poured out "into the rivers and the springs of waters; and they became blood" (v 4). This corresponds to the first plague upon Egypt, the changing of water into blood. Thus, all the water from the sea to the springs and to the rivers was turned into blood. Think what life would be like without water. We take it for granted. Even worse, what if a person turned on the kitchen faucet and it poured out red blood? It's awful even to think about it.

The reason for this particular plague was described in v. 6 as God's retribution against the apostate Jews: "for they poured out the blood of saints and prophets, and You have given them blood to drink. They deserve it." Here again the reference was to Israel and not particularly to Rome, although Rome was guilty of this too. The blood previously poured out by unbelieving Jews was the blood of the church. In vengeance, God would pour out their blood. Years ago I interpreted passages like this as a clear reference to the persecution by Rome. After all, I had been raised on the stories about the death of Christians in the Roman Coliseum. This was my focal point of interpretation. Later, after studying the Scriptures a great deal, I began to see that Rome was not the focal point of Revelation in regard to the persecution of Christians. Jerusalem was.

Comparing Scripture with Scripture, in Luke 11, we find this condemnation of the apostate Jews for shedding the blood of the saints where Jesus was speaking to the Pharisees: "Woe to you! For you build the tombs of the prophets, and it was your fathers who killed them. So you are witnesses and approve the deeds of your fathers; because it was they who killed them, and you build *their tombs*. For this reason also the wisdom of God said, 'I will send to them prophets and apostles, and *some* of them they will kill and some they will persecute, so that the blood of all the prophets, shed since the foundation of the world, may be charged against this generation...'" (vv. 47–50). Notice who was charged with the guilt of shedding the blood of the prophets according to Jesus. Even though the blood of the prophets had been shed by many previous generations, here Jesus brings charges "against this generation."

The *fourth* plague poured out from the fourth bowl of wrath was a scorching heat. "The fourth *angel* poured out his bowl upon the sun, and it was given to it to scorch men with fire" (v. 8). The final battle against the city occurred in the heat of the summer (ending probably in August of A.D. 70) when the heat was overwhelming. But much worse, think of men who were caught up in the fire that burned the city. Burning to death in the midst of fire was a horrible way to die.

The *fifth* plague was darkness. "Then the fifth *angel* poured out his bowl on the throne of the beast and his kingdom became darkened" (v.10a). This bowl of wrath corresponds to the ninth plague upon Egypt. Since I have identified the land beast as the Jewish priesthood, the throne of the beast here in this verse was the temple (the synagogue of Satan). The temple was the worship center of the priesthood.

In the book of Exodus the plagues happened separately, and then they were removed before another plague occurred. Pharaoh would plead for mercy and God removed the plague. Here in Revelation the plagues were cumulative. They continued to exist as one was added to another. Too, in regard to darkness, think of the whole city on fire, black smoke rising upward, and blocking the light of the sun. The sky was dark with black smoke. Here again, a metaphor is not incompatible with a literal interpretation.

The *sixth* bowl of wrath was poured out by the dragon and the beast and the false prophet. They are called unclean spirits. They are "three unclean spirits like frogs" (Rev. 16:13). The reference to frogs reminds me of the second plague upon Egypt; however, these were evil spirits. Before there were details given about the damage done by the wrath of the sixth bowl, we were told that its first effect was upon the River Euphrates; and we were told the purpose for this. "The sixth bowl is poured out on the great river, the Euphrates; and its water was dried up, so that the way would be prepared for the kings from the east" (v. 12). The River Euphrates was the eastern boundary of the Promised Land. It was to be dried up so that kings from the east would be able to cross over the dry land and come to aid the Romans in the destruction of Jerusalem. From Josephus, we know that Rome often used armies from the east to aid in their war engagements.

Again, notice the irony. When I think of curses here in this chapter, I also think of many of the former blessings of God. For example, at the birth of Christ the wise men came from the east to give gifts to Christ. Now, soldiers would come from the east to bring judgment on the city of Jerusalem.

Armageddon

John mentioned three unclean spirits like frogs in the pouring out of the sixth bowl (Rev. 16:13). The identity of these three unclean spirits should be evident by now. They were the dragon (Satan), the Beast (Rome), and false prophet (the Jewish priesthood). All of these forces would gather together for war in the presence of "the kings of the whole world…for the war of the great day of God, the Almighty" (v. 14). Rome would use all the forces of other nations at its disposal to bring down the city of Jerusalem. She would even use the Jewish priesthood. Satan is always there too.

The great war was called "Armageddon." The term Armageddon is another word that brings fear in the minds of many people. Most people don't know much about the Bible, but they are familiar with a couple of concepts like the number "666" and the word "Armageddon." Armageddon is usually associated with some battle in the future that will be the last battle on earth before the end of the world.

A popular view is that Iran will attack Israel, Russia will come down from the north to help, and this will bring about the end of the world. Prophecy experts are predicting when this will happen, which again, in their view, is in the generation of those who are alive today. Remember what I said — most every generation has been predicting this for their own generation since the death of Christ, and every one of them has been wrong. They missed it! Why should we expect Armageddon to happen in our own generation? Well, let me shock some of you again, and tell you that Armageddon is not something you have to fear, because it has already happened. Yes, you heard me correctly! The war at Armageddon has already happened. It happened about 2000 years ago.

The actual word Armageddon in the original Hebrew language consists of two parts from the Hebrew word "har-megiddo." If one were to read the word in the original Hebrew language (and as transliterated into the Greek text), that person would read the first part as "har" which means "mountain." The second part of the word is "megiddo" which is the name of a field in the plain of Palestine. Literally, the word Armageddon means "Mountain of Megiddo." This presents a puzzle because there is no mountain in the "Plain of Megiddo." It is flat land.

Why then did John refer to this particular place with no mountain? This place was famous to all Israelites for several reasons. It was a strategic location in the land of Israel for fighting off enemies. Wars often concluded here and were either won or lost. Think of it as the Jewish "Waterloo." It reminds me of a major defeat of a powerful kingdom. Think of the American Revolutionary War. It would be like using the word "Yorktown." In the American Civil War, it might be compared to "Gettysburg."

Armageddon was also the place where the last godly king of Judah died (King Josiah). Bible students will recognize the name of Josiah and Josiah's Reform. He was one of the greatest kings in the history of Israel. We associate names with places, and Josiah was associated with Armageddon. Similarly, in the history of the United States it would be like associating the death of Lincoln with Ford's Theater or like associating the death of JFK with Dallas. "In his days Pharaoh Neco king of Egypt went up to the king of Assyria to the river Euphrates. And King Josiah went to meet him, and when Pharaoh Neco saw him he killed him at Megiddo" (2 Kings 23:29). When I personally read of all the great deeds of Josiah and his righteous and godly character, I almost shed tears when I read of his death. The great leader was gone. His death appeared to be the end of the glory of Israel. He died at Meggido. Never forget Meggido! For an Israelite, it was like the end of the world. It signified the last great battlefield of an empire. Thus, Armageddon was a metaphor for the last great battle at Jerusalem. It was a reference to the destruction of the city of Jerusalem in the apostolic Age.

The Last Plague

Lastly, the *seventh* plague poured out by the seventh bowl was described in terms "of flashes of lightning and sounds and peals of thunder; and there was a great earthquake, such as there had not been since man came to be upon the earth, so great an earthquake was it, and so mighty" (16:18). Also, along with the earthquake were "huge hailstones, about one hundred pounds each, came down from heaven upon men" (v. 21a). This corresponded to the seventh plague of hailstones poured out upon Egypt.

Some Bible scholars believe that this was a picture of the heavy stones that were heaved upon Jerusalem by the Roman soldiers from outside the walls of Jerusalem using catapults. These caused the walls of Jerusalem to fall down, and resulted in the collapse of the city. With the final bowl of wrath poured out, a loud voice came out of the temple from the throne, saying, "It is done" (Rev. 16:17). This was the last gasp for life. It was time for the undertakers! John put it well in metaphorical form. "And every island fled away, and the mountains were not found" (Rev. 16:20). Everything was gone. There was nothing left.

Verse 19 is interesting. "The great city was split into three parts, and the cities of all the nations fell. Babylon the Great was remembered before God, to give her the cup of the wine of His fierce wrath." Josephus tells us that Jerusalem was divided into three factions of Jews who were killing each other before they were conquered by Rome. Possibly, apart from these factions, if Jerusalem had been united, she could have held off the advance of the Romans much longer.

However, before the Romans could finish off the city, the Jews in essence destroyed themselves. As Titus was approaching the city we are told by Josephus that "it so happened that the sedition at Jerusalem was revived and parted into three factions, and that one faction fought against the other, which partition in such evil cases may be said to be a good thing, and the effect of Divine justice" (*Wars* 5.1.1).

Thus, there is here the fulfillment of the prophecy of Jesus against apostate Israel as it is recorded for us in the Gospel of Luke. When Jesus approached Jerusalem, he saw the city and wept over it, saying, "If you had known in this day, even you, the things which make for peace! But now they have been hidden from your eyes. For the days will come upon you when your enemies will throw up a barricade against you, and surround you and hem you in on every side, and they will level you to the ground and your children within you, and they will not leave in you one stone upon another, because you did not recognize the time of your visitation" (Luke 19:41–44).

Conclusion

Lastly, before I leave this chapter of my book, it is proper to say something about the character of God. Even in the midst of judgment, God is also gracious in extending an offer of forgiveness upon repentance. In Revelation 14:6, God sent an angel to preach the gospel. "And I saw another angel flying in midheaven, having an eternal gospel to preach to those who live on the earth [land], and to every nation and tribe and tongue and people." Jerusalem was a global city, with people present from all over the known world who came to make pilgrimages to the holy city.

In 16:9, we find that after the fourth bowl was emptied, John said: "and they did not repent so as to give Him glory." In 16:11, after the fifth bowl was emptied, John said: "and they did not repent of their deeds." I have examined this concept before, but it does not hurt to remember it again. Until it is all over, God always has His hand extended out willingly to offer His grace of forgiveness. Even after many tragedies and suffering endured by men because of their own sin, up to the point of death itself, God stands ready and willing to forgive. It was true for the city of Jerusalem, and it is true for anyone who reads this book. All a person must do is repent of his sins and turn to Christ for forgiveness. This can be done at any time and at any place.

Now, we have covered the *three sevens*. We have followed John as he described the seven seals, the seven trumpets, and the seven bowls of wrath. It was all over! In John's vision, Jerusalem was a rubble of ashes. The enemy of the church who was called the false prophet was dead. God had predicted the collapse of the Roman Empire (Rev. 17:11). Nero was dead. The final end of Nero and of the false prophet will be revealed in Revelation 19. Chapter 20 of Revelation will describe the final end of Satan.

What happens after a war? Think of a funeral service. Think of a victory party. We will see these two events in the next chapter of my book. Then, in both chapters 21 and 22, (the last two chapters of Revelation) we will look at the future of the church after Jerusalem had been destroyed. The reader will see the promise of blessing both here on this earth and in the world to come (heaven) for those who worship at the feet of Christ.

10
A POST-MORTEM ANALYSIS AND THE VICTORY MARCH

"After these things I heard something like a loud voice of a great multitude in heaven saying, Hallelujah! Salvation and glory and power belong to our God; BECAUSE HIS JUDGMENTS ARE TRUE AND RIGHTEOUS; for He has judged the great harlot who was corrupting the earth with her immorality, and HE HAS AVENGED THE BLOOD OF HIS BOND-SERVANTS ON HER" (Rev. 19:1–2)

Introduction

In this chapter, which covers Revelation chapters 17 through 19, I will deal with what I call a *post-mortem analysis* of Jerusalem. A post-mortem analysis describes a person's condition after death. Jerusalem was dead. After death there usually is a funeral service which includes a eulogy. I will spend some time on what I view in the text as a eulogy. Also, after the defeat of Jerusalem there was a *victory march* in heaven that paid homage to Christ who was the great conqueror. In addition, John introduces another name for the false prophet — a harlot who is also called *Babylon the Great*. John will depict the final destiny of the great harlot (Jerusalem) and the beast (Nero). Both will be cast into the lake of fire. Later in Chapter 20, John tells us when the Devil will be cast into the lake of fire. Finally, looking ahead, Revelation ends with the theme of victory in chapters 21–22. Thus, the main elements that I shall cover in this chapter are the funeral eulogy, the victory march, the identity of the great harlot, and the final disposition of the great harlot and the beast.

Remember that in Rev. 16:17 "the seventh angel poured out his bowl upon the air, and a loud voice came out of the temple from the throne, saying, "It is done." My conclusion is that the city was totally destroyed at that particular time because John said: "And every island fled away, and the mountains were not found" (Rev. 16:20). Everything was gone. Nothing was left.

The Eulogy

A eulogy is a speech at a funeral remembering the dead. In our text, instead of a funeral remembering a great and wonderful person, there is the funeral of one who was cursed by God. Instead of being reminded of how good and decent the person was, the reader would be reminded of how despicable the person had been. This eulogy reminded the reader of how horrible the city of Jerusalem had become, and therefore why God was justified in destroying her.

In Rev. 18:2, John presented part of the eulogy. "And he cried out with a mighty voice, saying, 'Fallen, fallen is Babylon the great! She has become a dwelling place of demons and a prison of every unclean spirit, and a prison of every unclean and hateful bird.'" After the decimation of the city, it would be like a ghost town, but worse. It would be inhabited by evil spirits, wild animals, and birds like buzzards that eat the remaining flesh left on the bones of the dead.

All the normal sounds of happiness in a bustling city would be gone. No more music. No more craftsmen. No more weddings. No more buying and selling. "And the sound of harpists and musicians and flute-players and trumpeters will not be heard in you any longer; and no craftsman of any craft will be found in you any longer; and the sound of a mill will not be heard in you any longer; and the light of a lamp will not shine in you any longer; and the voice of the bridegroom and bride will not be heard in you any longer; for your merchants were the great men of the earth, because all the nations were deceived by your sorcery" (Rev. 18:22–23).

The economy that was dependent upon the lifestyle of idolatry was gone. Jerusalem had become rich through trade and mercantilism, but now Jerusalem was dead. "Then I saw an angel standing in the sun, and he cried out with a loud voice, saying to all the birds which fly in midheaven, come, assemble for the great supper of God, so that you may eat the flesh of kings and the flesh of commanders and the flesh of mighty men and the flesh of horses and of those who sit on them and the flesh of all men, both free men and slaves, and small and great" (Rev. 19:17–18). This was a description of what happened to Jerusalem. This was part of Jerusalem's eulogy.

It is interesting to compare the end of the literal Babylon in the Old Testament with the spiritual Babylon (Jerusalem) in Revelation. The Old Testament Babylon, too, had become a ghost town full of wild flesh-eating animals. In Isaiah 13 the prophet says the following:

> "Behold, I am going to stir up the Medes against them, who will not value silver or take pleasure in gold. And *their* bows will mow down the young men. They will not even have compassion on the fruit of the womb, *nor* will their eye pity children. And Babylon, the beauty of kingdoms, the glory of the Chaldeans' pride will be as when God overthrew Sodom and Gomorrah. It will never be inhabited or lived in from generation to generation, nor will the Arab pitch his tent there, nor will shepherds make *their flocks* lie down there. But desert creatures will lie down there, and their houses will be full of owls. Ostriches also will live there, and shaggy goats will frolic there. Hyenas will howl in their fortified towers and jackals in their luxurious palaces. Her *fateful* time also will soon come and her days will not be prolonged." (Isa. 13:17–22)

This description of Old Babylon exactly parallels the condition of the New Babylon, the city of Jerusalem after her destruction. The fire in the city of Jerusalem had finally burned out, and the only sounds remaining were those of wild beasts. God used a strange nation to bring judgment upon the people in both Old Babylon and New Babylon. Both cities became ghost towns occupied by wild animals. This was part of Jerusalem's eulogy.

This reminds me of a funeral I conducted once. I never knew the person, but a poor lady I had helped a great deal with charity asked me to preside over the funeral for her sister. I agreed to do it. Later I found out the woman in the coffin had been a prostitute, and she had died of an overdose of drugs. I did not really know that until after the service. In situations where I am asked to preside over a funeral, and where I do not know the deceased, I usually say very little about the person and just emphasize the gospel for those who are living. That was a sad funeral. To emphasize the potency of the text here in Revelation, think of a funeral for a wicked person. Think of a funeral for Hitler. This is what John was dealing with here. It is my view (which I shall justify below) that this Jerusalem was called "the Great Harlot" (Rev. 17:1). She was called "*BABYLON THE GREAT, THE MOTHER OF HARLOTS, AND OF THE ABOMINATIONS OF THE EARTH*" (Rev. 17:5).

Who was the "Mother of All Harlots"?

Who was this woman who was called both the Mother of All Harlots, and was also called Babylon the Great? This is a major question where good men disagree. It has been controversial in the church down through the ages. Oxford scholar and Revelation commentator Ian Boxall states that "over the centuries, Revelation's 'Babylon' has been associated both with imperial Rome and with historical fallen Jerusalem."[1] Henry Barclay Swete, Robert H. Mounce, David E. Aune, Craig S. Keener, and the majority of Revelation commentators identify her with Rome. Milton S. Terry, Philip Carrington, David Chilton, and Kenneth L. Gentry, Jr. identify her with Jerusalem. I agree with the latter.

I must confess that at one time I held the position that Babylon the Great (the Great Harlot or the Mother of Harlots) should be identified with the Roman Empire. That was my conviction as I preached some years ago through these latter chapters in Revelation. However, I was forced by two particular verses to change my mind. I hit a roadblock. I had to recant! I told my congregation that even the preacher has a right to change his mind, even in the middle of a sermon series. My gracious congregation understood. I had to backtrack through several previous sermons and revise a number of things. It was a humble test for me, but I believed that the truth was more important than my pride.

In what follows, I will argue for the position that the great harlot was Jerusalem. First, what did this harlot look like? I can tell a great deal about a woman by her dress and her lifestyle. "The woman was clothed in purple and scarlet, and adorned with gold and precious stones and pearls, having in her hand a gold cup full of abominations and of the unclean things of her immorality" (Rev. 17:4). I believe John's description was more than a description of a loose woman. I believe John was describing the priesthood of Jerusalem as represented by the high priest. Let us look at a few reasons why I draw this conclusion. Remember that Jerusalem and the priesthood can be used interchangeably, just like Hitler and Nazi Germany during World War II.

First, it is interesting here that the dress of the harlot resembles the dress of the Jewish high priest as he entered the temple's holy

---

[1] Ian Boxall, *The Revelation of St. John* (London: A & C Black, 2006), 239.

of holies once a year. He wore purple and scarlet clothing, and there were precious stones and pearls on his breastplate. The clothing of Aaron is described in the Book of Exodus. Notice how the clothing of the high priest resembles the great harlot.

> "These are the garments of which they shall make; a breastpiece and an ephod and a robe and a tunic of checkered work, a turban and a sash, and they shall make holy garments for Aaron your brother and his sons, that he may minister as priest to Me. They shall take the gold and the blue and the purple and the scarlet *material* and the fine linen. They shall also make the ephod of gold, and of blue and purple and scarlet *material* and fine twisted linen, the work of the skillfull workman." (Ex. 28:4–5)

> "You shall mount on it four rows of stones; the first row *shall be* a row of ruby, topaz and emerald; and the second row a turquoise, a sapphire and a diamond; and the third row a jacinth, and agate and an amethyst; and the fourth row a beryl and an onyx and a jasper; they shall be set in gold filigree." (Ex. 28:17–20)

Secondly, to demonstrate the connection between Jerusalem and the great harlot, there was one particular image I found in two separate verses that caused me to change my mind from identifying the harlot as Rome to identifying the harlot as Jerusalem. The image in the two verses is as follows:

> "And he *carried* [emphasis added] me away in the Spirit into a wilderness; and I saw a woman sitting on a scarlet beast, full of blasphemous names, having seven heads and ten horns." (Rev. 17:3).

> "And the angel said to me, 'Why do you wonder? I will tell you the mystery of the woman and of the beast that *carries* [emphasis

added] her, which has the seven heads and the ten horns'" (Rev. 17:7).

Notice a common image included in both verses. The beast with seven heads and ten horns *carried* the harlot. As we shall see below, the beast was obviously the Roman Empire. The harlot was being carried by the beast and therefore could not be the beast. They were two distinct persons. Thus, I concluded that the harlot could not be the Roman Empire. Some scholars have separated the identity of the city of Rome from the Roman Empire, and identified the beast as Rome and the harlot as the Roman Empire, but I do not believe this explanation is feasible. The harlot had to represent something other than Rome (or the Roman Empire) because the beast carried the harlot. Again, I believe the harlot represented Jerusalem, and more particularly, the leadership of Jerusalem or the Jewish priesthood.

Thirdly, notice that the mention of "Babylon" in chapter 17 (the city that was split into three parts) was a continuation of the "Babylon" first introduced in chapter 16, in the text where the seventh angel poured out the seventh bowl of wrath. There the object of the pouring out of the wrath of God was Jerusalem. A change in the identity of Babylon should not be expected between texts in such close proximity as Revelation 16:19 and Revelation 17:5. Thus, the Babylon of chapter 17 was the same as the Babylon of chapter 16. Both were Jerusalem.

Fourthly, in Rev. 17:16 John said: "And the ten horns which you saw, and the beast, these will hate the harlot and will make her desolate and naked, and will eat her flesh and will burn her up with fire." Jerusalem was desolate and naked after Rome's invasion. The ten horns represented the kings of other nations as a complete body under the authority of the Roman Empire that aided and abetted in the destruction of Jerusalem. Rome often recruited her vassal nations to aid in her military ventures. "The ten horns which you saw are ten kings who have not yet received a kingdom, but they receive authority as kings with the beast for one hour" (Rev. 17:12).

These kings had some power but they did not have the power of Caesar. They helped Rome for this particular "one hour" battle (a short, final battle compared to the long history of Israel). They, too, fully participated in the hatred of Jerusalem, and found pleasure in her destruction. "And the ten horns which you saw, and the beast, these will hate the harlot and will make her desolate and naked, and will eat her flesh and will burn her up with fire" (Rev. 17:16).

The allegiance of these ten kings to Rome, and their hatred of Israel were a result of the influence of God, who ordained that they would aid Rome in carrying out his secret will. God is sovereign! "For God has put it in their hearts to execute His purpose by having a common purpose, and giving their kingdom to the beast, until the words of God will be fulfilled" (Rev. 17:17). The prophecies of Jesus were fulfilled.

> "I say to you that many will come from the east and west, and recline *at the table* with Abraham, Isaac, and Jacob in the kingdom of heaven; but the sons of the kingdom will be cast out into the outer darkness; in that place there will be weeping and gnashing of teeth." (Matt. 8:11–12)

> "Therefore I say to you, the kingdom of God will be taken away from you and given to a people, producing the fruit of it. And he who falls on this stone will be broken to pieces; but on whomever it falls, it will scatter him like dust. When the chief priests and the Pharisees heard His parables, they understood that He was speaking about them." (Matt. 21:43–45)

In my opinion, it is inescapable that the great harlot was the priesthood who represented Jerusalem.

Fifthly, in demonstrating my view that the great harlot was Jerusalem and not Rome, in verse 18 of Chapter 17, John wrote, "The woman whom you saw is the *great city* [emphasis added], which reigns over the kings of the earth." We identified "the great city" in chapter 11:8: "And their dead bodies *will lie* in the street of *the great city* [emphasis added] which is mystically called Sodom and Egypt, where also their Lord was crucified." This was where the Lord was crucified. The *great city* was the city of Jerusalem.

No doubt you may ask the question: "if I take the position that Jerusalem was the great harlot, then how did Jerusalem reign over the kings of the earth?" The identity of the great harlot is wrapped up in this question. Let me explain this in the following.

John said Jerusalem was the one "with whom the kings of the earth committed *acts of* immorality, and those who dwell on the earth were made drunk with the wine of her immorality" (Rev. 17:2). These kings waged war against Christians. They too were drunk with passion in their desire to persecute Christians. "These will wage war against the Lamb, and the Lamb will overcome them, because He is Lord of lords and King of kings, and those who are with Him *are the* called and the chosen and faithful" (Rev. 17:14). Remember that the Greek word "earth" can be translated as the word "land." During the New Testament period before the fall of Jerusalem, there were a number of rulers who had influence over the land of Israel. They were all subservient to Caesar. They worshiped Caesar. However, and this is my main point, even though they were officially rulers of the land of the Jews, the Jewish priesthood, actually, ruled them. I've seen this in marriages. Officially, the husband is the head of his home, but unofficially, the wife "rules the roost."

The priesthood used their rulers to further their own purposes. In actuality, the priesthood ruled over the rulers; the best example being the manipulation of Pontius Pilate in the death of Christ. Herod Agrippa the First is held responsible for the death of James and the arrest of Peter. "Now about that time Herod the king laid hands on some who belonged to the church in order to mistreat them. And he had James the brother of John put to death. When he saw that it pleased the Jews, he proceeded to arrest Peter also" (Acts 12:1–3). Notice how the king did what was pleasing to the Jews! The Romans kings were officially over the land of Israel, but the harlot (the Jewish priesthood) manipulated these kings in the land of Israel.

In addition, notice that in Rev. 17:15, the great harlot sat on many waters. Later in chapter 17, an angel told John what that meant. Again, it is helpful when Revelation interprets itself. "And he said to me, "The waters which you saw where the harlot sits, are peoples and multitudes and nations and tongues"" (Rev. 17:15). This might appear to present some difficulty in identifying the harlot with the priesthood or Jerusalem, but actually, it presents no problem at all. Jerusalem was full of people from many nations who spoke many tongues.

> "Now there were Jews living in Jerusalem, devout men from every nation under heaven. And when this sound occurred, the crowd came together, and was bewildered because each one of them was hearing them speak in his own language. They were amazed and astonished, saying, 'Why, are not all these who are speaking Galileans? And how is it that we each hear them in our own language to which we were born? Parthians and Medes and Elamites, and residents of Mesopotamia, Judea and Cappadocia, Pontus, and Asia, Phrygia and Pamphylia, Egypt and districts of Libya around Cyrene, and visitors from Rome, both Jews and proselytes, Cretans and Arabs — we hear them in our own tongues speaking of the mighty deeds of God.'" (Acts 2:5–11)

Jerusalem was a cosmopolitan city especially during holy days. Some of the international Jews no doubt lived there permanently. It was the Mecca for Jews from all over the Roman Empire. It was the holy city for international and devout Jews who either lived there or made annual pilgrimages there. These multinational Jews were under the spell of the Jewish priesthood. This verse in Acts shows the connection between the Jewish priesthood with many nations and tongues.

Sixthly, in demonstrating that the harlot was Jerusalem (or the Jewish priesthood, or even the Jewish high priest), Rev. 18:4–5 reiterates that this was the city from which the elect Christians escaped before its destruction. "I heard another voice from heaven saying, 'Come out of her, my people, so that you will not participate in her sins and receive of her plagues; for her sins have piled up as high as heaven, and God has remembered her iniquities." God warned His elect to leave this place of harlotry. Thus, I believe this harlot was Jerusalem.

A *seventh* reason is derived from the timing issue again. Rome would not fall for several hundred years. Later, with the conversion of the Emperor Constantine to the Christian Faith, Rome would approve Christianity as a legal religion. Yet remember that the events in Revelation were to happen soon. The time is near. Jerusalem is the only option here. Christians must be ready to run from the city in the blink of an eye. In Revelation 16:15, it says: "(Behold, I am coming like a thief. Blessed is the one who stays awake and keeps his clothes, so that he will not walk about naked and men will not see his shame)."

Lastly, the city in this chapter was identified as the place where the prophets and saints were slain. The great harlot is "drunk with the blood of the saints, and with the blood of the witnesses of Jesus" (Rev. 17:6). Martyrdom certainly occurred in the city of Rome; but remember, Jerusalem is the focus of Revelation. Killing Christians was the major indictment of Jesus against the city of Jerusalem.

John made it clear that he was speaking of Jerusalem because it was in that city where the blood of the prophets and saints was shed. "And in her was found the blood of prophets and of saints and of all who have been slain on the earth" (Rev. 18:24). Remember John's words in Revelation 1:7 where he said: "BEHOLD, HE IS COMING WITH THE CLOUDS, and every eye will see Him, even those who pierced Him; and all the tribes of the earth [land] will mourn over Him. So it is to be. Amen." It was the Jewish people who were held responsible for piercing Christ using the instrument of the Romans rulers. These apostate Jews were charged with the guilt of the bloodshed of the saints in the past, of Christ in his death on the cross, and of the saints in the early church.

Thus, I conclude that the great harlot was Jerusalem. The three persons — the harlot, Babylon the Great, and the false prophet — are all one and the same.

The Response of Heaven

The saints of God in heaven were rejoicing over the destruction of Jerusalem. "Rejoice over her, O heaven, and you saints and apostles and prophets, because God has pronounced judgment for you against her" (18:20). In chapter 19, a great multitude in heaven sang: "Hallelujah! Salvation, glory and power belong to our God" (v. 1). Hallelujah means "Praise Jehovah." Notice that even though it was Rome who destroyed the city of Jerusalem, God was the one who received the praise. God brought judgment by using instruments on the earth, even such a great power as Rome. Rev. 19:2 further depicted the praises of God by the saints. "BECAUSE HIS JUDGMENTS ARE TRUE AND RIGHTEOUS; FOR HE HAS AVENGED THE BLOOD OF HIS BOND-SERVANTS ON HER." This was followed by a second Hallelujah. "And a second time they said, Hallelujah! HER SMOKE RISES UP FOREVER AND EVER." (v.3). The word "Hallelujah" was used four times in the first six verses of this section of chapter 19. Including the two previous uses there follows: "Amen, Hallelujah!" (v.4). "Hallelujah! For the Lord our God, the Almighty, reigns" (v.6). God rules in the affairs of men.

The Victory March

There was in Rev. 17:11–19, a picture of a victory march of Christ after the defeat of Jerusalem. After World War II was over, there were victory celebrations all over the world. Hitler was dead. The war was over and the wretched enemy had been defeated. Americans rejoiced in New York City. Sailors kissed the girls, and the girls did not mind. The armies returned home, and the people gathered on the streets to greet their heroes.

It was common in Rome after a victory of the army over some particular enemy that the military general led his soldiers into the city before crowds who celebrated the victory. The Arch of Titus, which can be visited in Rome today, is a monument to his victory marches. It was constructed around A.D. 82 by the Roman Emperor Domitian shortly after the death of his older brother Titus to commemorate Titus' victories, including the Siege of Jerusalem in A.D. 70. In the victory march, the conquered enemy was put on display as the army marched into the city. The conquered walked in chains behind the horses. Their wealth was carried and displayed on wagons.

This victory march in Revelation took place in heaven, the home of the victors. John tells us this when he said: "and I saw heaven opened" (Rev. 19:11). This victory march was led by the Great General of heaven. We meet him in chapter 19. He is called the King of Kings and the Lord of Lords. "And on His robe and on His thigh He had a name written, KING OF KINGS, AND LORD OF LORDS" (Rev. 19: 16). He is Jesus Christ. "And I saw heaven opened, and behold, a white horse, and He who sat on it is called Faithful and True, and in righteousness he judges and wages war" (Rev. 19:11). He was followed by his soldiers who also rode on white horses.

"And the armies which are in heaven, clothed in fine linen, white and clean, were following Him on white horses" (Rev. 19:14).

Not only had he won this war, but he will win all wars in the future with all nations. "From His mouth comes a sharp sword, so that with it He may strike down the nations, and He will rule them with a rod of iron; and He treads the wine press of the fierce wrath of God, the Almighty" (Rev. 19:15). I believe the scope of the kingship of Christ is expanded here from his victory over Jerusalem to his eventual victory over all the nations of the world through the preaching of the gospel (the sharp sword from the mouth of Christ).

We are reminded in Psalm 2, that Jesus actually will rule over all the nations of the entire earth (as seen from the moon). Look out, Rome! Look out, all nations that arrogantly take counsel against God! "You shall break them with a rod of iron. You shall shatter them like earthenware. Now therefore, O kings, show discernment; Take warning O judges of the earth. Worship the Lord with reverence and rejoice with trembling. Do homage to the Son that He not become angry and you perish *in* the way. For His wrath may soon be kindled. How blessed are all who take refuge in Him" (Psalm 2: 9–12). Thus, these last two verses in Psalm 2 envisioned God's eventual victory over Rome. In chapter 19 of Revelation, there may have been a reference both to the defeat of Jerusalem, and also to the defeat of all the nations down through history by the King of kings.

The crowds in heaven saw the evidence of Christ's battle with the enemy. "He is clothed with a robe dipped in blood, and His name is called the Word of God" (Rev. 19:13). Christ was a General who actually fought in the midst of battle. He did not stand at a far distance and watch. This symbolizes that he was there in the midst of the fighting, in the midst of death and blood. It has been pointed out to me that in the Old Testament, kings always led their armies into battle. Of David, it is said that he failed to go to war when he committed sin with Bathsheba. He was AWOL. So it was explained in 2 Samuel 11:1: "Then it happened in the spring, at the time when kings go out *to battle*, that David sent Joab and his servants with him and all Israel, and they destroyed the sons of Ammon and besieged Rabbah. But David stayed at Jerusalem." David stayed home. From there he saw Bathsheba bathing and everything went downhill. If modern politicians, who are so quick to send our troops into war, were required to lead them onto the battlefield, then there would be fewer wars. There are just wars, but not all wars are justifiable. This is something to think about! However, this General (Jesus Christ) who was also a King, had the blood of his enemies dripping from his own garments. Again, it is confirmed here that this King riding on a white horse was Jesus Christ. He was called the Word of God.

The Final Destiny of the Great Harlot

Most every funeral has a burial service. There must be some disposition of the body. John here describes the final burial service of both the false prophet and the beast (Rev. 19:20). However, this was not just the burial of a physical body. This was a burial of the soul. This passage in Revelation spoke not only of a burial service but also of the eternal condition of both the false prophet and the beast.

The beast here was probably a reference to Nero since John also made a reference to the mark of the beast in verse 20. Nero was dead. He committed suicide in A. D. 68. Jerusalem was in ashes. The Jewish priesthood was dead. The final destination of the false prophet and the beast was the lake of fire. In the next chapter of Revelation, John will tell us when the Devil, too, shall be thrown into the lake of fire.

Conclusion

This concludes the *post-mortem analysis* which included the funeral of Jerusalem, the eulogy, the identity of the harlot, and the final burial. It also included the victory march of Christ after the war. The Jewish priesthood (or the high priest himself), who was also the great harlot, had been destroyed and cast into the lake of fire. Nero (the beast) had been cast into the lake of fire.

God divorced the harlot — Old Jerusalem. Jesus was ready to take a new bride — the church. Jesus rode in a procession of celebration in the midst of heaven itself. This was his victory march after the war. He had come home to take a new wife. There would be a great wedding feast. He rode on a white horse. Everyone in his army rode on a white horse. Everyone in heaven, including the martyrs, greeted them with joy. They were happy and singing. Not only was Jesus victorious over Jerusalem, but he will be victorious over all the nations that stand against him. This will come through the preaching of the gospel. Those who reject Christ will face his judgment as did Jerusalem. Only a few hundred years later, the great empire of Rome would fall into the hands of barbarians. Christianity would capture Rome. Christianity would begin its march to conquer Europe and the West.

The leaders of modern nations need to read history. Whether it is America or the rising empires of other nations, these nations must be reminded that if they turn their backs on God and the Christian faith, eventually Christ will destroy them with a rod of iron. Americans often think this cannot happen here. America thinks she is invincible. This was the belief of Jerusalem. Oh, how everyone needs to study the past! Oh, how there is a need to study about Jerusalem, Rome, and all the other empires down through history! For those who turn their faces against Jesus Christ, their days will be numbered. God is a God of love, but he is also a Holy God who will not tolerate those who arrogantly deny him.

This leads now into the final two chapters of my book. In the next chapter, I will cover the ultimate doom of Satan which is described in Chapter 20. He too, like the false prophet and the beast, will be sent to the lake of fire. In the last chapter of my book, I shall consider the future of God's church and the wonderful future of every individual Christian. This glorious future is revealed in chapters 21 and 22.

11
THE FINAL JUDGMENT

"And the devil who deceived them was thrown into the lake of fire and brimstone, where the beast and the false prophet are also; and they will be tormented day and night forever and ever." (Rev. 20:10)

Introduction

Chapter 20 of Revelation is one of the more controversial chapters in the book. One thing for certain, among almost all interpreters there is agreement that chapter 20 describes the final defeat of the Devil. He will be thrown into the lake of fire alongside the beast and the false prophet and tormented forever and ever (v.10).

Also, in this chapter there are both the death of death itself, and the final end of all those who do not belong to Christ. "And death and Hades were thrown into the lake of fire. This is the second death. And if anyone's name was not found written in the book of life, he was thrown into the lake of fire" (Rev 20:14–15). I will return to this later in this chapter.

A Little Review

Thus far in this book I have covered the prophecy of the *three sevens*. The seven-sealed book was opened. In it was the edict of God against the apostate Jews with its focal point of Jerusalem. Following the edict, the seven trumpets blew, and God gave the warning that he always gives before he brings judgment. Then, there was the execution of that judgment in the pouring out of the seven bowls of wrath. I identified the sea beast as Rome. I identified the land beast as Jerusalem or the Jewish priesthood. The land beast was also called the false prophet. He was also called Babylon and the great harlot. At the end of chapter 19, John told us about the end of the false prophet (Jewish priesthood) and the beast (Nero). "And the beast was seized, and with him the false prophet who performed the signs in his presence, by which he deceived those who had received the mark of the beast and those who worshiped his image; these two were thrown alive into the lake of fire which burns with brimstone" (Rev. 19:20). Thus, as I begin dealing with chapter 20 remember at this point, that the beast and the false prophet have already been cast into the lake of fire.

However, this still leaves the Devil. He is the worst of the three enemies of the church. In the minds of the Christians in the seven churches, he was alive and well on planet earth. Yet John describes his end here in Chapter 20. He too shall be cast into the lake of fire. What transpires in chapter 20, before Satan is cast into the lake of fire, has always been a matter of controversy.

Remember the Time-Restrictions

I have presented the case that the time-restrictions of the events described in Revelation are limited to the time-frame around A.D. 70. Remember the time-limitation passages at the beginning of Revelation: "the time is near" (1:1) and the "time is at hand" (1:3). Remember too my description of the time-limitation passages at the end of Revelation. John did not shift gears at all. He still maintained, even to the last chapter, that the events he described would occur soon. He says in Rev. 22:6, that these things "must soon take place." As we have seen before, he repeats this time-restriction four more times in Chapter 22. As I have previously mentioned, I believe the integrity of John and God himself depends upon interpreting these time-restrictions literally. When John says "soon," he must have meant that these events described in Revelation would happen quickly.

Transcending the Time-Restrictions

I believe the time-restrictions in Revelation must be taken seriously. However, since I am dealing with the future of Satan in chapter 20, I also believe this chapter in particular moves outside of these time-restrictions and gives us a picture of what happens to Satan far into the future. His final destruction obviously did not happen 2000 years ago. Hyper-preterists accuse me of being inconsistent here because I interpret this chapter as occurring outside of the time-restrictions. They interpret all the events in chapter 20 as if they occurred in A.D. 70. They believe the resurrection of the dead, the final judgment, and the end of Satan occurred in A.D. 70. I do not believe this.

Thus I must grant that this is one chapter in Revelation that *transcends* the time-restrictions; it takes us on a journey far into the future, which to this day has not been totally fulfilled. In this particular chapter, John lifts the reader up from the time-restrictions of the rest of the book and gives him a bird's eye view of what will happen to Satan when the world will come to an end. John also deals with the final judgment. When the readers of the seven churches heard the number "one-thousand years," I believe they would have been compelled to think more long-term in regard to the events mentioned in this particular chapter. This may not be a literal one-thousand years, but it certainly implies a long period of time. This justifies a long-term view here in this chapter. I will demonstrate this more clearly in other sections to follow.

Even though the lake of fire existed in A.D. 70, Satan would not be finally cast into it until sometime into the future. In the midst of the events that would shortly take place (around A.D. 70), John hands the reader a device that will show him what will happen to

Satan far into the future. Think of a submarine ship where men are moving along in certain deep waters with only a limited view of their interior submarine environment; then the captain looks through a periscope and gets a look above the waters. With the periscope the captain can see above and beyond the sight limitations of the submarine. This device enables men to see great distances. The destruction of Jerusalem and Nero is only a partial comfort for Christians in any age. What about Satan? When will he be cast into the lake of fire? Chapter 20 gives the reader a clear picture of the final end of Satan in the future. It is the final guarantee of victory and comfort for all Christians living in every age.

Returning to Chapter 20

The beginning verse of chapter 20 speaks of the angel coming down from heaven. "Then I saw an angel coming down from the heaven, holding the key of the abyss and a great chain in his hand" (Rev. 20:1). In chapter 19, following the eulogy of Jerusalem, there was the victory march of Christ along with his army in heaven. Chapter 20 transports the reader back to earth.

The Abyss

The angel held the key of the abyss, and also had a great chain in his hand. The key was an instrument of power. The key opened and closed the abyss, the dwelling place of Satan. This angel had the power to cast Satan into the abyss, and he had the power to let Satan out of the abyss. It is my belief that this angel was Christ. It is evident from the Bible that Christ ultimately has the power over both heaven and hell. Christ is the person in John's vision in the first chapter of Revelation, and there John plainly tells us that Christ had the keys of death and Hades. "When I saw Him, I fell at His feet, like a dead man. And He placed His right hand on me, saying, 'Do not be afraid; I am the first and the last, and the living One; and I was dead and behold, I am alive forevermore, and I have the keys of death and of Hades'" (Rev. 1:17–18). John wrote to the Church at Philadelphia the following concerning Christ: "He who is holy, who is true, who has the key of David, who opens and no one will shut, and who shuts and no one opens" (Rev. 3:7).

Satan will be cast into the abyss and bound with a chain for a thousand years. "And he laid hold of the dragon, the serpent of old, who is the devil and Satan, and bound him for a thousand years" (20:2). Of course, this is a metaphor since Satan is a spirit. A spirit cannot be bound with a literal chain. Notice the angel *laid hold* of the dragon. The dragon did not lay hold of the angel. The angel was in total control. Using common parlance, the angel kicked him in the seat of his pants and put a headlock on him. God is in total control.

One Thousand Years

Satan will be bound for a thousand years (v.2). After this period, he will be unchained. Satan will be limited in what he can do for this one-thousand year period, and then he will be released for a short period of time: "and he threw him into the abyss, and shut *it* and sealed *it* over him, so that he would not deceive the nations any longer, until the thousand years were completed; after these things he must be released for a short time" (Rev. 20:3). Satan will not prevent the spread of the gospel to the Gentiles. This is the purpose of binding him in the abyss.

All right, here are some more big issues! Are one-thousand years to be taken literally? What is the time period in history that they cover? These are two major issues that I will discuss.

First, is the one-thousand year period to be taken literally? I believe the number one-thousand is not a reference to a literal period of one-thousand years. The Bible is full of symbolic numbers.

Christians are to forgive "seven times seventy" (Matthew 18:22). There were 144,000 of God's elect who had the seal of God on their forehead (Rev. 7:4). The horsemen of the Romans who came up against the city of Jerusalem were 200 million (Rev. 9:16). It is very difficult for me to take such passages as these as literal. As I mentioned in a previous chapter, in Psalm 50, the psalmist said that God owns the cattle on a thousand hills, yet the psalmist knew the world contained more than a thousand hills with cattle on them. He knew God owned the cattle on all the hills of the whole world. I view the number one-thousand as symbolic from the onset.

When Will Satan Be Bound?

Now, the second question is, when will this period occur when Satan is bound? This certainly is a more difficult question. He will be bound during most of the one-thousand years. He will only be released at the end of this period for a short period of time (Rev. 20:7). It would be most consistent with my time-restrictions to interpret this period as happening sometime around A.D. 70. However, as I mentioned above, since this chapter involves the casting of Satan into the lake of fire and the final judgment, then it appears that this time-limitation should be transcended.

There are Gentiles that are yet to be called into the Church. There must be yet a major conversion of the Jews. Satan has not yet been cast into the lake of fire, thus the one-thousand year period cannot be limited to the apostolic period. Remember, here in chapter 20 the periscope is up, and the skipper in the submarine is looking far beyond what he can see inside the submarine.

Many interpreters of the Bible who hold to the futurist view believe this time period will be in the future. According to them, it will follow a rapture of the church out of this world, and the descent of Christ who will rule the earth for a literal one-thousand years.

The Binding of Satan

Others believe the period from the first coming of Christ to the second coming of Christ is identical with the one-thousand years. Still others believe that this period will come as a glorious period on earth a thousand years preceding the second coming of Christ. I believe that the Millennium (1,000 years) covers the era of the Christian church from the first coming of Christ to the second coming of Christ; however, toward the end of this period, I believe the gospel will be so effective that a glorious period will climax this age.

From this perspective, the church is now in that one-thousand period. Satan is bound now. The success of the gospel demonstrates the binding of Satan. He is alive but *not well* on Planet Earth. This may sound strange with so much evil in the world, but if you read the language of the Bible, it is difficult to come to a different conclusion. Also, students of church history should find credence in this view.

Biblical Credence

Look at how the Scriptures speak of the condition of Christians in this present world. The Bible gives strong evidence that Christians actually are living in the Millennium and that Satan is bound. According to the Scriptures, the binding of Satan began when Christ came to earth. When Jesus was asked if he was using Satan's power to control the demons of Satan, he answered them as follows: "But if I cast out demons by the Spirit of God, the kingdom of God has come upon you. Or how can anyone enter the strong man's house and carry off his property, unless he first binds the strong *man*? And then he will plunder his house" (Mat. 12:28–29).

The Lord also gave this power to the disciples, and they were amazed at how they could control the demons. The seventy returned with joy, saying: "Lord, even the demons are subject to us in Your name. And he said to them, 'I was watching Satan fall from heaven like lightning. Behold, I have given you authority to tread on serpents and scorpions, and over all the power of the enemy, and nothing will injure you'" (Luke 10:17–19). Jesus spoke of his own death as the casting out or the binding of Satan. Satan was bound during the life of Christ, and at his death. "Now judgment is come upon this world; now the ruler of this world will be cast out. And I, if I am lifted up from the earth, will draw all men to Myself" (John 12: 31–32). The spread of the gospel to the Gentiles is evidence of the binding of Satan.

Paul told the Colossians that Christ "disarmed the rulers and authorities" (Colossians 2:15). Peter spoke of demons as those whom God "cast them into hell and committed them to pits of darkness, reserved for judgment" (2 Peter 2:4). Jude spoke of the same thing. "And angels who did not keep their own domain, but abandoned their proper abode, He has kept in eternal bonds under darkness for the judgment of the great day" (Jude 6). This does not mean that the demons were not active in the apostolic age or that they still are not active today. It means they are limited in their activities. They are bound. Neither Satan nor his demons will prevent the gospel from spreading to all the nations. The purpose of this binding is to limit Satan so that "he would not deceive the nations any longer" (Rev. 20:3a). Christ told the Apostle Paul that he was to preach the gospel "to open their eyes so that they may turn from darkness to light and from the dominion of Satan to God." (Acts 26:18a).

Finally, in the Great Commission Jesus says: "all authority has been given to Me in heaven and on earth" (Matthew 28:18). From the fact that all authority has been given to Christ, the church should go and preach the gospel to all the nations "baptizing them in the name of the Father and the Son and the Holy Spirit, teaching them to observe all that I commanded you; and lo, I am with you always, even to the end of the age" (Matthew 28:20). This does not sound like defeat to me. This gives me reason to hope in the success of the gospel as Christ conquers all the nations for himself.

Notice also the calling of Christians to a place of rule and royalty, a position of preeminence over Satan. For example, Christians are seated with Christ in heavenly places (Ephesians 2: 5–6). He has made us to be a kingdom (Rev. 1:6). We are a royal priesthood (1 Peter 2:9). All things belong to us (1 Corinthians 3: 21–22). We overcome the world (I John 5:4–5).

God will build his kingdom, and the gates of hell will not prevail against it (Matthew 16:18). Gates do not attack the enemy. They protect the occupants behind the gates. As the gospel goes forth into the world, those behind the gates of hell will not prevail against the great offensive power of the gospel. Whatever Christians bind on earth shall be bound in heaven, and whatever they loose on earth will be loosed in heaven (Matt. 18:18). This text is applicable to more than church discipline. "If we endure we will also reign with Him" (2 Tim. 2: 12b). Does this sound like Christians are losers now? I hardly think so! Satan is bound today. Gentry describes the Millennium as follows:

> "John's Millennium is an image of Christ's present rule with his people. He established his kingdom in the first century, because the prophetic time was "fulfilled" and the time of the kingdom was "at hand" (Mark 1:15). Since he has all authority "in heaven and on earth" (Matt 28:29), his people in heaven and on earth share in his rule. His kingdom also involved the binding of Satan so that the gospel may go to all nations, and the spiritual resurrection which occurs at the moment of salvation. The Millennium is John's symbol for the era of the new covenant, the

church age, the kingdom of heaven, i.e., the period of current, worldwide gospel proclamation."[1]

Historical Credence

As a student of history, I have learned that over the long period since the resurrection of Christ, the Church actually has made great advances. Satan has been bound. Christianity captured the seat of the Roman Empire in less than 400 years. The Roman Empire legalized Christianity at the conversion of Constantine in A.D. 313. Who would have ever predicted this ascendancy of Christianity in Rome when Nero was killing believers? The last laugh would be on Nero. The last laugh would be on Rome.

What secular historians call the "Dark Ages" actually can be viewed as a time of great advance in the church. For example, Alfred the Great (who ruled from A.D. 871 to A.D. 901) is considered by many scholars to have been the ablest and most remarkable of all English kings; he was a dedicated Christian ruler who was greatly influenced by his faith in Christ. This faith enabled him to make much beneficial advancement for his people.

The Protestant Reformation (ca.1517) influenced most of Europe, including the British Empire (the Church of England), and eventually spread to America. In many places in America today, there is a church steeple on almost every street. Christianity has had influence in every area of life including science, economics, politics, and education. Looking at the advance of the Kingdom of God over the last 2,000 years, the church has made great and glorious strides.

Yes, at certain periods in history, it is true that Christianity sees dark days. Sometimes it appears that death is knocking at the door of the church. Even today, in certain parts of the world, Christians

---

[1] Kenneth Gentry, *The Book of Revelation Made Easy* (Powder Springs: American Vision, 2008), 113.

are dying for their faith. As Judge Robert Bork said, America is certainly "slouching toward Gomorrah." However, history teaches us that it is during such times that Christ is at work preparing for a greater manifestation of his glory. The darkness is often most black just before the burst of the morning sun.

Some Christians believe that history began when they were born or when their local church was founded. It escapes their notice that the New Testament church began over two-thousand years ago. Taking the long-view of history, it seems obvious to me, that the church has made great progress. From twelve disciples came a great multitude of Christians, even in the midst of much opposition. We should never set aside the long-term view of the progress of the church even in the midst of her darkest days.

The Christian can be assured of the victory of God before the final end of Satan. God's rule through the work of the Holy Spirit is demonstrated in his kingdom on earth. It began with the cross, and it will end with the final blow that will be given to the head of Satan. That Kingdom will grow like a small mustard seed into a large tree (Matt. 13:31–32). In Habakkuk 2:14, the prophet tells us: "For the earth will be filled with the knowledge of the glory of the Lord, as the waters cover the sea." Thus, Jesus taught us to pray with such hope in the Lord's Prayer: "Your kingdom come, Your will be done on earth as it is in heaven" (Matthew 6:10). The Kingdom of God begins with change in the hearts of men, which changes the way they live. This changes cultures. A Christian culture is the evidence of the presence of the Kingdom of God.

The great hymn-writer Isaac Watts expressed an optimistic view of the future in his *Jesus Shall Reign*. The first verse exhibits this hope for the Kingdom of God on this earth before the Second Advent: "Jesus shall reign where'er the sun does his successive journeys run; his kingdom stretch from shore to shore, till moons shall wax and wane no more."

Every time I am ridiculed for believing that I live in a golden age, I ask my critic to think of one thing. Think of life without a dentist! Oh, how I am thankful for a dentist when I have a toothache. We actually live in a golden age. There are some good men who believe in a golden period yet to come. Others believe we are in the midst of that age and that we shall see it grow even more in the future. This is my belief.

Is Satan Chained Today?

Certainly there is a sense in which Satan is chained today. He can only do what God allows him to do. The purpose of chaining something is not to annihilate it but to limit it. As an example, I am afraid of dogs because I was bitten by a dog as a young child. I have overcome that fear to some degree, but I am still nervous in the presence of any dog. I often hear from dog owners who tell me their dog (pit bulls, etc.) will not harm anyone. They all believe this! I sometimes think that my grave headstone will say: "They said the dog wouldn't bite." What I like is a dog on a chain. Think of Satan as a dog on a chain. He can't hurt you as a person as long as you are beyond the reach of the chain. Satan cannot hurt a Christian as long as he walks in the paths of righteousness. God may give Satan permission to claw you (like Job), but even this is for testing to prove the character of the Christian's faith.

To put it bluntly, in my view, the only reason the world is in such bad shape as it is in today is because Christians have not walked in the paths of righteousness. We have not lived by a biblical faith that seeks to conquer the world through the preaching of the gospel and the application of the law of God to all areas of life. We have not truly prayed "Thy Kingdom Come." May God soon send us both revival and reformation! Let us pray for a greater manifestation of triumph over Satan by God's people.

The First Resurrection

It is also seen in this text that during this one-thousand year period, these saints of God who had been martyred will reign with Christ from heaven itself for this period. This takes the reader back to the time-period around A.D. 70 because John described the martyrs as those who had not worshiped the beast or his image and had not received the mark on their forehead and on their hand. "Then I saw thrones, and they sat on them, and judgment was given to them. And I *saw* the souls of those who had been beheaded because of their testimony of Jesus and because of the word of God, and those who had not worshiped the beast or his image, and had not received the mark on their forehead and on their hand; and they came to life and reigned with Christ for a thousand years" (Rev. 20:4). It is important to note that all martyrs who die for Christ shall reign with him as those did in the apostolic church. Let us not forget this.

What is the first resurrection mentioned here in Revelation (Rev. 20:5)? I think it is clear that the first resurrection is the conversion of Christians that brings them from death to life. It happens to every Christian. "Truly, Truly, I say to you, he who hears My word, and believes Him who sent Me, has eternal life, and does not come into judgment, but has passed out of death into life" (John 5:24). For this reason, Paul tells the Romans to live like those risen from the dead. "Therefore do not let sin reign in your mortal body so that you obey its lusts, and do not go on presenting the members of your body to sin *as* instruments of unrighteousness; but present yourselves to God as those alive from the dead, and your members *as* instruments of righteousness to God" (Romans 6:12–13). One of the evidences of spiritual resurrection is the love of the brethren. "We know that we have passed out of death into life, because we love the brethren. He who does not love abides in death" (I John 3:14).

The first resurrection precedes the first death. The first death, the grave, still has power over believers, but John makes it clear that the second death (hell) has no power over believers. "Blessed and holy is the one who has a part in the first resurrection; over these the second death has no power, but they will be priests of God and of Christ and will reign with Him for a thousand years" (Rev. 20:6). The grave (the first death) still has power even over Christians; however, following the first death, every martyred saint of the apostolic age will take his place beside God and reign for one-thousand years. Other saints will also reign with Christ into eternity.

The Second Resurrection

If the spiritual resurrection is the first resurrection, then the second resurrection is the resurrection of the physical body. This has been a neglected teaching in the church. We often hear at funerals and at the burial service that the departed soul has entered into his final rest. This is just not true! The dead in Christ go to the grave awaiting the second and final resurrection of the body. The Westminster Confession of Faith puts it plainly in chapter 23, section 1:

> "The bodies of men after death return to dust, and see corruption; but their souls, (which neither die nor sleep,) having an immortal subsistence, immediately return to God who gave them. The souls of the righteous, being then made perfect in holiness are received into the highest heavens, where they behold the face of God in light and glory, *waiting for the full redemption of their bodies...* " [emph. added].

Jesus spoke of both resurrections when he said that the dead will hear the Son of God and live both now and into the future.

"Truly, truly, I say to you, an hour is coming and *now is* [emphasis added] when the dead will hear the voice of the Son of God, and those who hear will live. For just as the Father has life in Himself, even so He gave to the Son also to have life in Himself; and He gave Him authority to execute judgment, because He is the Son of Man. Do not marvel at this; for an hour is coming in which all who are in the tombs will hear His voice, and will come forth; those who did the good *deeds* to a resurrection of life, and those who committed the evil *deeds* to a resurrection of judgment" (John 5:25–29).

The modern church must never substitute "walking on streets of gold" (which is a metaphorical phrase) for the physical resurrection of the dead where Christians will dwell on a new earth "because we are looking for a new heaven and a new earth where righteousness dwells" (2 Peter 3:13). I fully expect in heaven to walk on *terra firma* and get my feet and hands dirty. I expect my wife to be working in her rose garden (without thorns).

The Release of Satan

Once this millennium period is over, then Satan will be released for a short period of time before his final destruction. "And when the thousand years are completed, Satan will be released from his prison" (v.7).

Typically, as most people read about the release of Satan, they think of a horrible age when Satan is not chained and will cause great destruction. Actually, if you read the passage closely, just the opposite is true. Even though Satan will have some success, it will be short-lived. John described the activity of Satan during this short period in verses 8–9: "and [he] will come out to deceive the nations which are in the four corners of the earth, Gog and Magog, to gather them together for the war, the number of them is like the sand of the seashore. And they came up on the broad plain of the earth and surrounded the camp of the saints and the beloved city, and the fire came down from heaven and devoured them."

Gog and Magog are symbolic of God's enemies (see Ezekiel 39:1–2). Satan will have some success in opposing the church. Satan and his demons will have the church of the nations surrounded at some point in the future; however, notice that it is Satan and his demons that are destroyed. The goal of Satan in his arrogance will be to deceive the church of nations, but actually it will be Satan who will be deceived. The people of God will witness the execution of Satan and all those who follow him.

The point of the release of Satan for a short period of time is not to put fear in the people of God about a great and terrible age to come. The point is that Satan will be crushed! The purpose of the release of Satan is for God to destroy him completely. If I release a rattlesnake intentionally from a pen, my purpose is not to let him harm other people but is to let him stretch out so that I can cut off his head with an axe. Likewise, God releases Satan not to cause havoc to the church but to give Satan enough rope to hang himself. Somehow, this picture of victory has been turned into a picture of fear for God's people. It ought not to be!

The Final Judgment

In verses 11–15 of chapter 20, John speaks of the final judgment by God. In the time in which I live, it seems that few people, even in the church, believe in a final judgment and the existence of a lake of fire. If the modern church does still believe in it, then she certainly is silent about it. There is no doubt that there is here, in the latter part of chapter 20, the reality of the final judgment of all men and the casting of some souls into the lake of fire.

Some might ask whether the lake of fire is to be taken literally. Since much of Revelation is symbolic, then maybe this too is a metaphor? I would not bet my life on it! If it is not to be taken literally, then whatever it is, it is just as bad (if not worse) than the metaphor. I interpret it literally because man in his person is both spirit and body. The Bible teaches that all the bodies of the dead shall be raised from the grave, and their spirits will be reunited with their physical bodies. They will appear before the judgment seat of God and spend all eternity in either heaven or in hell. I believe the lake of fire is hell. This is historic biblical Christianity. If there is no hell, there is no need for a gospel, and if there is no need for a gospel, then there is no need for the death of Christ. Christ becomes superfluous. In an age where the concept of sin has disappeared from our vocabulary and there is no threat of hell, no wonder morality has dipped so low.

Hell: The Lake of Fire

Jesus spoke of hell as a place where unbelieving souls are "cast out into the outer darkness, in that place there shall be weeping and gnashing of teeth" (Matthew 8:12). He spoke of hell as a place of "unquenchable fire [WHERE THEIR WORM DOES NOT DIE AND THE FIRE IS NOT QUENCHED]" (Mark 9:43–44). Jesus told the story of a certain rich man who went to hell. While there, he was in much misery. He lifted up his eyes and cried out: "Father Abraham, have mercy on me, and send Lazarus, that he may dip the tip of his finger in water and cool off my tongue, for I am in agony in this flame" (Luke 16:24). Jude tells us in Jude 6 that "angels who did not keep their own domain, but abandoned their proper abode, he has kept in eternal bonds under darkness for the judgment of the great day."

Regardless of how we interpret the text, hell is a horrible place. God does not enjoy punishing people, but he is a God of justice who hates sin. The good news is that if anyone becomes a follower of Christ, that person shall be delivered from hell. Men need not fear such a place if they repent and turn to Jesus for the forgiveness of their sins, trusting in his shed blood on the cross to make them right with God.

The judgment place of God is called the great white throne. "Then I saw a great white throne and Him who sat upon it, from whose presence earth and heaven fled away, and no place was found for them" (Rev. 20:11). White symbolizes purity. Because of the purity or holiness of God, none of us can stand in his presence unless Jesus goes before us.

John next saw the dead standing. Everyone will stand before God on the Judgment Day. No one will be sitting. God will be respected by everyone. No one will escape the judgment of God regardless of what position one held on earth and regardless of how one died. "And I saw the dead, the great and the small, standing before the throne (v.12a). And the sea gave up the dead who were in it, and death and Hades gave up the dead which were in them" (v. 13a). Whether kings or beggars, all men shall appear before the judgment seat of God. Whether a person was buried at sea or buried on land, that person shall appear before the judgment seat of God.

Even cremation of the body will not prevent this resurrection. The disposal of the body by cremation has increased over the years. For some people, it may be a financial decision. For others, it may be an attempt to prevent their appearance before God on the Judgment Day. It may be a denial of the resurrection and the continuation of life. I certainly respect people's decisions to dispose of their bodies as they see proper, but for me, I plan to be buried in a grave of dirt, which symbolizes my hope in the resurrection of the body. I want what was once called a Christian burial.

The Book of Life

There are additional books here in these verses. Remember, Revelation has already presented the seven-sealed book (5:1) and the little book that was digested by John (Rev. 10:2). Here we find several books, and among them is the book of life. "And I saw the dead, the great and the small standing before the throne, and books were opened; and another book was opened, which is the book of life" (v. 12a). The book of life is a list of the elect of God who have responded in faith and repentance to Christ. If your name appears there, you are safe from the lake of fire. "And if anyone's name was not found in the book of life, he was thrown into the lake of fire" (v. 15). It would appear that God keeps books (again a metaphor) or an account of all the deeds of men. Jesus said in Matthew 12:36: "But I tell you, that every careless word that people shall speak, they shall give an accounting for it in the day of judgment." All that we do is written in the books. This again is why we need to flee to Christ for salvation.

The Death of Death

Notice too that not only are unbelievers thrown into the lake of fire, but death and Hades (the grave) were thrown into the lake of fire. "And death and Hades were thrown into the lake of fire. This is the second death, the lake of fire" (v. 14). This will be the end of death. This will be the end of the grave. No more dying and death! No more funerals!

Conclusion

A period (1000 years) of great blessing will come for the church. The fullness of the Gentiles will be added to the Church, and we should expect a great conversion of Jews to Christ. At the end of this period, Satan will be released only for the purpose of providing God an excellent target. The false prophet, the beast, and Satan will all be in the lake of fire. This was no doubt a great comfort to the

Christians in the seven churches. It should be a comfort for all Christians who read this book.

As I move into the last two chapters of Revelation, the reader will see that God has a glorious future for his church. That too should give great comfort to all Christians. In addition to that, John will take all his metaphors describing the future church from the nature and character of heaven. This will teach us about the future of the church here on earth, but too, indirectly, this will teach us about heaven, the great and final hope for all believers.

12
THE FUTURE OF GOD'S PEOPLE

"And He who sits on the throne said, 'Behold I am making all things new.' And He said, 'Write for these words are faithful and true.'" (Rev. 21:5)

Introduction

The last two chapters of Revelation contain language that definitely is descriptive of heaven. For example, these chapters speak of a place where there shall no longer be any curse (22:3), death, mourning, crying, pain (21:4), and night (22:5). These descriptions certainly identify the characteristics of heaven. This will be the ultimate place of joy for every believer. Our ultimate hope in this life is that someday we will be delivered from death, pain, sorrow, and trials. This is the hope that should be proclaimed at every Christian funeral. What a wonderful day that will be!

Actually, the Bible does not say a great deal about the nature of heaven. Jesus spoke of heaven as his Father's house with many mansions. "In My Father's house are many dwelling places [mansions]; if it were not so, I would have told you; for I go to prepare a place for you. If I go and prepare a place for you, I will come again and receive you to Myself, that where I am, there you may be also" (John 14:2–3). The Greek word which is often translated "mansions" is actually better translated "dwellings." Dwellings are temporary places. Jesus appears to be speaking about a temporary place after death and before the resurrection of the body. This temporary state is often called Paradise. Jesus said to the thief on the cross "Truly I say to you, today you shall be with Me in Paradise" (Luke 23:43). Following the resurrection and the reuniting of the body with the spirit, there will be a more permanent dwelling place — a new heavens and a new earth.

Jesus appeared with Moses and Elijah on the Mount of Transfiguration (Luke 9:28–36). Both Moses and Elijah had been dead for a long time but were personally identified by John. Also, the Apostle Paul was caught up in what he called the Third Heaven which he identified as Paradise. He did not give any details. He just let us know that he heard something wonderful while he was there. He tells us that what he heard was impossible to put into human words. "I know a man in Christ who fourteen years ago — whether in the body I do not know, or out of the body I do not know, God knows — such a man was caught up to the third heaven, and I know how such a man — whether in the body or apart from the body I do not know, God knows — was caught up into Paradise and heard inexpressible words, which a man is not permitted to speak" (2 Corinthians 12:3–4).

I can say, with the authority of the Bible behind me, that in heaven God will make all things well, and every Christian shall know indeed the blessings described here in Revelation. John also spoke of heaven in Rev. 7:16–17 where he said: "They will hunger no longer, nor thirst anymore, nor will the sun beat down on them, nor any heat; for the Lamb in the center of the throne will be their shepherd, and will guide them to springs of the water of life, and God will wipe every tear from their eyes." I think maybe the most important thing Christians can learn from the Bible about heaven is simply that it is a place where they shall be with Jesus in all his glory.

A Dilemma

The reader may think at this point that I am going to handle the last two chapters of Revelation as I did chapter 20, using the periscope method. It would be easy for me to conclude that chapters 21–22 are about heaven and are not limited by the time-restrictions of Revelation. All I need to do is to put up the periscope from our submarine and look far into the future. However, I cannot in good conscience deal with the last two chapters as I did with chapter 20 where there was described a one-thousand year period, the final end of Satan, and the final Day of Judgment. In chapter 20, there were reasons within the chapter itself that prohibited limiting the text to the time-restrictions (such at 1,000 years). There was every reason to transcend those time limits. However, here in chapters 21–22, there are numerous reasons in the text itself that compel me to limit the time-restrictions to the apostolic period. My method of approaching chapters 21–22 will be different than my approach to chapter 20. It appears that the time-restriction verses of chapter 22 limit the text to the apostolic church. However, the language seems to be speaking of heaven. This appears to be a dilemma.

Solving the Dilemma

It could be argued that the last two chapters of Revelation are a picture of heaven, and that the warnings and gospel offerings are directed to those who are yet on earth and not in heaven. However, this would appear to contradict the time-restriction texts. Whatever John is describing in the last two chapters must be coming soon! What then is the answer to this dilemma? The time-restriction verses of chapter 20 did force me to conclude that John was speaking about the distant future of the apostolic church. Not so here in chapters 21–22. The topic in these two chapters was not heaven, but the primary topic was the Christian church on earth. What about the heavenly language? Are chapters 21–22 descriptive of heaven or the church on earth? That is the dilemma that I face; however, I do believe there is a solution to this dilemma.

Even though the topic of these two chapters is the Christian church on earth beginning with the churches in the apostolic age, yet the metaphorical language used to describe the church is from the nature and character of heaven itself. The language of heaven is the illustrative language used by John to describe the glory of the church on earth. Remember the nature of a metaphor. A metaphor has two parts. It has the basic truth, and it has the illustration or image that helps a person understand the basic truth.

I've used an example before, but I will use another one here. If I told my grandson that my old pocket knife is a million-dollar knife to me, this tells him two things. First, it tells him that my old pocket knife is important to me (the basic truth). Secondly, it tells him how important it is because he understands the value of a million dollars (the illustration). Actually, I would probably depart with the old knife for much less than a million dollars!

Likewise, John tells Christians that the church on earth is important (the basic truth); and secondly, John tells Christians how important the church is by using the language of a reality that has immense value — heaven. Thus, John uses heavenly language to describe the hope of the church on earth for believers in the apostolic age and, by extension, for those in the church until the completion of the 1,000 years. Certainly, the blessings of the church on earth would begin shortly for those Christians living in the apostolic age, for the time was near; but those blessings will continue until the end of the millennial age — and actually, into eternity

This "double meaning" is illustrated in the nature of biblical prophecy. The Bible often uses what I call *diplopia* (double vision). Often one event has two references. For example, David spoke of himself in Psalm 22:18, when he said: "They divide my garments among them, and for my clothing they cast lots." With these words he also spoke of Christ on the cross who would experience the same thing. "And they crucified Him, and divided up His garments among themselves, casting lots for them *to decide* what each man should take" (Mark 15:24). Diplopia is not my invention. It is a legitimate method of interpreting the Bible. Diplopia is similar to a metaphor. Diplopia sees two objects. Remember, a metaphor has two parts — the reality and the illustration. The reality (the church) is illustrated by something greater (heaven). Heavenly language is used to speak of the hope of the church on earth. The principle used in applying chapters 21–22 of Revelation to both the church and to heaven is not something new in the Bible.

In 1 Corinthians 2:9, Paul spoke of: "THINGS WHICH EYE HAS NOT SEEN AND EAR HAS NOT HEARD, AND WHICH HAVE NOT ENTERED THE HEART OF MAN, ALL THAT GOD HAS PREPARED FOR THOSE WHO LOVE HIM." This text is usually interpreted as a reference to heaven, and I think rightly so. However, taken in context, Paul spoke of "these things" as something already revealed to him and the disciples. "For to us God revealed *them* through the Spirit; for the Spirit searches all things, even the depths of God" (1 Corinthians 2:10). Again, this is an example of diplopia.

Another example of this diplopia is found in 2 Samuel 7:12–13 where David is planning to build a temple. God tells David that he will not build the temple, but his son Solomon will. In this promise about Solomon, we see what is undoubtedly a reference to both Solomon and Jesus Christ. "When your days are complete and you lie down with your fathers, I will raise up your descendent after you, who will come forth from you, and I will establish his kingdom. He shall build a house for My name, and I will establish the throne of his kingdom forever." One passage can have two references. This is what I am calling diplopia which is similar to the concept of a metaphor.

Earthly Descriptions

It appears from much of the content of these two chapters that John was still speaking of life on this earth prior to heaven. I have already mentioned the five time-restrictions in Chapter 22 that appear to limit the events to the apostolic age. However, chapters 21–22 use language that definitely does not describe heaven. For example: "Let the one who does wrong, still do wrong; and the one who is filthy, still be filthy" (Rev. 22:11a). This does not describe heaven. Because of the time-restrictions, neither can it be a warning from heaven to those on earth. Also, there is the warning of future judgment.

> "Behold, I am coming quickly, and My reward is with Me, to render to every man according to what he has done" (22:12).

> "But for the cowardly and unbelieving and abominable and murders and immoral persons and sorcerers and idolaters and all liars, their part will be in the lake that burns with fire and brimstone, which is the second death" (21:8).

In describing the nature of the place or location in chapter 22, there is the language of endurance: "and let the one who is righteous, still practice righteousness; and the one who is holy, still keep himself holy" (22:11b). There is the language of perseverance: "He who overcomes shall inherit these things, and I will be his God and he will be My son" (21:7). There is the presentation of the gospel in two places:

> "Then He said to me, 'It is done. I am the Alpha and the Omega, the beginning and the end. I will give to the one who thirsts from the spring of water of life without cost" (21:6).

"The Spirit and the bride say, 'Come.' And let the one who hears say, 'Come.' And let the one who is thirsty come; let the one who wishes take the water of life without cost" (22:17).

Notice in 21:1, that John is definitely *not* speaking of heaven here as the location of the church. He said the New Jerusalem came down out of heaven. He is speaking of the bride of Christ which is the church on earth. "And I saw the holy city, New Jerusalem, coming down out of heaven from God, made ready as a bride adorned for her husband." The source or the power for the church on earth comes from heaven. I believe this is the message John is seeking to communicate by speaking of the New Jerusalem coming down from heaven. God has divorced his former wife because she became a harlot, and now he is prepared to take a new wife — the church of the New Testament.

A New Creation

Also notice that in 21:1, there will be a new heaven and a new earth for the dwelling place of this New Jerusalem. Is this a reference to the church or to heaven? Here we grapple with the same problem. Isaiah appears to apply the language of a new heavens and a new earth (Rev. 21:1) to the beginnings of the New Covenant Church. "For behold, I create a new heavens and a new earth…and there will no longer be heard in her the voice of weeping and the sound of crying. No longer will there be in it an infant who lives but a few days, or an old man who does not live out his days; for the youth will die at the age of one hundred and the one who does not live out his days of one hundred will be thought to be accursed" (Isa. 65:17–20). Notice, this passage in Isaiah is not a description of heaven because old men still die there. Isaiah was not using metaphorical language. This must be a description of the church under the New Covenant, although the language is certainly heavenly.

Peter's reference to a new heavens and a new earth in 2 Peter 3 may again refer to the coming of Christ in judgment upon Jerusalem. If I am correct, however, regarding my theory of diplopia, he is taking his image from the future final day of the world when Christ will return, and there will indeed be a physically transformed new heaven and a new earth.

> "But the day of the Lord will come like a thief, in which the heavens will pass away with a roar and the elements will be destroyed with intense heat, and the earth and its works will be burned up. Since all these things are to be destroyed in this way, what sort of people ought you to be in holy conduct and godliness, looking for and hastening the coming of the day of God, because of which the heavens will be destroyed by burning, and the elements will melt with intense heat! But according to His promise we are looking for a new heavens and a new earth, in which righteousness dwells." (2 Pet. 3:10–13)

My point is that even though the New Jerusalem here in Revelation should be identified with the church on earth, this does not nullify the hope that someday after death, Christians will walk with Jesus where there is a new heavens and a new earth. Remember, John is using heavenly concepts to describe an earthly church in these last two chapters of Revelation. Remember the term diplopia (double vision).

Back to the Seven Churches

It is important to remember that the message in these two chapters was written to the seven churches. At the end of Revelation, the reader is reminded of the letters to the seven churches in the beginning of the book (chapters 2 and 3). Most people tend to read these last two chapters in Revelation as if they only apply to Christians living today. However, it should be remembered that even though the Bible was written for us, it was not written to us. The recipients of the book of Revelation were the seven churches; therefore, the recipients of chapters 21–22 were the seven churches. "I, Jesus, have sent My angel to testify to you these things *for the churches* [emphasis added]. I am the root and the descendant of David, the bright morning star" (22:16). However, as I have mentioned before in chapter 1 of my book, Revelation was definitely written as well for Christians who live today.

Even though I believe that I have demonstrated above that John is primarily speaking about the church on earth using heavenly language, yet I will support this view by listing below a few more reasons why I take this position. The language of these two chapters is definitely the New Testament language that speaks of the church on earth.

The Church as the Bride of Christ

As I previously stated, the New Jerusalem came down out of heaven. Notice that the New Jerusalem is also called the "bride adorned for her husband." The bride of Christ is language used to describe the New Testament church. The husband-bride language is not a term only reserved for heaven. Note the following two verses for example:

> "FOR THIS REASON A MAN SHALL LEAVE HIS FATHER AND MOTHER AND SHALL BE JOINED TO HIS WIFE, AND THE TWO SHALL BECOME ONE FLESH. This mystery is great; but I am speaking with reference to Christ and the church" (Eph. 5:31–32).

> "For I am jealous for you with a godly jealousy; for I betrothed you to one husband, so that to Christ I might present you as a pure virgin" (2 Cor. 11:2).

God Dwells in His Church

"And I heard a loud voice from the throne, saying, 'Behold, the tabernacle of God is among men, and He will dwell among them and they shall be His people, and God Himself will be among them'" (Rev. 21:3). This language certainly can be applied to heaven, but it can also be applied to the church on earth. God dwells among his people on earth. One thing that separates the New Covenant from the Old Covenant is the fact that God no longer dwells in a temple made with hands. God dwells in the hearts of his people. As the dwelling place of God's Spirit, we are his temple.

There is no temple in this new city. "I saw no temple in it, for the Lord God the Almighty and the Lamb are its temple" (Rev. 21:22). Jesus told the woman at the well about the coming New Covenant change and how God will tabernacle among men. Jesus said to her: "Woman, believe Me, an hour is coming when neither in this mountain nor in Jerusalem will you worship the Father. You worship what you do not know; we worship what we know, for salvation is from the Jews. But an hour is coming, and now is, when the true worshipers will worship the Father in spirit and truth; for such people the Father seeks to be His worshipers" (John 4:21–23).

Peter spoke of Christians as a spiritual house and as a new priesthood: "you also, as living stones, are being built up as a spiritual house for a holy priesthood, to offer up spiritual sacrifices acceptable to God through Jesus Christ" (1 Peter 2: 5). Paul wrote to the Corinthians: "Do you not know that you are a temple of God and *that* the Spirit of God dwells in you?" (1 Corinthians 3:16). He also told the Corinthians: "For we are the temple of the living God, just as God said, I will dwell in them and walk among them, and I will be their God and they shall be my people" (2 Corinthians 6:16).

Stephen preached that: "the Most High does not dwell in houses made by human hands" (Acts 7:48a). Paul preached likewise on Mars Hill the following: "The God who made the world and all things in it, since He is Lord of heaven and earth, does not dwell in temples made with hands" (Acts 17:24b). These references are not to Christians in heaven but to Christians in the various local congregations of the church on earth.

These words were very offensive to the apostate Jews and to the Jewish priesthood. The temple was the focal point of their religion. It was their life. God was telling Christians in the seven churches that all this *has* changed, and this *will officially be changed* with the destruction of the Temple in Jerusalem. He will not dwell in some physical building; on the contrary, he will dwell in the hearts of his people. Thus, I believe the New Jerusalem in Revelation is all about the church of the Lord Jesus Christ on earth. However, it is so glorious that only heavenly language can do justice to her description.

The Church is the Jerusalem Above

In the book of Galatians, Paul speaks of the Old Jerusalem and the New Jerusalem when comparing them to the Old Covenant and the New Covenant. The Old Jerusalem was seeking to please God by doing the works of the law. The "Jerusalem above" (which I believe is the New Jerusalem) is justified by faith and is therefore free. "Now this Hagar is Mount Sinai in Arabia and corresponds to the present Jerusalem, for she is in slavery with her children. But the *Jerusalem above* [emphasis added] is free, she is our mother" (Galatians 4:25–26). The New Jerusalem is free from the curse of the law, and she presently is our mother.

Likewise, the writer of the book of Hebrews speaks of the "heavenly Jerusalem" as the assembly and church of the firstborn who have come to God through the mediator Jesus Christ. This Jerusalem is heavenly because it comes down out of heaven and is accessible by faith. This is in contrast to the Old Jerusalem that came to the mountain where God gave the law to Moses.

> "But you have come to Mount Zion and to the city of the living God, the heavenly Jerusalem, and to myriads of angels, to the general assembly, and church of the firstborn who are enrolled in heaven, and to God, the Judge of all, and to the spirits of the righteous made perfect, and to Jesus, the mediator of a new covenant, and to the sprinkled blood, which speaks better than the blood of Abel" (Hebrews 12:22–24).

Notice that Christians have *already come* to the heavenly Jerusalem (or the New Jerusalem), the church. This is a description of the New Covenant Church.

A Taste of Heaven

Hebrews 6:4–5 speaks of believers tasting "the heavenly gift and the good word of God and the powers of the age to come." Even though the church has always been imperfect, yet it does taste of the reality of heaven on earth. Even though a taste is not the same as full consumption by the digestive system, a taste partakes of the real thing. This taste of heaven will begin in the apostolic church and will continue into the era of the New Testament church, and that includes the day in which we live.

Thus, I am constrained to apply these words in chapters 21–22 of Revelation first as a message of hope to the seven churches and secondly as a message of hope for us today. It is both a message about the glorious future of the Christian church and also a message about the joy of heaven, because the language of heaven is used to describe the New Covenant church.

The New Jerusalem in Detail

I am not going to deal with the details of this description. Remember, this book is a primer. However, I will quote a passage from the Old Testament which appears to be John's source as he describes the New Jerusalem in detail in chapter 21. This text in Revelation is an expansion of Isaiah's words. In speaking of God's future blessing on the New Jerusalem, Isaiah spoke as follows:

> "Violence will not be heard again in your land, nor devastation or destruction within your borders; but you will call your walls salvation, and your gates praise. No longer will you have the sun for light by day, nor for brightness will the moon give you light; but you will have the Lord for an everlasting light, and your God for your glory. Your sun will no longer set, nor will your moon wane; for you will have the Lord for an everlasting light, and the days of your mourning will be over. Then all your people will be righteous; they will possess the land forever, the branch of My planting, the work of My hands, that I may be glorified. The smallest one will become a clan, and the least one a mighty nation. I, the Lord, will hasten it in its time." (Isa. 60:18–22)

Thus, the basic material that John used to describe the New Jerusalem was not original with him. I believe it was prophetic of the New Testament church.

The Gentiles and the New Jerusalem

My point is that everything that John says in chapters 21–22 can be applied to the church. The New Jerusalem is the church on earth. John also saw this New Jerusalem as glorious because it included the success of the gospel among the Gentiles. He said in 21:24: "The nations shall walk by its light, and the kings of the earth shall bring their glory into it." The holy city will be open to all. The gates shall never be closed. "And in the daytime (for there will be no night there) its gates shall never be closed; and they shall bring the glory and the honor of the nations into it; and nothing unclean and no one who practices abomination and lying, shall ever come into it, but only those whose names are written in the Lamb's book of life" (21:25–27). This is first and primarily a picture of the church.

The church, in addition to being composed of godly Jews, will be composed of the Gentiles and the kings of the earth. In the Old Testament, the church (or the congregation of God's people) was made up largely of the Jewish people. However, the ultimate goal of God dwelling among His people was to draw all nations to worship Him. In the New Covenant this has actually happened. This is the glory of the New Covenant — it is inclusive of both Jew and Gentile. Isaiah spoke of this clearly. Notice how the language corresponds to the language in Revelation 21:24 about the blessing upon the nations:

> "Arise, shine; for your light has come, and the glory of the Lord has risen upon you. For behold, darkness will cover the earth and deep darkness the peoples; but the Lord will rise upon you and His glory will appear upon you. Nations will come to your light, and kings to the brightness of your rising" (Isa. 60:1–3).

> "Your gates will be open continually; they will not be closed day or night, so that *men* may bring to you the wealth of the nations, with their kings led in procession" (Isa. 60:11).

Also, Paul made the inclusion of the Gentiles clear in Ephesians 2:11–13, where he said: "Therefore remember that formerly you, the Gentiles in the flesh, who are called 'Uncircumcison' by the so-called 'Circumcision,' which is performed in the flesh by human hands — remember that you were at that time separate from Christ, excluded from the commonwealth of Israel, and strangers to the covenants of promise, having no hope and without God in the world. But now in Christ Jesus, you who formerly were far off have been brought near by the blood of Christ."

In today's egalitarian society, people may not think of this as being glorious because they live in a culture that thinks it deserves all it gets and even more. It has not always been this way. There was a time when a person who was a Gentile (non-Jew) was excluded from the promises and blessings of God. He was an outcast. Now, he has every right to be a part of the New Jerusalem — the church. The doors of the church are open all day and all night for those who come in by the way of Christ. The nations will be able to enter because they have been made holy "and nothing unclean, and no one who practices abomination and lying, shall ever come into it, but only those whose names are written in the Lamb's book of life" (Rev. 21:27). This is not perfect holiness without sin, but it is a picture of a sanctified people who have been separated from the ways of the world.

The Healing of the Nations

God's healing grace shall flow from His church to all the nations. Whatever sin or grief you bear, whatever guilt you carry, whatever anxiety you have — there is healing flowing from the throne of God and the Lamb. "And he showed me a river of the water of life, clear as crystal, coming from the throne of God and of the Lamb" (22:1). John used the image of the tree of life from the Garden of Eden to explain this glorious truth. "On either side of the river was the tree of life, bearing twelve *kinds* of fruit, yielding its fruit every month; and the leaves of the tree were for the healing of the nations" (22:2). Again, it appears that this language finds it origin in the book of Ezekiel where the prophet is speaking of the future church on earth under the New Covenant.

> "Then he brought me back to the door of the house; and behold, water was flowing from under the threshold of the house toward the east, for the house faced east. And the water was flowing down from under, from the right side of the house, from south of the altar." (Eze. 47:1)

"By the river on its bank, on one side and on the other, will grow all *kinds* of trees for food. Their leaves will not wither and their fruit will not fail. They will bear every month because their water flows from the sanctuary, and their fruit will be for food and their leaves for healing." (Eze. 47:12)

This tree that continually bears fruit every month cures us of all our diseases. As we grow older and have to deal sometimes with the difficult process of aging in this life, this certainly makes us yearn for heaven. Oh! — here I am speaking about heaven — when the topic is the church on earth. I'm contradicting myself. Excuse me — but again — don't excuse me! I am speaking of both heaven and earth!

John referred to "living water" in 21:6: "Then He said to me, 'It is done, I am the Alpha and the Omega, the beginning and the end. I will give to the one who thirsts from the spring of the water of life without cost.'" It is also interesting that in the Gospel of John, the same John who wrote Revelation records the words of Jesus where he compared the living waters to the work of the Holy Spirit in the lives of Christians. "Now on the last day, the great day of the feast, Jesus stood and cried out, saying, 'If anyone is thirsty, let him come to Me and drink. He who believes in Me, as the Scripture said, from his innermost being will flow rivers of living water.' But this He spoke of the Spirit, whom those who believed in Him were to receive; for the Spirit was not yet given, because Jesus was not yet glorified" (John 7:37–39).

Zechariah had made a reference to the healing of the waters many years earlier. "And in that day living waters will flow out of Jerusalem, half of them toward the eastern sea and the other half toward the western sea. It will be in summer as well as in winter" (Zechariah 14:8). Notice that Zechariah said the living waters shall flow out of Jerusalem. Jesus said that living waters will flow from the innermost being of believers. It appears that Jesus associated

Zechariah's Jerusalem with the body of the church — the New Jerusalem.

Some Closing Remarks

I have covered a great deal in this book. There is much that is difficult to understand, but I have tried to make it understandable. Many readers may disagree with my interpretations at various points, but that is all right. My purpose has been to present to you a legitimate interpretation of Revelation — the only one that I believe is faithful to the text. Also, my purpose is to encourage you to explore more about these important issues. To be honest, there is much yet for me to learn.

There are many who believe the book of Revelation is just a fable. There are many who will doubt the truth of the words of John just as they doubt the entire Bible. Faith operates in the hearts of God's people, and the Holy Spirit causes Christians to believe these things. Do I believe what must seem impossible and even ridiculous to others? I do indeed!

John makes the point (or Jesus speaking through John) that I must believe that the words I read in Revelation are true, and — by extension — that the words I read in the entire Bible are true. They are true because Jesus is true. Jesus is a person of integrity and truth. Christians can bet their lives on what Jesus says. Actually, that is what we do. Christians hang on to every word that proceeds from the mouth of God in the Holy Scriptures. John was told in 21:5: "Write, for these words are faithful and true." Again, in 22:6 John was told: "These words are faithful and true." Maybe some in the seven churches were doubtful? Jesus reassured them that all he said was true.

A Personal Testimony

Often, people ask me why I personally believe in some things that seem impossible. I answer that we all believe in things that seem impossible. For example, there are those who believe the world began with an explosion and from that chaos came order. It takes great faith to believe this. From an explosion came the rotation of the earth around the sun, the four seasons, the flow of blood in the human body, the coordination of all the muscles and bones to enable a man to move from one place to another, and other things such as the complexity of the human eye? Need I say anymore! This faith system (that order and complexity came from a big bang) seems impossible to me.

Actually, everything is really a matter of faith. It is just the faith of one man versus the faith of another man. It's not science versus faith. I choose to believe in a God who created the earth and who providentially governs the world on a day-to-day basis. I choose to believe there is life after death. I choose to believe there is a heaven and a hell. I choose to believe that I am a sinner, and the only hope I have as I face the Judgment of God is the shed blood of a great Savior — Jesus Christ. I choose to believe these things because the Holy Spirit works in me to convince me that these things are true.

A Final Warning

The words of Revelation are so important that Jesus warns all of those who handle them that they must not change them. If a person adds to the words of this book, then he shall have the plagues added to him. "I testify to everyone who hears the words of the prophecy of this book: if anyone adds to them, God shall add to him the plagues which are written in this book" (22:18).

Remember the plagues from the pouring out of the seven bowls of wrath? The wise man Agur spoke of this danger in the book of

Proverbs: "Every word of God is tested; he is a shield to those who take refuge in Him. Do not add to His words or He will reprove you, and you will be proved a liar" (Proverbs 30:5). This is not intended to make us fearful to read or interpret Revelation, but it is intended to teach us that we must handle it with respect and care.

Also, to take away from the book is just as dangerous as adding to the book. The warning is strong: "and if anyone takes away from the words of the book of this prophecy, God shall take away his part from the tree of life and from the holy city, which are written in this book" (Rev. 22:19). Again, this is not meant to scare the child of God. Let unbelievers who deny the authority of God's Word be warned. Also, these final words in Revelation alone are enough to make me think twice about even writing a primer on the book of Revelation. I have endeavored to cover it carefully. God is my witness!

The Gospel Call

John closed the book of Revelation with the gospel, and that is how any book on Revelation should be closed. "And the Spirit and the bride say, 'Come'. And let the one who hears say, 'Come.' And let the one who is thirsty come; let the one who wishes take the water of life without cost" (22:17). This is an invitation to everyone who reads this book and who may be troubled about the things I have written. God gives an invitation to all men to come to him and to be a part of this glorious body — the church, regardless of what you have done or thought in your life. You are never too old. You don't have to belong to the right race. You don't have to bring any goodness of your own. You may think you are not good enough. That's all right. This only makes you eligible to come. The invitation is unlimited. The invitation is for the sick. The invitation is for the sinner. Just come!

Revelation repeats the invitation given throughout the Scriptures. In the Old Testament, Isaiah said in 55:1: "Ho, everyone who thirsts, come to the waters; and you who have no money come, buy and eat. Come, buy wine and milk without money and without cost." In John 7:37 Jesus said: "Now on the last day, the great day of the feast, Jesus stood and cried out, saying, 'If any man is thirsty, let him come to Me and drink. He who believes in Me, as the Scripture said, from his innermost being shall flow rivers of living water.'"

The gospel is greatly misunderstood today. The only thing we need in order to be saved is a hunger and thirst that causes us to flee to Christ. We don't need good works. We don't need a religious experience. We don't need some prequalification. All we need is a hunger and thirst for Christ in order to be forgiven and to be changed. We have made a mess of life, and we need God's grace. We can bring all of our trash that we have accumulated over the years, and dispose it at the door of the church. The invitation still stands today. It will stand as long as men have life on this earth.

Amen!

The last words in Revelation are: "The grace of the Lord Jesus be with all. Amen" (22:21). This is a good way to end any book, even this my book. I hope you have profited from what I have written. I hope you will think about all that I have said.

I pray you will experience the same joy that I have had in writing this book. I hope you now drink of the water of life — Jesus Christ. After a long and sometimes difficult study of Revelation, I have been blessed. If you have been afraid of Revelation, I pray that you are no longer afraid to read it. We need not fear all of the awful scenarios that are out there now in what I call the prophecy cult. Ultimately, the book of Revelation is a book about Jesus and his grace. The seven churches suffered a great deal. The martyrs in heaven cried out for justice and vengeance. God heard their cries, and God answered because God is just and good. He will do the same for you. This is what the book of Revelation is all about. Amen!

SUMMARY

"Write the things which you have seen, and the things which are, and the things which will take place after these things." (Rev 1:19)

Summary

Remember my illustration of *the three sevens*. If you are like me when I was in school, you tended to memorize everything for a test; and then you tended to forget most of what you memorized. Often, I needed a memory device such as a mnemonic or a catchphrase. Think of the three sevens as a catchphrase. It should help you maintain a broad outline of the Book of Revelation. My goal here in this short summary is to remind you of some of the main points I have covered in this book.

The greatest obstacle for me to overcome in Revelation was the time-restriction texts. John said at the beginning, in the middle, and at the end of Revelation that the events he described must happen soon. The time is near. Now, here is my problem. He was writing to the seven churches, and if these things did not happen soon in their own generation, then this causes me to doubt the integrity of John. Soon must mean *soon*. Either John (and God too) were mistaken or they were not telling the truth. God forbid! This drove me to interpret the events in Revelation (except for chapter 20) as happening in the days of the apostles. It seems rather simple, but it makes a profound difference in how the reader interprets the book.

My view of the interpretation of Revelation is associated with what traditionally has been called the preterist view (or what some prefer to call the partial-preterist view). Most of the events of Revelation occurred in the past during the apostolic age. Not only does this seem credible because of the time-restrictions, but also it seems plausible because of the ability to correlate the events in Revelation with actual historical events and entities in the apostolic age, especially with the Roman Empire.

My approach of limiting the events to the apostolic age is based upon the principle of historical limitation. I covered this in *chapter one* of this book. The Bible was not written to us but for us. I used a number of texts from the Bible to demonstrate this. In *chapter two*, I applied the principle of historical limitation to the time-limitation texts. These things must soon take place. The time is near. These time-limitations were also found in the middle and at the end of Revelation.

In *chapter three,* I looked at some other principles that are needed to interpret Revelation. I demonstrated that not everything in the Bible can be taken literally. For example, the image of Jesus' coming with the clouds represents a judgment of God that is distinct from the Second Advent of Christ. I looked at how the Greek term often translated "earth" can be also translated "land." Also, I looked at the nature of a metaphor. In the first chapter of Revelation, Jesus gave a metaphor, and he interpreted it to help the reader understand its nature.

In *chapter four,* I looked at the letters to the seven churches. The persecuted church needed to be comforted and to be told that this persecution would shortly be mitigated. Christ would destroy their enemy — Jerusalem. The church was reminded to clean up her own act first because judgment begins with the household of God.

In *chapter five,* I presented the seven-sealed book that only Jesus could open. I developed the theory that the seven-sealed book was an edict of judgment against Jerusalem. Three separate sevens were the subject of the following chapters of Revelation (chapters 6 through 16). These three sevens would reveal the following: 1) the edict of judgment against Jerusalem in the seven-sealed book (*chapter six*), 2) the warning against Jerusalem in the blowing of the seven trumpets (*chapter seven*), and 3) the execution of judgment against Jerusalem in the pouring out of the seven bowls of wrath (*chapter nine*).

As I moved through chapters 4-16 of Revelation, there were several scenes of heaven with God upon his throne. God is in total control of everything. God is sovereign. He is constantly being worshiped. We were granted a peek into heaven. One of the prominent images was a scene of the martyrs who died at the hands of the Jews and who were crying out for vengeance. God promised he would execute that judgment and asked them to be patient just a little while longer. Jewish Christians would escape from Jerusalem before her destruction.

Also in chapters 4-16 of Revelation, I presented the necessity of witnesses before the execution could be carried out (*chapter seven*). There must be two or three witnesses before a person can be convicted. These came in the form of a drama witness and finally in the form of two personal witnesses. The drama showed John eating a book that tasted like honey but became bitter in the stomach.

John then introduced the beast from the sea (Rome or Nero) that would carry out this vengeance against Jerusalem (*chapter eight*). The mark of the beast whose number was six hundred and sixty-six was identified with Nero. John also introduced the land beast who was called both the false prophet and the great harlot. I identified this beast as the Jewish priesthood which represented apostate Jerusalem. God used various names to describe Jerusalem such as Egypt, Sodom, Babylon, the false prophet, and the great harlot. Even though Rome eventually destroyed Jerusalem, the priesthood of Israel manipulated Rome to persecute and kill Christians. The great harlot was carried by the beast, yet the great harlot manipulated the beast, just as the Scribes and Pharisees manipulated Pontius Pilate in the death of Christ.

In chapters 17-19 of Revelation, we were reminded of the death of both the beast (Nero) and the false prophet (the Jewish priesthood or the high priest himself). They were thrown into the lake of fire. We performed a post-mortem analysis of the false prophet, and then we looked at the victory march of Christ as King before the saints of heaven. His new bride (the church) was waiting for him as he returned from war (*chapter 10*).

In *chapter 11* of my book, I covered chapter 20 of Revelation. I lifted the reader above the time-limitations. There John introduced a thousand years, the final judgment, and the end of Satan. Satan would be bound for a thousand years and then be released only to be destroyed. The end of Satan, as well as the false prophet and the beast, was the lake of fire. All those who did not have the mark of God on their forehead would also be cast into the lake of fire. Both death and the grave, too, would be cast into the lake of fire.

In *chapter 12* of my book I covered chapters 21-22 of Revelation. I presented descriptions that can only be a picture of heaven. However, this presented a dilemma because the time-restrictions were so prevalent in the last chapter of Revelation (chapter 22). Much of the language of these two chapters could not be used to describe heaven. All the language and images had to be set within the time-restrictions. This appeared to be a dilemma. I resolved this dilemma by suggesting that even though the last two chapters of Revelation described the future of the church, yet John used the language of heaven in his description. Heaven is a real place and the language used to describe the church is derived from the very nature and character of heaven.

Finally, John closes Revelation with a warning to all those who read the book. No one must add to or subtract from the words. The consequences of tampering with the book are ominous.

Also, Revelation closes with the preaching of the gospel. If the book frightens the reader, then the only real answer to that fear is to flee to Christ. With this I conclude again with the final words of Revelation — Amen!

APPENDIX
Recommended Reading

Adams, Jay, *The Time Is At Hand*
Boettner, Loraine, *The Millennium*
Bray, John L., *Matthew 24 Fulfilled*
Campbell, Roderick, *Israel and the New Covenant*
Chilton, David, *Days of Vengeance*
DeMar, Gary, *Last Days Madness*
Gentry, Kenneth L., Jr. *Before Jerusalem Fell*
_____ *He Shall Have Dominion*
_____ *The Beast of Revelation*
_____ *The Divorce of Israel* (forthcoming)
Kelly, Douglas F., *Revelation, A Mentor Expository Commentary*
Kik, Marcellus, *An Eschatology of Victory*
_____ *Matthew 24*
Mathison, Kenneth L., *Postmillennialism*
Murray, Iain, *The Puritan Hope*
Rushdoony, Rousas J., *Thy Kingdom Come: Studies in Daniel and Revelation*
Sproul, R. C., *Last Days according to Jesus*
Stuart, Moses, *A Commentary on the Apocalypse*
Terry, Milton S., *Biblical Apocalyptics*

SCRIPTURE INDEX

Genesis
1   4
15:16   160

Exodus
19:4 140
19:16   120
28:4–5   178
28:17–20   178
28:36–38   112

Deuteronomy
6:6   112
6:8   101
19:15   127
20:10   82
28:26   102
28:27   163
28:53   100
28:56–57   100–01

Joshua
6:4–5   83

2 Samuel
7:12–13 215
11:1 187

1 Kings
9:6–9   93–94

2 Kings
23:29   168

Esther
1:19–21 90
8:8   86

Job
1:6, 7   137
1:8–11   138
2:7   163

Psalms
2   69, 133
2:9–12   186
22:18   214
50:10   110, 196
104:1–3   50

Proverbs
21:1   58
27:6   74
30:5   229

Isaiah
6:2   80
6:9   82
13:1, 10   107
13:17–22   175
19:1–2   49
29:9–16   88
40:30–31   141
55:1   230
58:1   83
60:1–3   224
60:11   224
60:18–22   223
65:17–20   217

Jeremiah
1:7   82
6:16–19 83

Lamentations
4:8   100

Ezekiel
1:10–11 79
1:1 4 80
2:3–4 82
2:8–3:4 129
2:9–10 88
2:10 84
3:1–3 129
3:14 129
4:1–3 130
9:1–3 162
9:4–9 162
12:7 130
39:1–2 206
47:1 225
47:12 226

Daniel
6:8–9 90
12:4 89
12:7 141
12:9, 10 89

Joel
2:1 84
2:31 106

Habakkuk
1:5–6 48
2:4 201

Zechariah
1:8, 10 101
14:8 226

Matthew
2:20–21 51
5:31–32 46
6:10 201
7:22–23 149

8:11 94
8:12 207
12:28–29 198
12:36 209
12:43–45 121
13:31–32 201
16:18 199
16:19 71
17:20 44
18:15–16 127
18:18 199
18:22 196
21:43 93
21:43–45 180
23:34–36 103–04
23:37–38 48
23:39 49
24 13
24:1, 2 104
24:15–22 139
24:16–18 109
24:21 124
24:29–41 30
24:32 25
24:34 13, 14, 30, 104
26:59 147
26:63–64 49
28:18 198
28:20, 29 199

Mark
1:15 199
9:43–44 207
10:11 46
13:37 11
15:24 215

Luke
8:31 121
9:28–36 212

10:17–19	198	*7:48a*	220
11:47–50	165	*7:52*	95
12:22	11	*8:1*	38
12:33	10, 12, 13	*12:1–3*	182
12:40, 41	11	*17:7*	148
16:24	207	*17:24b*	221
18:22	9	*21:10–11*	131
19:41–44	31, 92, 170	*25:4*	25
21:20–22	92	*26:18a*	198
22:43	211		
23:28–30	92	Romans	
23:30	105	*2:9*	95
		4:11	111
John		*6:12–13*	203
2:18–21	43	*9:14*	32
3:3	43	*11:25–26*	95
4:1 4	67	*11:30–32*	96
4:21–23	220	*15:4*	17
5:24	203		
5:25–29	205	1 Corinthians	
5:31–32	126	*2:9, 10*	215
5:39–40	127	*3:16*	220
7:37	230	*3:21–22*	199
7:37–39	226		
8:12	44	2 Corinthians	
10:11	44	*6:16*	220
11:47–48	149	*11:2*	219
14:2–3	211	*12:3–4*	212
15:5	44	*12:10*	71
16:2–4	147	*13:1, 2*	127
19:12–15	146–47		
19:15	95	Galatians	
		3:28	15
Acts		*4:25–26*	221
1:9, 11	47		
2:5–11	182	Ephesians	
2:20	107	*1:13–14*	111
2:23f	52, 95	*2:5–6*	199
5:30	95	*2:11–13*	224
7	103	*5:31–32*	219

Colossians
2:15   198

1 Thessalonians
2:15   95
2:16   160
4:16   47

1 Timothy
2:12   15
2:13   16
4:16   78
5:19   127
5:20   69

2 Timothy
2:11–13 74
2:12b   199
3:16   3
3:16–17   xi, 1
4:11   9
4:13   7, 9

Philemon
1:22   8

Hebrews
6:4–5   222
9   87
10:32–34   146
10:34   65
12:22–24   222
13:2   80
13:11–12   159

James
1:1   139

1 Peter
1:7   73
2:5   220
2:9   199
4:7   75
4:12–13   60
4:17 61

2 Peter
1:5–8   68
1:21 4
2:4   198
3   218
3:8   26
3:9   84
3:10–13   218
3:13   205

1 John
2:18   29
3:14   203
5:4–5   199

Jude
1:3   xii
1:6   198, 207

Revelation
1   41, 60
1:1   23, 24, 85, 86, 192
1:1–3   19, 32
1:3   xi, 23, 24, 15, 192
1:5   5, 8
1:6   59, 199
1:7   4, 46, 50,51, 52, 53,55, 95,103, 184
1:9   59, 85
1:12–20   54–55
1:17–18   195
1:19   233
1:20   55
2   24, 57, 72

2, 3	218	4:6	78
2:1	57	4:8–11	94
2:2–3	63	4:10	79, 80
2:3	59	5	77, 80, 81, 89, 110, 157
2:4, 5	64	5:1	84–85, 208
2:6	63	5:3	85
2:7	64	5:4	77, 84
2:8–9	65	5:6–7	93
2:9	149	5:8	157
2:10	25, 59, 65	5:9	93
2:12a	58	6	108
2:13	59, 66	6–8:5	108
2:14–15	66	6–16	234
2:16	66	6:1	97
2:17, 19	67	6:2, 4b	99
2:20–21	68	6:5, 6	100
2:22–23	68	6:8	82, 84, 98
2:23a	69	6:9	102, 105
2:24	68	6:9–11	103
2:25	59	6:10	26, 85, 102, 163
2:26–29	69	6:11	26, 71, 102
3	24, 57	6:12–13	106
3:2, 3	70	6:16–17	105
3:4	69	7	108, 109, 113
3:5–6	70, 71	7:1–3	108
3:7	195	7:3	110
3:9	59, 72, 74, 93	7:4	109, 196
3:10–11	72	7:9	115
3:11	25	7:9–17	113
3:12	72	7:14	109
3:15–16	73	7:16–17	212
3:17	73	8:1	114
3:18, 19	73	8:1–13	117
3:20	74	8:2	117
3:21–22	74	8:3, 5	114
4	77, 78, 79	8:5, 6	97, 108
4–16	235	8:7	84, 119, 120
4:1	78	8:8, 9, 10, 11, 12	119, 120
4:4	79	8:13	121
4:5	78, 79	9	124

9–11	117	12:13–14	136
9:1–12	117	12:14–16	140
9:4, 5	122	12:16	141
9:6	124	12:17	136, 140
9:11	121	13	113, 142, 156, 157
9:12, 13	125	13:1	141, 142, 144
9:13–21	117	13:2	144
9:15,16	125	13:3	143
9:15, 18	119	13:4	142
9:16	159, 196	13:5	145
9:17a	125	13:5, 6	144
9:19	126	13:8	135
10	117, 128, 129, 131	13:10	144
10,11	126	13:11	156
10:1–2	128	13:11, 12a	146
10:2	209	13:11, 12, 13, 14, 15, 16	145
10:2, 5	52	13:14	148
10:4	128	13:15	147
10:9–10	129	13:16	148
11	128, 132	13:17	146
11:1–14	117	13:18	141, 150, 151, 153
11:2, 3	122	14	157
11:6	132	14, 15	155
11:8	37, 119, 134, 181	14:1	156
11:10	132	14:4	158
11:14	126	14:6	170
11:15–19	118, 133	14:8	156
11:18	133	14:9–10, 11a	157
11:19	134	14:12, 13, 14, 15, 17, 18	158
12–14	134, 135	14:19, 20	159
12	136	14:20	160
12:1–2	138	15	134, 156
12:3	136	15:1, 3a	160
12:3–4	44	15:4, 6	161
12:4	136, 137	15:7	155, 161
12:6	139	15:8	162
12:9a	136	16	97, 117, 135, 155, 156, 160, 162, 179
12:10	136, 137, 138	16:1	161
12:12	140	16:2	163
12:13	137		

16:3, 4, 6   164
16:8, 10a   165
16:9, 11   170
16:12   166
16:13   148, 166
16:14   167
16:15   183
16:17   84, 169, 174
16:18   168
16:19   179
16:19, 20   169
16:20   169, 174
17   91, 179
17–19   173, 235
17:1, 5   176
17:2   181
17:3   178
17:4   177
17:5   179
17:6   44, 183
17:7   179
17:9   37
17:9–10 142
17:10   38, 143
17:11   143, 171
17:11–19   185
17:12   180
17:14   181
17:15   182
17:16   179, 180
17:17   180
17:18   181
18:2   174
18:4–5   183
18:20   184
18:22–23   175
18:24   184
19   99, 171, 186, 194
19:1–2   173
19:1, 2, 3   184

19:4, 6, 11   185
19:13   186
19:14, 15   186
19:16   185
19:17–18   175
19:20   148, 149, 187, 192
20   121, 171, 173, 189, 191, 192, 193, 194, 196, 206, 212, 213, 233, 236
20:1   194
20:2, 3   195
20:3a   198
20:4, 5   203
20:6   204
20:7   196, 205
20:8–9   205
20:10   191
20:11   208
20:11–15   206
20:12a   209
20:12a, 13a 208
20:14   209
20:14–15   191
20:15   209
21   171, 223
21–22   173, 187, 213, 215, 216, 219, 222, 223, 236
21:1   217
21:3   220
21:5   211, 227
21:6   216, 226, 227
21:7, 8   216
21:16   44
21:22   220
21:24   223, 224
21:25–27   224
21:27   87, 225
22   171, 192
22:1, 2   225
22:3–4   111, 211

22:5 211
22:6 192
22:6–7 27
22:10, 12 28
22:11 216
22:12 216
22:16 219
22:17 217, 229
22:18 228
22:19 229
22:21 230

Subject and Name Index

Abaddon, 121
Abomination of Desolation, 139
Abyss, 194-195
Arch of Titus, 185
Antipas, 59
Apocalypse, 22
Apollyon, 121
Armageddon, 166-168
Asia Minor, 38, 58, 66

Babylon the Great, 156, 169, 173, 184
— High priesthood and, 177-181
Balaam, 66,
Balak, 66
Bahnsen, Greg, 1, 152
Bible Inspiration, 3-6
Book of Life, 191, 208-209
Bork, Robert, 201
Bowls of wrath (Seven) 81-82
Burial service, 187, 155-171

Caesar, 60, 109, 143
Call to suffer, 60
Cannibalism, 100-101
Chained (Satan), 195, 202
Chaldeans, 48
Chilton, David, 177
Church:
— as bride, 219
— as dwelling of God, 220
— fudgment and, 61
— sometimes pitiful, 61-62
— three enemies of, 135
Coming with (on) the Clouds, 41, 46-49, 60, 184
Riding on the Clouds, 50, 53
— Clouds as his chariot, 50

Comparing Scripture with Scripture, 42, 45-46, 53, 56
Constantine, 183, 200
Covenant:
— Nature and, 69
— Old Covenant, 90, 97, 106, 139, 220-221
— as New Covenant, 92, 106, 217, 220-221, 224-225
Creation ordinance, 15
Credence:
— Biblical, 197-200
— Historical, 200-202
Cremation, 208
Crockett, Davy, 45
Crystal Sea, 78

Daniel, 89-90, 141
Darius, 90
Dark Ages, 200
Dating of Revelation, 36-38
Days, "1260," 139
Day of Judgment, 213
Death of death, 209
DeMar, Gary, 14
Diplopia, 214-215
Divorce, 92, 94
Domitian, 36
Dragon, 140
Dwellings in heaven, 211

Earth:
— *Ge*, 51
— Geography, 52
— *Graphikos*, 52
— Land, 51- 53, 103, 181, 234
— New, 218
Edict of judgment, 90-94, 191
Eighth part, 143

Egalitarianism, 15
Elders, twenty-four, 79-80
Egypt, 37, 49-50, 120
Ephesus church, 63-65
Esther, 90
Eulogy, 174
Euphrates River, 125
Eyes of those who pierced Him, 52

False Prophet, 148, 184, 236
Final Judgment, 191-193, 206
First Resurrection, 203-204
Flavius, 35
Four horsemen 98-102, 115
Four living creatures, 79
Futurist view, 34, 37

Gates of Hell, 199
Generation, this, 13
Gentiles, 222-224
Gentry, Kenneth, 1, 26-27. 37-38, 92, 99, 177, 199
God and Magog, 206
Gospel call, 229
Great Commission, 198-199
Great Harlot, 187

Hades, 194, 208
Healing of the nations, 225-227
Heaven, 214, 217, 236
— Taste of, 222
— New, 218
Hell, 207-208
Herod Agrippa, 181
Henry, Matthew, 74-75
Henty, G. A., 35-36
Hermeneutics, 42
Historical limitation, 8-9, 10-17, 28, 30, 36, 41-42, 56, 234
Historical view, 33

Holy of Holies, 67, 78
Hyper-preterists, 34, 193

Idealist view, 33
Imminent return, 27-29
Inerrant Bible, 3-4, 6, 42
Imprecatory prayers, 115
Incremental judgment, 98, 136
Infallible Bible, 3-4, 6, 42
Interlude, 108, 126
Israel, 94-96

Jerusalem:
— Destruction of, 11-12, 29-30, 34-38, 48-49, 51-53, 91-92, 97, 102, 108-109, 126, 156, 159, 169, 234
— Above, 221
— Identity, 119
— Internal Conflict, 122-125
— Great City, 181
— Great Harlot, 177, 181
— New, 44, 72, 217-219, 222
— Persecuting, 58-59
— Target of vengeance, 91
Jezebel, 68
Jewish Church, 139
Jewish High Priests, 135, 177, 182
Jews, 12, 30, 85, 89, 91, 97
— Future salvation of, 95-96
— Twelve Tribes, 139
Job, 137-138, 202
John, 77-78
  weeping of, 84-86
Josephus, 34-35, 38, 100
Judaism, 38
Jurassic Park, 19
Justification, 21

Keys of Death, 195
Kingdom, 39, 200-202

Lake of Fire, 191, 206-207, 236
Lamb of God, 156
Land Beast, 145-149
Laodicea church, 58, 72-75
Liberal church, 29, 30
Literalism, 42-44, 56
Little while longer, 26, 103

Male Child, 137-138
Mark of the Beast, 150-151
Mark on forehead:
— Christians and, 108-113
— Unbelievers and, 162
Martyrs in Heaven, 104-105
Materialism, 12
Medes and Persians, 91
Megiddo, 167
Menorah, 79
Metaphor, 23, 32, 37-38, 53-55, 107, 120, 159, 214, 217, 234
— Meta-pherein, 53
Months
— Forty-two, 122
Mother of Harlots (Great), 177-184
Mount of Transfiguration, 212
Mt. Sinai, 78, 120
Mt. Zion, 155-157

NASB, 6
Nations, 224,
— Healing, 225
Near, 24-26, 31
— *engus*, 25
Neo-orthodoxy, 16
Nero, 109, 141-145, 187, 235
— *Nrwn Qsr*, 153
New Babylon, 176

New Creation, 217
Nicolaitans, 63-64, 66
Number:
— "144,000", 109-110, 156-157, 196
— "666" (of the man), 150-154, 167
— "1600" Stadia, 160
— "1000" Years, 193, 195-196

Old Babylon, 176
One-thousand years, 195, 213-214
— Millennium, 197

Pax Romana, 99
Pergamum church, 57, 66-67
Persecution of the church, 59
Philadelphia church, 24, 25, 58, 71-72, 75
Pilate, 95
Pontius Pilate, 181
Post-mortem analysis, 173-189
Precious stones, 78
Preterist view, 33-34, 36-37,
— Hyper-preterist, 34
— Partial-preterist, 34
Presuppositions, 1, 2
Protestant Reformation, 200
Puritans, 21

Reapers, 158-160
Red dragon, 136
Rome (Roman), 29, 30, 53, 58-60, 85, 95, 109, 235
— Armies of, 51, 99, 102, 125
— Empire, 103, 177, 182, 200
— Persecutor of church, 135
Rich Young Ruler, 9

Sardis Church, 69-71
Satan (Devil), 135-141, 191, 193-195
— Bound, 195-197
— Dwelling place of, 194
— Release of, 205-206
— End of, 213, 236
Second Advent (Coming), 11, 27-31, 41, 47-48, 87
Science verses Faith, 43
Sea Beast, 141-145
Seals (Seven):
— Book, 77, 84-86, 97-98, 108, 234
— First four, 98-102
— Fifth, 102-105
— Sixth, 105-106
— Seventh, 114
Second Resurrection, 204-205
Seven Angels, 161
Seven bowls of wrath (plagues), 155-171
Seven heads, 37, 142
Seven mountains, 37-38, 142-143
Singing in Heaven, 79-80, 113, 160-161
Song of Moses, 161
Sproul, R. C., 30
Smyrna church, 25, 58, 65, 71, 75
Sodom, 37
Soon (Shortly), 24-26, 36, 48, 50, 67
— *en tachei*, 25
— Personal Example, 31-32
Spiritualized, 10-13

Temple, 104, 221
Temporal expectation, 19-39
Three sevens, 81, 97, 134
Three enemies of Church
— Satan, 135-1141
— Rome, (Sea Beast), 141-145

— Jewish Priesthood, (Land Beast), 145-149
Throne:
— Of God, 77-80
— Great White, 208
Thyatira Church, 67-69
Titus, 35, 169, 185
Time-Restrictions, 193-194, 213, 236
Times, Time, Times, Half-time, 140
Tongues (as languages), 182
Tree of Life, 225-227
Tribes:
— of the Earth, 41, 52, 55
— of Israel, 110
Trumpets, 81, 117, 134
— First four, 119-120
— Fifth, 121-122
— Sixth, 125-126
— Seventh, 133-134
Old Testament, 118-119

Vespasian, 35, 109
Victory march, 185

Walls of Jericho, 83
Watts, Isaac:
— "Jesus Shall Reign," 201
Westminster Confession of Faith, 62
Witnesses:
— Drama, 128-132, 235
— Modern day, 131-132
— Two or three, 126-128, 132
Woes:
— First, 121
— Second, 125-126
— Third, 133-134
Women and ordination, 16

Years:
   — Three and one-half, 122

Related Victorious Hope Publications

Gentry, Kenneth L., Jr., "The Climax of the Book of Revelation: A Study of Revelation 19-22"

DVD conference lectures on the glorious climax of Revelation. Engages much introductory material for Revelation, as well.

Gentry, Kenneth L., Jr., *The Greatness of the Great Commission: The Christian Enterprise in a Fallen World.*

Book demonstrating the Christian worldview-calling of the Christian and the Church, along with the hope of its full accomplishment in the spread of the gospel in the discipling of all nations.

Gentry, Kenneth L., Jr., "Keys to the Book of Revelation"

DVD conference lectures highlighting the basic concepts necessary for interpreting the Book of Revelation.

Gentry, Kenneth L., Jr., *Navigating the Book of Revelation: Special Studies on Important Issues*

Book containing fifteen important studies on issues arising from a preterist interpretation of the Book of Revelation.

Gentry, Kenneth L., Jr., *Perilous Times: A Study in Eschatological Evil*

Book containing in-depth studies of key prophetic chapters, analyzing them from a preterist perspective. Chapters cover Daniel's Seventy Weeks, the Olivet Discourse, Paul's "Man of Sin," the Beast of Revelation, and the Harlot of Revelation

Gentry, Kenneth L., Jr., "Survey of the Book of Revelation"

DVD class lectures of 35 minutes each, designed for Sunday schools and small group studies. Comes with a pdf containing a reproducible syllabus for note-taking.

Gentry, Kenneth L., Jr., *Tongues-Speaking: The Meaning, Purpose, and Cessation of Tongues*

Book demonstrating that the gift of tongues was a first-century phenomenon that pointed to the coming destruction of the temple and the ending of the old covenant.

www.ingramcontent.com/pod-product-compliance
Lightning Source LLC
Chambersburg PA
CBHW070530090426
42735CB00013B/2928